The Wind on the Heath

A Gypsy Anthology

HEAD OF A GITANA
BY AUGUSTUS JOHN

The Wind on the Heath

A GYPSY ANTHOLOGY

CHOSEN BY

John Sampson

With a Frontispiece in colour by
AUGUSTUS JOHN, R.A.
and
Fourteen designs by John Garside

PRINTED IN GREAT BRITAIN
BY T. AND A. CONSTABLE LTD.
AT THE UNIVERSITY PRESS
EDINBURGH

To all the Affectionated

Preface

THIS little work is an attempt to interpret to gentile (and I trust to gentle) readers something of the glamour that enwraps the Gypsy race, of their strange choice of ways in their earthly pilgrimage, and of that life romantic which Lavengro eulogized as the ' happiest under Heaven, the true Eden-life.'

I call this *Wind on the Heath* a Gypsy anthology ; but it is rather an anthology of the Gypsy spirit, since I include some pieces which are not definitely Romani, and exclude others as ' Counterfeit Egyptian,' whose sole claim is the use of the name Gypsy, and a few words purloined from Borrow.

The Gypsies are in truth a touchstone to the personality of a man. Just as one person may see in an ancient battered coin merely a worthless piece of metal, of no utility as currency, so to another it may conjure up visions of famous men and bygone civilization, and even seem a thing of worth and beauty in itself. The reaction of great minds to this theme is an interesting chapter in literary history. It covers a wide field, from the myth-makers of the Middle Ages to the Elizabethans with their happy acceptance of these fellow romantics as part of the multi-coloured pageant of life ; the be-wigged philosophy of the eighteenth century, disapprobatory, judicial or cynical; and the various views, artistic, sympathetic or philanthropic, of the present day. The sentiments of these worthies differ as notably as the costume of their period.

Our Gypsies meanwhile have gone on in their old way serenely indifferent to opinion. ' Are you aware, Rosaina,' I asked a picturesquely clad young Romani, ' that Wordsworth, the great Mr. Wordsworth, has called you a " wild outcast of Society " ? ' ' There are two societies, Raia,' was the disdainful reply. Yes, certainly, there are two Societies, and which is the happier remains a question. Do we not find Shakespeare — through the mouth of Amiens—Hazlitt, Kinglake, Stevenson, Housman, Masefield, and many another, sometimes wondering whether Madam Civilization may not have put her money on the wrong horse?

I have divided the book into twelve sections which are designed to bring to light the chief facets of Gypsy life. And if one dare advise a reader as to how he should read, may I say that it were better if he read these consecutively, since the pieces are arranged in an ordered sequence, and gain by their neighbourhood. I have tried to hang my pictures with judgment, and should it be charged against me that I have not everywhere succeeded, and that there is in fact too much Borrow, it should be borne in mind that such a painter can hardly be over-represented in the Gypsy Gallery, even though he has a tendency to throw others into the shade; just as Turner's single blob of vermilion (affixed to his own picture on varnishing day) obliterated his rivals' work in the exhibition.

While these extracts include some of the fine flower of literature, it will be perceived that this anthology is not merely a collection of classical pieces *in vacuo*. Some of my flora—weeds doubtless in the eyes of the horticulturist—have been chosen for their historical and archaeological interest, or as real illustrations of Gypsy life and thought. Yet the same wind blows over them all, and it is hoped may welcome with an invigorating gale the adventurer on our Gypsy heath.

* * *

I thank my old friend and brother Rai, Augustus John, for his generous gift of the frontispiece of the Gitana, and for a vivid sketch in words of foreign Gypsies at Marseilles. I owe to the loved and revered Robert Bridges, who since this preface first was written has set in glory like the sun, two passages from the *Testament of Beauty*, which he graciously gave me before the publication of that noble poem. I tender my thanks to my friends: Arthur Symons for a poem from *Images of Good and Evil*, and extracts from two articles in the *Journal of the Gypsy Lore Society*; Oliver Elton for a translation from the Russian of Pushkin; Mrs. Joseph Pennell for two passages from *To Gipsyland*, and several extracts from the *Life* and various works of Charles Godfrey

Leland; Mrs. Watts-Dunton for permission to quote two of her husband's poems and a passage from *Aylwin*; William Meredith and the Trustees of George Meredith for permission to reprint *The Orchard and the Heath* and three short passages from *Harry Richmond* (Messrs. Constable & Co. Ltd., Lond., and Messrs. Charles Scribner's Sons, N.Y.); T. W. Thompson and D. F. de l'Hoste Ranking for articles from the *J. G. L. S.*; Sir Donald MacAlister for permission to quote a stanza from his Romani version of Stevenson's ' Vagabond '; Miss M. E. Lyster, Miss F. Marston and Miss D. E. Yates for extracts from articles in the *J. G. L. S.*; and J. Glyn Davies for a translation of a Welsh poem by Eifion Wyn (Foyle's Welsh Depot), and of a couplet from Dafydd ab Gwilym.

My cordial thanks are also offered to the following authors and publishers for kind permission to use poems or extracts from their works : A. E. Housman for one of his *Last Poems*; John Masefield for a poem from *Salt Water Ballads* and a passage from *The Everlasting Mercy* (Sidgwick & Jackson); John Galsworthy for a passage from *In Chancery*; George Bernard Shaw for two passages from *Cashel Byron's Profession*; Edmund Blunden for a poem from *The Shepherd* (Cobden-Sanderson); Miss Sackville-West for a passage from *The Land* (Heinemann), and for three poems from *Orchard and Vineyard* (John Lane); Mrs. Hardy for an extract from *The Early Life of Thomas Hardy*; Sacheverell Sitwell for two passages from *The Visit of the Gypsies*; Gipsy Smith for an extract from his *Life* (National Council of the Evangelical Free Churches); Arthur B. Talbot for a quatrain from his translation of *Omar Khayyam* (Elkin Mathews); the executor of the late Sir James Yoxall and Messrs. Longmans Green & Co. for a passage from *The Rommany Stone*; Mr. John Murray for an extract from *The Girlhood of Queen Victoria*; Messrs. Chatto & Windus for two passages from the *Works* of R. L. Stevenson; Messrs. William Heinemann for the passage from Swinburne's *Tale of Balen*, and three stanzas by Sarojini Naidu; Messrs. Kegan Paul Trench Trubner & Co. for an extract from A. G. and E. Warner's translation of Firdausi; Messrs. Longmans for three passages from Richard Jefferies' *Field and Hedgerow*;

Messrs. Dent for a passage from W. H. Hudson's *Hampshire Days*; Messrs. Sampson Low for an extract from Francis Hitchman's *Life* of Sir Richard Burton; Messrs. Abel Heywood & Son for a passage from *Jannock* by Edwin Waugh; and the poet's family and the Oxford University Press for a stanza from Gerard Hopkins' ' Inversnaid.'

Acknowledgments for permission to reprint copyright poems and prose passages are due to : Miss Gwen Clear and Messrs. Longmans Green & Co. for a sonnet from *The Eldest Sister*; the executrix of the late Kuno Meyer and Messrs. Constable & Co. for two translations from *Ancient Irish Poetry*; Messrs. Methuen for three passages from W. H. Hudson's *A Shepherd's Life*; Messrs. Ingpen & Grant for three poems of the late Edward Thomas; Messrs. Macmillan for a passage from Henley's *Views and Reviews*, and two of Ralph Hodgson's poems ; and to the owners of copyright for two extracts from Mrs. Ewing's ' Father Hedgehog and his Neighbours ' (*Brothers of Pity and Other Tales*).

J. S.

CONTENTS

II. THE ROAMING LIFE

CONTENTS

III. FIELD AND SKY

IV. GYPSIES AND GENTILES

V. THE ROMANY CHYE

CONTENTS

PAGE

VI. GYPSY CHILDREN

IX. A GYPSY BESTIARY

b

X. EGIPTE SPECHE

XI. SCHOLAR GYPSIES

XII. ENVOY

I

THE DARK RACE

A

I

The Dark Race

Lords of the Universe

WE are the Lords of the Universe, of fields, fruits, crops, forests, mountains, of the rivers and springs, of the stars and all the elements. Having learned early to suffer, we suffer not at all. We sleep as calmly and easily on the ground as on the softest bed, and our hard skin is an impregnable armour against the assaults of the air. We are insensible to pain ; the cruellest torment does not make us tremble ; and we shrink from no form of the death which we have learned to scorn. When we see fit, we make no difference between *yes* and *no* ; well can we be Martyrs, but Confessors never. We sing loaded with chains and irons, and in the deepest dungeons, but in Gehenna we are ever mute. Our sole livelihood is to take to ourselves the goods of others, and, since to gain our ends we need no betraying witnesses, we busy ourselves from policy in some petty work, and it is by night that we ply our true craft. Fame, honour, and ambition have no power over us ; we are therefore free from that base servitude in which most of the Great are illustrious and unhappy, nay rather, very slaves. But our Palaces are the tents we carry with us, and nothing can be compared to the elegance of these moving houses. For these have such beauty as nature herself displays, and are far above the sumptuous hangings and gilded furniture, which man's silly pride and effeminate weakness have devised. We dwell in these tents, busied in the present, and without overmuch care for the future. We look indifferently upon what may come, and living by our toil, abandon ourselves blindly to our star, and avoid only three things ;—the Church, the Sea, and the King's Court.

Cervantes.

In Praise of Gypsies

THEY are changeless ; the world has no power over them. They live by rote and by faith and by tradition, which is part of their blood. They go about in our midst, untouched by us, but reading our secrets, knowing more about us than we do about ourselves, prophets, diviners, soothsayers. They are our only link with the East, with mystery, with magic. They dance and play for money ; they dance in Spain, they play in Hungary ; they are better dancers than the Spaniards in their national dances, and they play Hungarian music better than the Hungarians. They do few things, but they do these things better than others. They create nothing ; they perpetuate. They make theirs whatever is of use to them, they reject whatever their instinct forbids them to take. They reach their own ends by scheming and are the deftest flatterers on the earth. . . .

Can the world repress this race which is so evasive and slips through its gross fingers like wind ? ' Like one on a secret errand,' they pass through the world. They are the symbols of our aspirations, and we do not know it. They stand for the will for freedom, for friendship with nature, for the open air, for change and sight of many lands. The Gypsy represents nature before civilisation. He is the wanderer whom all of us, who are poets or love the wind, are summed up in. He does what we dream. He is the last romance left in the world. His is the only free race. . . .

The Gypsies are nearer to the animals than any race known to us in Europe. They have the lawlessness, the abandonment, the natural physical grace in form and gesture, of animals. Only a stealthy, wary something in their eyes makes them human. Their speech which is their own, known to them, known to few outside them, keeps them to themselves. Their lilting voices are unacquainted with anything but the essential parts of speech for the open air needs.

Then they are part of the spectacle of the world, which they pass through like a great procession to the sound of passionate and mysterious music. They are here to-day and there to-morrow ; you cannot follow them for all the leafy tracks that they leave for each other on the ground. They are distinguishable from the people of every land which they inhabit. There is something in them finer, stranger, more primitive, something baffling to all who do not understand them through a natural sympathy. The sullen mystery of Gypsy eyes, especially in the women, their way of coiling their hair, of adorning themselves with bright colours and many rings and long earrings are to be found whenever one travels east or west. Yet it is eastward that we must go to find their least touched beauty, their original splendour.

Arthur Symons.

Honestest of the Human Race

TO my thinking he is, in the first place, quite the least of impostors now abroad. He proclaims to you, by his or her, to both convenient, not immodest, not insolent, dress that he belongs to an outcast tribe, yet patient of your rejection—unvindictive—ready always to give you good words and pleasant hopes for half a crown, and sound tinkering of pot or kettle for less money. He wears no big wigs—no white ties ; his kingship is crownless, his shepherding unmitred ; he pins on his rough cloak no astrology of honour. Of your parliamentary machineries, are any a Gipsy's job ?—of your cunningly devised shoddies, any a Gipsy's manufacture ? Not against the Gipsy's blow you iron-clad yourself ;—not by the Gipsy's usury do your children starve. Honestest, harmlessest of the human race —under whose roof *but* a Gipsy's may a wandering Madonna rest in peace ?

John Ruskin.

The Nomades

SCYTHIANS, with Nature not at strife,
Light Arabs of our complex life,
They build no houses, plant no mills
To utilise Time's sliding river,
Content that it flow waste for ever,
If they, like it, may have their wills.

An hour they pitch their shifting tents,
In thoughts, in feelings, and events ;
Beneath the palm-trees, on the grass,
They sing, they dance, make love and chatter,
Vex the grim temples with their clatter,
And make Truth's fount their looking-glass.

James Russell Lowell.

The Cuckoo

'YOU should learn to read, Jasper.'
    'We have not time, brother.'
' Are you not frequently idle ? '
'Never, brother ; when we are not engaged in our traffic, we are engaged in taking our relaxation, so we have not time to learn.'
' You really should make an effort. If you were disposed to learn to read, I would endeavour to assist you. You would be all the better for knowing how to read.'
' In what way, brother ? '
' Why, you could read the Scriptures, and by so doing learn your duty towards your fellow-creatures.'
' We know that already, brother ; the constables and justices have contrived to knock that tolerably into our heads.'
' Yet you frequently break the laws.'
' So, I believe, do now and then those who know how to read, brother.'
' Very true, Jasper ; but you really ought to learn to read, as by so doing you might learn your duty towards yourselves, and your chief duty is to take care of your own souls ; did not the preacher say : " In what is a man profited, provided he gain the whole world ? " '
' We have not much of the world, brother.'
' Very little, indeed, Jasper. Did you not observe how the eyes of the whole congregation were turned towards our pew, when the preacher said : " There are some people who lose their souls, and get nothing in exchange ; who are outcast, despised, and miserable." Now, was not what he said quite applicable to the gypsies ? '

' We are not miserable, brother.'

' Well, then, you ought to be, Jasper. Have you an inch of ground of your own ? Are you of the least use ? Are you not spoken ill of by everybody ? What 's a gypsy ? '

' What 's the bird noising yonder, brother ? '

' The bird ! Oh, that 's the cuckoo tolling ; but what has the cuckoo to do with the matter ? '

' We 'll see, brother ; what 's the cuckoo ? '

' What is it ? you know as much about it as myself, Jasper.'

' Isn't it a kind of roguish, chaffing bird, brother ? '

' I believe it is, Jasper.'

' Nobody knows whence it comes, brother ? '

' I believe not, Jasper.'

' Very poor, brother, not a nest of its own ? '

' So they say, Jasper.'

' With every person's bad word, brother ? '

' Yes, Jasper, every person is mocking it.'

' Tolerably merry, brother ? '

' Yes, tolerably merry, Jasper.'

' Of no use at all, brother ? '

' None whatever, Jasper.'

' You would be glad to get rid of the cuckoos, brother ? '

' Why, not exactly, Jasper ; the cuckoo is a pleasant, funny bird, and its presence and voice give a great charm to the green trees and fields ; no, I can't say I wish exactly to get rid of the cuckoo.'

' Well, brother, what 's a Romany chal ? '

' You must answer that question yourself, Jasper.'

' A roguish, chaffing fellow, a'n't he, brother ? '

' Ay, ay, Jasper.'

' Of no use at all, brother ? '

' Just so, Jasper ; I see——'

' Something very much like a cuckoo, brother ? '

' I see what you are after, Jasper.'

' You would like to get rid of us, wouldn't you ? '

' Why, no, not exactly.'

' We are no ornament to the green lanes in spring and summer time, are we, brother ? and the voice of our chies with their cukkerin and dukkerin don't help to make them pleasant ? '

' I see what you are at, Jasper.'

' You would wish to turn the cuckoos into barn-door fowls, wouldn't you ? '

' Can't say I should, Jasper, whatever some people might wish.'

' And the chals and chies into radical weavers and factory wenches, hey, brother ? '

' Can't say that I should, Jasper. You are certainly a picturesque people, and in many respects an ornament both to town and country; painting and lil-writing too are under great obligations to you. What pretty pictures are made out of your campings and groupings, and what pretty books have been written in which gypsies, or at least creatures intended to represent gypsies, have been the principal figures. I think if we were without you, we should begin to miss you.'

' Just as you would miss the cuckoos, if they were all converted into barn-door fowls. I tell you what, brother, frequently as I have sat under a hedge in spring or summer time and heard the cuckoo, I have thought that we chals and cuckoos are alike in many respects, but especially in character. Everybody speaks ill of us both, and everybody is glad to see both of us again.'

George Borrow.

Wildness and Wet

. . . WHAT would the world be, once bereft
Of wet and of wildness ? Let them be left,
O let them be left, wildness and wet ;
Long live the weeds and the wilderness yet.

Gerard Hopkins.

The Oldest Race on Earth

THE gipsy loves the crescent moon, the evening star, the clatter of the fern-owl, the beetle's hum. He was born on the earth in the tent, and he has lived like a species of human wild animal ever since. Of his own free will he will have nothing to do with rites or litanies ; he may perhaps be married in a place of worship—to make it legal, that is all. At the end, were it not for the law, he would for choice be buried beneath the ' fireplace ' of his children's children. He will not dance to the pipe ecclesiastic, sound it who may—Churchman, Dissenter, priest, or laic. Like the trees, he is simply indifferent. All the great wave of teaching and text and tracts and missions and the produce of the printing-press has made no impression upon his race any more than upon the red deer that roam in the forest behind his camp. The negroes have their fetich, every nation its idols ; the gipsy alone has none—not even a superstitious observance ; they have no idolatry of the Past, neither have they the exalted thought of the Present. It is very strange that it should be so at this the height of our civilisation, and you might go many thousand miles and search from Africa to Australia before you would find another people without a Deity. That can only be seen under an English sky, under English oaks and beeches.

Are they the oldest race on earth ? and have they worn out all the gods ? Have they worn out all the hopes and fears of the human heart in tens of thousands of years, and do they merely live, acquiescent to fate ? For some have thought to trace in the older races an apathy as with the Chinese, a religion of moral maxims and some few joss-house superstitions, which they themselves full well know to be nought, worshipping their ancestors, but with no vital living force, like that which drove Mohammed's bands to zealous fury, like that which sent our own Puritans over the sea in the *Mayflower*. No living faith. So old, so very, very old, older than the Chinese, older than the Copts of Egypt, older than the Aztecs ; back to those dim Sanskrit times that seem like the clouds on the far horizon of human experience, where space and chaos begin to take shape, though but of vapour. So old, they went through civilisation ten thousand years since ; they have worn it all out, even hope in the future ; they merely live acquiescent to fate, like the red deer. The crescent moon, the evening star, the clatter of the fern-owl, the red embers of the wood fire, the pungent smoke blown round about by the occasional puffs of wind, the shadowy trees, the sound of the horses cropping the grass, the night that steals on till the stubbles alone are light among the fields—the gipsy sleeps

in his tent on mother earth ; it is, you see, primeval man
with primeval nature.

Richard Jefferies.

The Youthful Ruskin speaks

BUT, midst the wandering tribe, no reverenced shrine
Attests a knowledge of the Power Divine.
By these alone, of mortals most forlorn,
Are priest and pageant met with only scorn. . . .
' Ye abject tribes, ye nations poor and weak ! '
(Thus might, methinks, the haughty wanderer speak),
' Yours be the life of peace, the servile toil ;
Yours be the wealth, its despicable spoil ;
Stoop to your tyrant's yoke with mildness meet,
Cringe at his throne, and worship at his feet ;
Revere your priesthood's consecrated guilt ;
Bow in the temples that your dreams have built ;
Adore your gods—the visionary plan
Of dotards grey, in mockery of man :—
To me the life hath wildest welcoming,
That fears nor man, nor spirit, priest, nor king.
Be mine no simple home, no humble hearth,—
My dome, the heaven,—my dwelling, all the earth.
No birth can bind me, in a nation's cause,
To fight their battles, or obey their laws.
The priest may speak, and women may grow pale ;
Me he derides not with his ghastly tale ;
Virtue and vice, the names by which the wise
Have governed others, I alike despise.
No love can move me, and no fear can quell,
Nor check my passions, nor control my will.
The soul, whose body fears no change of clime,
Aims at no virtue, trembles at no crime ;
But, free and fearless as its clay, shall own
No other will upon its fiery throne.
When fate commands it, come the mortal strife !
I fear not dying, nor an after life.
Such as it hath been must my spirit be,—
Destroyed, not shackled,—if existent, free.

John Ruskin.

Fantastical Personages

I HAVE a great toleration for all kinds of vagrant, sun-
shiny existence, and must confess I take a pleasure in
observing the ways of gipsies. . . . I like to behold their
clear olive complexions, their romantic black eyes, their
raven locks, their lithe, slender figures, and to hear them, in
low, silver tones, dealing forth magnificent promises, of
honours and estates, of world's worth, and ladies' love.
Their mode of life, too, has something in it very fanciful
and picturesque. They are the free denizens of nature, and
maintain a primitive independence, in spite of law and
gospel, of county gaols and country magistrates. It is
curious to see the obstinate adherence to the wild, unsettled
habits of savage life transmitted from generation to generation, and preserved in the midst of one of the most cultivated, populous, and systematic countries in the world.
They are totally distinct from the busy, thrifty people about
them. They seem to be like the Indians of America, either
above or below the ordinary cares and anxieties of mankind.
Heedless of power, of honours, of wealth ; and indifferent
to the fluctuations of the times, the rise or fall of grain, or
stock, or empires, they seem to laugh at the toiling, fretting
world around them. . . .

In this way they wander from county to county, keeping
about the purlieus of villages, or in plenteous neighbour-
hoods, where there are fat farms and rich country seats.
Their encampments are generally made in some beautiful
spot ; either a green shady nook of a road ; or on the
border of a common, under a sheltering hedge ; or on the
skirts of a fine spreading wood. They are always to be
found lurking about fairs and races, and rustic gatherings,
wherever there is pleasure, and throng, and idleness. They
are the oracles of milkmaids and simple serving girls ; and
sometimes have even the honour of perusing the white
hands of gentlemen's daughters, when rambling about their
fathers' grounds. They are the bane of good housewives
and thrifty farmers, and odious in the eyes of country
justices ; but, like all other vagabond beings, they have
something to commend them to the fancy. They are

among the last traces, in these matter-of-fact days, of the
motley population of former times ; and are whimsically
associated in my mind with fairies and witches, Robin
Goodfellow, Robin Hood, and the other fantastical person-
ages of poetry.   *Washington Irving.*

Children of the Wilderness

NOW, in that part of merry England, at the time of our
story, gipsies were not an unusual sight. In summer
time, these dusky wanderers might be seen encamped upon
the commons, or on the sprawling borders of some quiet
road, beneath a sheltering hedge, with the wild bird, the
mole, the weasel, and the field-mouse for their only neighbours ; or lounging, with furtive grace, among the bustle
of some country fair, plying the hereditary arts of their
race, as tinkers, besom-makers, musicians, beggars, and
fortune-tellers ; or creeping along some lonely rustic way,
in slow nomadic trail, towards another camping-ground.
Gipsies were a familiar sight in that green nook of the
bonny north.   From the great rural plain of the Fylde, on
the west coast of Lancashire, up to the wild hills and beautiful vales of the Scottish border, gipsies were well known.
    . . . And who are these children of the wilderness,
roving ' homeless, ragged, and tanned, under the changeful
sky,' as free as the wild bird that flits at will from bough to
bough ; and despising alike the trammels and the comforts
of settled life ? These tawny, trinketed aliens, clad in
gaudy tatters,—so poor and yet so proud,—found amongst
all peoples of the earth, yet belonging to none—and among
all such changes of climes and nations, clinging with such
tenacity to the habits, and the language, and the superstitions of their forefathers—who are they ? Whence
come these ragged, landless, vagabond lordlings of the
waste,—these wild-eyed dwellers in tents, gliding about the
solitudes of the land, like half-tamed panthers ; and streak-
ing the conventional web of western civilisation with a
weird thread of lurid hue ?   What burning tract of Egypt,
or of Hindostan, was the ancient home of this mysterious
race of restless outlaws ?   *Edwin Waugh.*

Gais Bohémiens

SORCIERS, bateleurs ou filous,
    Reste immonde
    D'un autre monde,
Sorciers, bateleurs, ou filous,
Gais Bohémiens, d'où venez-vous ?

D'où nous venons ? l'on n'en sait rien.
    L'hirondelle
    D'où vous vient-elle ?
D'où nous venons, l'on n'en sait rien ;
Où nous irons, le sait-on bien ?

Sans pays, sans prince et sans lois,
    Notre vie
    Doit faire envie.
Sans pays, sans prince et sans lois,
L'homme est heureux un jour sur trois.

Tous indépendans nous naissons,
    Sans église
    Qui nous baptise,
Tous indépendans nous naissons,
Au bruit du fifre et des chansons.

Nos premiers pas sont dégagés,
    Dans ce monde
    Où l'erreur abonde,
Nos premiers pas sont dégagés
Du vieux maillot des préjugés.

Au peuple en butte à nos larcins,
    Tout grimoire
    En fait accroire ;
Au peuple, en butte à nos larcins,
Il faut des sorciers et des saints.

Trouvons-nous Plutus en chemin,
  Notre bande
  Gaîment demande.
Trouvons-nous Plutus en chemin,
En chantant nous tendons la main.

Pauvres oiseaux que Dieu bénit,
  De la ville
  Qu'on nous exile ;
Pauvres oiseaux que Dieu bénit,
Au fond des bois pend notre nid.

A tâtons l'amour, chaque nuit,
  Nous attèle
  Tous pêle-mêle ;
A tâtons l'amour, chaque nuit,
Nous attèle au char qu'il conduit.

Ton œil ne peut se détacher,
  Philosophe
  De mince étoffe,
Ton œil ne peut se détacher
Du vieux coq de ton vieux clocher.

Voir, c'est avoir.   Allons courir !
  Vie errante
  Est chose enivrante.
Voir, c'est avoir ; allons courir ;
Car tout voir, c'est tout conquérir.

Mais à l'homme on crie en tout lieu,
  Qu'il s'agite,
  Ou croupisse au gîte,
Mais à l'homme on crie en tout lieu :
' Tu nais, bonjour ! tu meurs, adieu ! '

Quand nous mourons, vieux ou bambin,
  Homme ou femme,
  A Dieu soit notre âme !
Quand nous mourons, vieux ou bambin,
On vend le corps au carabin.

Nous n'avons donc, exempts d'orgueil,
De lois vaines,
De lourdes chaînes ;
Nous n'avons donc, exempts d'orgueil,
Ni berceau, ni toit, ni cercueil.

Mais croyez-en notre gaîté,
Noble ou prêtre,
Valet ou maître ;
Mais croyez-en notre gaîté :
Le bonheur, c'est la liberté.

Oui, croyez-en notre gaîté,
Noble ou prêtre,
Valet ou maître,
Oui, croyez-en notre gaîté :
Le bonheur, c'est la liberté.

Béranger.

Arabs of Europe

WHETHER from India's burning plains,
Or wild Bohemia's domains,
Your steps were first directed ;
Or whether ye be Egypt's sons,
Whose stream, like Nile's, for ever runs
With sources undetected :

Arabs of Europe ! Gipsy race !
Your Eastern manners, garb, and face
Appear a strange chimera ;
None, none but you can now be styled
Romantic, picturesque, and wild,
In this prosaic era.

Ye sole freebooters of the wood,
Since Adam Bell and Robin Hood :
Kept everywhere asunder
From other tribes,—King, Church, and State
Spurning, and only dedicate
To freedom, sloth, and plunder ;

Your forest-camp,—the forms one sees
Banditti-like amid the trees,
    The ragged donkeys grazing,
The Sybil's eye prophetic, bright
With flashes of the fitful light
    Beneath the caldron blazing,—

O'er my young mind strange terrors threw :
Thy History gave me, Moore Carew l
    A more exalted notion
Of Gipsy life ; nor can I yet
Gaze on your tents, and quite forget
    My former deep emotion.

For 'auld lang syne ' I 'll not maltreat
Yon pseudo-tinker, though the cheat,
    As sly as thievish Reynard,
Instead of mending kettles, prowls,
To make foul havoc of my fowls,
    And decimate my hen-yard.

Come thou, too, black-eyed lass, and try
That potent skill in palmistry,
    Which sixpences can wheedle ;
Mine is a friendly cottage—here
No snarling mastiff need you fear,
    No Constable or Beadle.

'Tis yours, I know, to draw at will
Upon futurity a bill,
    And Plutus to importune ;—
Discount the bill—take half yourself,
Give me the balance of the pelf,
    And both may laugh at fortune.

Horace Smith.

Where do we come from ?

WHERE we comes from, the dear Lord only knows,
and He 's too high and mighty to tell the likes of us.

Charley Smith, a Gypsy.

The Region of Chal

THE region of Chal was our dear native soil,
  Where in fulness of pleasure we lived without toil;
Till dispersed through all lands, 'twas our fortune
    to be—
Our steeds, Guadiana, must now drink of thee.

Once kings came from far to kneel down at our gate,
And princes rejoic'd on our meanest to wait;
But now who so mean but would scorn our degree—
Our steeds, Guadiana, must now drink of thee.

For the Undebel saw, from his throne in the cloud,
That our deeds they were foolish, our hearts they were
    proud;
And in anger he bade us his presence to flee—
Our steeds, Guadiana, must now drink of thee.

Our horses should drink of no river but one;
It sparkles through Chal, 'neath the smile of the sun;
But they taste of all streams save that only, and see—
Apilyela gras Chai la panee Lucalee.

George Borrow.

How Bahrám Gur brought the Gipsies from India to Persia

THEREAFTER he sent letters to each arch'mage,
  Gave clothing to the mendicants, and asked:—
' In all the realm what folk are free from toil,
And who are mendicants and destitute?
Tell me how things are in the world, and lead
My heart upon the pathway toward the light.'
  An answer came from all the archimages,
From all the nobles, and the men of lore:—

B

'The face of earth appeareth prosperous,
Continuous blessings are in every part,
Save that the poor complain against the ills
Of fortune and the Sháh. " The rich," they say,
" Wear wreaths of roses in their drinking-bouts,
And quaff to minstrelsy, but as for us
They do not reckon us as men at all.
The empty-handed drinketh with no rose
Or harp."   The king of kings should look to it.'
   The Sháh laughed heartily at this report,
And sent a camel-post to king Shangul
To say thus : ' O thou monarch good at need !
Select ten thousand of the Gipsy-tribe,
Both male and female, skilful on the harp,
And send them to me.   I may gain mine end
Through that notorious folk.'
                              Now when the letter
Came to Shangul he raised his head in pride
O'er Saturn's orbit and made choice of Gipsies,
As bidden by the Sháh who, when they came,
Accorded them an audience and gave each
An ox and ass, for he proposed to make
The Gipsies husbandmen, while his officials
Gave them a thousand asses' loads of wheat,
That they might have the ox and ass for work,
Employ the wheat as seed for raising crops,
And should besides make music for the poor,
And render them the service free of cost.
The Gipsies went and ate the wheat and oxen,
Then at a year's end came with pallid cheeks.
The Sháh said : ' Was it not your task to plough,
To sow, and reap ?   Your asses yet remain,
So load them up, prepare your harps, and stretch
The silken chords.'
                              And so the Gipsies now,
According to Bahrám's just ordinance,
Live by their wits ; they have for company
The dog and wolf, and tramp unceasingly.

                                      Firdausi.

The Family of Ham

THERE also we saw a race outside the city, following the Greeks' rite, and asserting themselves to be of the family of Ham. They rarely or never stop in one place beyond thirty days, but always wandering and fugitive, as though accursed by God, after the thirtieth day remove from field to field with their oblong tents, black and low like the Arabs', and from cave to cave.

Symon Simeonis (1322).

A very Odd Sort of Gentry

ONE day there came to Rheims a very odd sort of gentry. They were beggars and truands, strolling about the country, led by their duke and their counts. Their faces were tawny, their hair all curly, and they 'd rings of silver in their ears. The women were still uglier than the men. Their faces were darker, and always uncovered ; they wore a sorry kirtle about their body ; an old piece of linen cloth interwoven with cords bound upon their shoulder ; and their hair hanging like a horse's tail. The children scrambling under their feet would have frightened an ape. An excommunicated gang ! They were all come in a straight line from lower Egypt to Rheims, through Poland. The Pope had confessed them, it was said, and had ordered them by way of penance to wander through the world for seven years together without sleeping in a bed ; and so they called themselves penancers, and stank. It seems they 'd formerly been Saracens, and that 's why they believed in Jupiter, and demanded ten Tours pounds from all archbishops, bishops, and abbots that carried crosier and mitre. It was a bull of the Pope gave them this right. They came to Rheims to tell fortunes in the name of the King of Algiers and the Emperor of Germany. You may suppose that was quite enough for them to be forbidden to enter the town. Then the whole gang encamped of their own accord near the Braine gate, upon that mound where there 's a windmill, close by the old chalkpits. Then none of the folk in Rheims could rest till they 'd been to see them. They looked into your hand and told you mar-

vellous prophecies—they were bold enough to have foretold to Judas himself that he should be pope.   At the same
time there were shocking ſtories told about them—of child-
ſtealing, purse-cutting, and eating of human flesh.   The
wise folks said to the foolish ones, 'Don't go ! ' and then
went themselves by ſtealth.   It was quite the rage.   The
faǿt is that they said things enough to aſtonish a cardinal.

Viǿtor Hugo.

Of Gypsies

GREAT wonder it is not, we are to seek, in the original
of Æthiopians, and natural Negroes, being also at a loss
concerning the original of Gypsies and counterfeit Moors,
observable in many parts of Europe, Asia, and Africa.

Common opinion deriveth them from Egypt, and from
thence they derive themselves, according to their own
account hereof, as Munſter discovered in the letters and
pass which they obtained from Sigismund the Emperour.
That they firſt came out of lesser Egypt, that having de-
feǿted from the Chriſtian rule, and relapsed unto Pagan
rites, some of every family were enjoined this penance to
wander about the world.   Or, as Aventinus delivereth,
they pretend for this vagabond course a judgement of God
upon their forefathers, who refused to entertain the Virgin
Mary and Iesus, when she fled into their country.

Which account notwithſtanding is of little probability :
for the generall ſtream of writers, who enquire into their
originall, insiſt not upon this ; and are so little satisfied in
their descent from Egypt, that they deduce them from
several other nations.   Polydore Virgil accounting them
originally Syrians ; Philippus Bergomas fetcheth them
from Chaldea ; Æneas Sylvius from some part of Tartary ;
Bellonius no further then Wallachia and Bulgaria ;   nor
Aventinus then the confines of Hungaria.

That they are no Egyptians, Bellonius maketh evident :
who met great droves of Gypsies in Egypt, about Gran
Cairo, Mataerea, and the villages on the banks of Nilus,
who notwithſtanding were accounted ſtrangers unto that
nation, and wanderers from foreign parts, even as they are
eſteemed with us.

That they came not out of Egypt is also probable, because their first appearance was in Germany, since the year 1400; nor were they observed before in other parts of Europe, as is deducible from Munster, Genebrard, Crantsius and Ortelius.

But that they first set out not far from Germany, is also probable from their language, which was the Sclavonian tongue; and when they wandred afterward into France, they were commonly called Bohemians, which name is still retained for Gypsies. And therefore when Crantsius delivereth, they first appeared about the Baltick Sea; when Bellonius deriveth them from Bulgaria and Wallachia, and others from about Hungaria, they speak not repugnantly hereto : for the language of those nations was Sclavonian, at least some dialect thereof.

But of what nation soever they were at first, they are now almost of all : associating unto them some of every country where they wander. When they will be lost, or whether at all again, is not without some doubt ; for unsettled nations have out-lasted others of fixed habitations. And though Gypsies have been banished by most Christian Princes, yet have they found some countenance from the great Turk, who suffereth them to live and maintain a publick stews near the Imperial City in Pera, of whom he often maketh a politick advantage, imploying them as spies into other nations, under which title they were banished by Charles the Fift.   *Sir Thomas Browne.*

The Lone People

CITIES have fallen and empires passed away,
    Earth's giant forms waxed hoary with decay,
Since the lone people 'mid our moors and glades
Looked heedless round, as on a world of shades !
By German streams, through England's good green woods,
In Spain's deep vales, by India's ocean floods,
By desert moor, huge cliff, or willow grey,
Still the dark Wanderers meet us on our way ;
Amid glad homes for ever doomed to roam
In lonely woe, themselves without a home !
                    Arthur Penrhyn Stanley.

An Epitaph

IN strenger Wanderschafft bracht ich mein Leben hin,
Zwey Reime lehren dich, wer ich gewesen bin.
Aegypten, Ungern, Schweitz, Beelzebub und Schwaben,
Hat mich genennt, erzeugt, genährt, erwürgt, begraben.

Christian von Hofmannswaldau.

De Ceux qu'on appelait Bohêmes ou Egyptiens

IL y avait alors une petite nation aussi vagabonde, aussi méprisée que les Juifs, et adonnée à une autre espèce de rapine : c'était un ramas de gens inconnus, qu'on nommait Bohêmes en France, et ailleurs Égyptiens, Giptes, ou Gipsis, ou Syriens ; on les a nommés, en Italie, Zingani et Zingari. Ils allaient par troupes d'un bout de l'Europe à l'autre, avec des tambours de basque et des castagnettes ; ils dansaient, chantaient, disaient la bonne fortune, guérissaient les maladies avec des paroles, volaient tout ce qu'ils trouvaient, et conservaient entre eux certaines cérémonies religieuses dont ni eux ni personne ne connaissait l'origine. Cette race a commencé à disparaître de la face de la terre depuis que, dans nos derniers temps, les hommes ont été désinfatués des sortilèges, des talismans, des prédictions et des possessions ; on voit encore quelques restes de ces malheureux, mais rarement : c'était très-vraisemblablement un reste de ces anciens prêtres et des prêtresses d'Isis, mêlés avec ceux de la déesse de Syrie. Ces troupes errantes, aussi méprisées des Romains qu'elles avaient été honorées autrefois, portèrent leurs cérémonies et leurs superstitions mercenaires par tout le monde. Missionaires errants de leur culte, ils couraient de province en province convertir ceux à qui un hasard heureux confirmait les prédictions de ces prophètes, et ceux qui, étant guéris naturellement d'une maladie légère, croyaient être guéris par la vertu miraculeuse de quelques mots et de quelques signes mystérieux. Le portrait que fait Apulée de ces troupes vagabondes de prophètes et de prophétesses est l'image de ce que les hordes errantes appelées Bohêmes ont été si longtemps dans toutes

les parties de l'Europe : leurs castagnettes et leurs tambours de basque sont les cymbales et les crotales des prêtres
isiaques et syriens.   Apulée, qui passa presque toute sa vie
à rechercher les secrets de la religion et de la magie, parle
des prédictions, des talismans, des cérémonies, des danses
et des chants de ces prêtres pèlerins, et spécifie surtout
l'adresse avec laquelle ils volaient dans les maisons et dans
les basses-cours.   *Voltaire.*

A Singular Race

I WAS thus employed in drawing a species of Indictment
against the errors, follies, selfishness and vices of my
fellow-men, while I passed along a pleasant foot-path, which
conducted me from Brick-stables to the carriage-road from
Mortlake to Kew.   On arriving at the stile, I saw a colony
of the people called Gipsies, and gratified at falling in with
them, I seated myself upon it, and hailing the eldest of the
men in terms of civility, he approached me courteously,
and I promised myself from the interview a fund of information relative to the economy of those singular people. . . .
   Policy so singular, manners so different, and passions so
varied have for so many ages characterized the race of
Gipsies, that the incident of meeting with one of their
little camps agreeably awoke me from that reverie on
Matter and its modifications into which I had fallen.   What
can be more strongly marked than the gipsy physiognomy ?
Their lively jet-black eyes—their small features—their
tawny skins—their small bones—and their shrill voices,
bespeak them to be a distinct tribe of the human race, as
different from the English nation as the Chinese, the North
American Indians, or the woolly-head Africans.   They
seem in truth, as distinct in their bodies, and in their instincts from the inhabitants of England and other countries
in which they live, as the spaniel from the greyhound, or as
the cart-horse from the Arabian.   Our instincts, propensities, or fit and necessary habits, seem to lead us like the
ant, to lay up stores ; theirs like the grasshopper to depend
on the daily bounties of nature ;—we with the habits of
the beaver build fixed habitations ; and they, like the deer

range from pasture to pasture ;—we with an instinct all
our own cultivate arts ; they content themselves with
picking up our superfluities ;—we make laws and arrange
governments ; they know no laws but those of personal
convenience, and no government beyond that of muscular
force growing out of the habits of seniority ;—and we
cherish passions of ambition and domination, consequent
on our other arrangements, to which they are utter
strangers. Thus, we indulge our propensities, and they
indulge theirs. Which are the happiest beings might be
made a question. . . .

As I stood conversing with these people I could not help
marvelling that, in the most polished district of the most
civilized of nations, with the grand pagoda of Kew Gardens
in full view on one hand, and the towers of the new Bastile
Palace in view on the other—I should thus have presented
under my eyes a family of eleven persons in no better condition than the Hottentots in their kraals, the Americans
in their wigwams, or the Tartars in their equally rude tents.
. . . I felt that the manners of these Gipsies were assimi-
lated to those of the shepherd tribes of the remotest antiquity, and that in truth I saw before me a family of the
pastoral ages, as described in the Book of Genesis. They
wanted their flocks and herds, but the possession of these
neither accorded with their own policy, nor with that of the
country in which they reside. Four dogs attached to their
tents, and two asses grazing at a short distance, completed
such a grouping as a painter would I have no doubt have
found in the days of Abraham in every part of Western
Asia, and as is now to be found among the same people at
this day in every country in Europe. They exhibit that
state of man in which thousands of years might pass away
without record or improvement ; and whether they are
Egyptians, Arabs, Hindoos, Tartars or a peculiar variety
of our species, whether they exhibit man in the rude state,
which according to Lord Monboddo, most nearly approxi-
mates the Ourang-Outang of the oriental forests, or whether
they are considered in their separated character—they form
an interesting study for the philosopher, the economist, and
the antiquary.

Sir Richard Phillips.

Houseless Birds

I CANNOT, for the life of me, bring myself to despise them, for they seem to me like the houseless birds whom God feedeth, and for whom He cares. They appear more than any other human beings to depend on Him alone for daily bread. They know not, it is true, much of Him : the wisest of us know but little more. They, however, may view Him in his wonders, and love to live amidst his works, and if they less adore, they probably less offend.

Samuel Roberts.

A Divine Purpose

THE poor Gypsies would seem to a humourist to have been created by the Devil, whose name they almost use for God, a living parody and satanic burlesque of all that human faith, hope, or wisdom, have ever accomplished in their highest forms. All over the world this black and God-wanting shadow dances behind the solid Theism of the ' People.' How often have we heard that the preservation of the Jews is a phenomenon without equal ? And yet they both live—the sad and sober Jew, the gay and tipsy Gypsy, Shemite and Arian—the one so ridiculously like and unlike the other, that we may almost wonder whether Humour does not enter into the Divine purpose, and have its place in the destiny of man.

Charles Godfrey Leland.

Mr. Petulengro and the Jew of Fez

SO it came to pass that one day I was scampering over a heath, at some distance from my present home : I was mounted upon the good horse Sidi Habismilk, and the Jew of Fez, swifter than the wind, ran by the side of the good horse, Habismilk, when what should I see at a corner of the heath but the encampment of certain friends of mine ; and the chief of that camp, even Mr. Petulengro, stood before the encampment, and his adopted daughter, Miss Pinfold, stood beside him.

MYSELF. Kosko divvus, Mr. Petulengro! I am glad
to see you : how are you getting on ?

MR. PETULENGRO. How am I getting on ? as well as
I can. What will you have for that nokengro ?

Thereupon I dismounted, and delivering the reins of the
good horse to Miss Pinfold, I took the Jew of Fez, even
Hayim Ben Attar, by the hand, and went up to Mr. Petulengro, exclaiming, 'Sure, ye are two brothers.' Anon the
Gypsy passed his hand over the Jew's face, and ſtared him
in the eyes : then turning to me, he said, 'We are not dui
palor ; this man is no Roman ; I believe him to be a Jew ;
he has the face of one ; besides, if he were a Rom, even
from Jericho, he could rokra a few words in Rommany.'

George Borrow.

Gypsy or Israelite ?

MY father belonged to that rank which is meaneſt and
moſt despised of all the families in the land. . . .

After I had been thus for some considerable time,
another thought came into my mind ; and that was,
whether we were of the *Israelites*, or no ? For finding in
the Scriptures that they were once the peculiar people of
God, thought I, if I were one of this race, my soul muſt
needs be happy. Now again, I found within me a great
longing to be resolved about this queſtion, but could not
tell how I should. At laſt I asked my father of it ; who
told me—No, we were not. Wherefore then I fell in my
spirit as to the hopes of that, and so remained.

John Bunyan.

cA Covey of Gipsies

TOWNSHEAD. Well said, Tom Fool : why thou simple
parish ass, thou, didſt thou never see any gipsies ? These
are a covey of gipsies, and the braveſt new covey that ever
conſtable flew at ; goodly, game gipsies, they are gipsies of
this year, of this moon in my conscience.

CLOD. Oh, they are called the Moon-men, I remember
now.

Ben Jonson.

Moone-Men

A discovery of a strange wilde people, very dangerous to townes and country villages.

A MOONE-MAN signifies in English a mad-man, because the Moone hath greatest domination (above any other Planet) over the bodies of Frantick persons. But these Moone-men (whose Images are now to be carved) are neither absolutely mad, nor yet perfectly in their wits. Their name they borrow from the Moone, because as the Moone is never in one shape two nights together, but wanders up and downe Heaven, like an Anticke, so these changeable-stuffe-companions never tary one day in a place, but are the only base Ronnagats upon earth. And as in the Moone there is a man, that never stirres without a bush of thornes at his backe, so these Moone-men lie under bushes, and are indeed no better then Hedge creepers.

They are a people more scattred then Iewes, and more hated: beggerly in apparell, barbarous in condition, beastly in behaviour: and bloudy if they meete advantage. A man that sees them would sweare they had all the yellow Iawndis, or that they were Tawny Moores bastardes, for no Red oaker man caries a face of more filthy complexion; yet are they not borne so, neither has the Sunne burnt them so, but they are painted so: yet they are not good painters neither, for they do not make faces, but marre faces. By a by-name they are called Gipsies, they call themselves Egiptians, others in mockery call them Moone-men.

If they be Egiptians, sure I am they never descended from the tribes of any of those people that came out of the Land of Egypt: Ptolomy (King of the Egiptians) I warrant never called them his Subiects, no nor Pharao before him. Looke what difference there is betweene a civell cittizen of Dublin and a wilde Irish Kerne, so much difference there is between one of these counterfeit Egiptians and a true English Begger. An English Roague is iust of the same livery.

They are commonly an army about foure-score strong. Yet they never march with all their bagges and baggages together, but (like boot-halers) they forrage up and downe countries, four, five, or six in a company. As the Swizer has his wench and his Cocke with him when he goes to the warres, so these vagabonds have their women, with a number of litle children following at their heeles : which young brood of Beggers, are sometimes carted (like so many greene geese alive to a market) in payres of panieres, or in dossers like fresh fish from Rye that comes on horsebacke (if they be but infants). But if they can ſtradle once, then as well the shee-roagues as the hee-roagues are horſt, seaven or eight upon one iade, ſtrongly pineond, and ſtrangely tyed together.

One Shire alone and no more is sure ſtil at one time to have these Egiptian lice swarming within it, for like flocks of wilde-geese, they will evermore fly one after another : let them be scattred worse then the quarters of a traitor are, after hees hanged, drawne, and quartred, yet they have a tricke, (like water cut with a swoord) to come together inſtantly and easily againe : and this is their pollicy, which way soever the formoſt ranckes lead, they ſticke up small boughes in severall places, to every village where they passe ; which serve as ensignes to waft on the reſt.

Their apparell is od and phantaſticke, tho it be never so full of rents : the men weare scarfes of Callico, or any other base ſtuffe, hanging their bodies, like Morris-dancers, with bels, and other toyes, to intice the country people to flocke about them, and to wounder at their fooleries or rather rancke knaveryes. The women as ridiculously attire themselves, and (like one that plaies the Roague on a ſtage) weare rags, and patched filthy mantles upermoſt, when the under garments are hansome and in fashion.

Thomas Dekker.

cA Vision of Hell

ONE fair evening of warm, sunny summer, I took a ſtroll to the top of one of the mountains of Wales, carrying with me a telescope to assiſt my feeble sight by bringing diſtant objeɗs near, and magnifying small ones. Through the thin, clear air, and the calm and luminous heat, I saw many delightful prospeɗs afar across the Irish

Sea. At length after feasting my eyes on all the pleasant
objects around me, until the sun had reached his goal in the
west, I lay down upon the green grass, reflecting how fair
and enchanting from my own country the countries appeared, whose plains my eyes had glanced over, how
delightful it would be to obtain a full view of them, and
how happy those were who saw the course of the world in
comparison with me. Weariness was the result of all this
toiling with my eyes and my imagination, and in the shadow
of weariness, Mr. Sleep came stealthily to enthrall me, who
with his keys of lead, locked the windows of my eyes, and
all my other senses securely. But it was in vain for him to
endeavour to lock up the soul, which can live and toil in-
dependently of the body, for my spirit escaped out of the
locked body upon the wings of Fancy, and the first thing
which I saw by the side of me was a dancing ring, and a
kind of rabble in green petticoats and red caps dancing
away with the most furious eagerness. I stood for a time
in perplexity whether I should go to them or not, because in
my flurry I feared they were a gang of hungry gipsies, and
that they would do nothing less than slaughter me for their
supper, and swallow me without salt : but after gazing
upon them for some time, I could see that they were better
and handsomer than the swarthy, lying Egyptian race. So
I ventured to approach them, but very softly, like a hen
treading upon hot embers, that I might learn who they
were ; and at length I took the liberty of addressing them
in this guise, with my head and back lowered horizontally :
' Fair assembly, as I perceive that you are gentry from
distant parts, will you deign to take a Bard along with you,
who is desirous of travelling ? ' . . .
    At this moment twenty devils with packs on their
shoulders, like Scotchmen, mounted before the throne of
Despair, and what had they got, on enquiry, but gipsies.
' Ho ! ' said Lucifer, ' how did ye know the fortunes of
others so well, without knowing that your own fortune was
leading ye to this prison.' But the gipsies said not a word
in reply, being confounded at beholding faces here more
ugly than their own. ' Hurl them into our deepest dun-
geon,' said Lucifer to the fiends, ' and don't starve them ;
we have here neither cats nor rush-lights to give them, but

let them have a toad between them, every ten thousand
years, provided they are quiet, and do not deafen us with
their gibberish and clibberty clabber.'

Ellis Wynne.

A Vagabond and Useless Tribe

I SEE a column of slow-rising smoke
   O'ertop the lofty wood that skirts the wild.
A vagabond and useless tribe there eat
Their miserable meal.   A kettle, slung
Between two poles upon a stick transverse,
Receives the morsel—flesh obscene of dog,
Or vermin, or at best of cock purloined
From his accustomed perch.   Hard-faring race !
They pick their fuel out of every hedge,
Which, kindled with dry leaves, just saves unquenched
The spark of life.   The sportive wind blows wide
Their fluttering rags, and shows a tawny skin,
The vellum of the pedigree they claim.
Great skill have they in palmistry, and more
To conjure clean away the gold they touch,
Conveying worthless dross into its place ;
Loud when they beg, dumb only when they steal.
Strange ! that a creature rational, and cast
In human mould, should brutalize by choice
His nature ; and though capable of arts,
By which the world might profit, and himself,
Self-banished from society, prefer
Such squalid sloth to honourable toil !
Yet even these, though feigning sickness oft . . .
Can change their whine into a mirthful note
When safe occasion offers ; and with dance,
And music of the bladder and the bag,
Beguile their woes, and make the woods resound.
Such health and gaiety of heart enjoy
The houseless rovers of the sylvan world ;
And, breathing wholesome air, and wandering much,
Need other physic none to heal the effects
Of loathsome diet, penury, and cold.

William Cowper.

The Black Zigan

FOR the root that 's unclean, hope if you can ;
No washing e'er whitens the black Zigan :
The tree that 's bitter by birth and race,
If in paradise garden to grow you place,
And water it free with nectar and wine,
From streams in paradise meads that shine,
At the end its nature it still declares,
For bitter is all the fruit it bears.
If the egg of the raven of noxious breed
You place 'neath the paradise bird, and feed
The splendid fowl upon its nest,
With immortal figs, the food of the blest,
And give it to drink from Silisbel,
Whilst life in the egg breathes Gabriel,
A raven, a raven, the egg shall bear,
And the fostering bird shall waste its care.

Firdausi.

Catch them who can

GYPSIES have a fine faculty of evasion, catch them who
can in the same place or story twice ! Take them ;
teach them the comforts of civilisation ; confine them in
warm rooms, with thick carpets and down beds ; and they
will fly out of the window—like the bird, described by
Chaucer, out of its golden cage.

William Hazlitt.

Seeking after Gypsies

'TIS no use to go seeking after Gypsies. When you
wants to see them, 'tis impossible to find one of
them ; but when you are thinking of other matters you see
plenty, plenty of them.

George Borrow.

A Gypsy Appointment

Scene : The Gypsy Encampment

Enter DIEGO

DIEGO.   Where are the Gypsies ?

CARDOCHIA.   Gone.

Thomas Middleton.

II
THE ROAMING LIFE

C

II

The Roaming Life

Mens avet vagari

IAM ver egelidos refert tepores,
  Iam caeli furor aequinoctialis
Iucundis Zephyri silescit auris . . .
Iam mens praetrepidans avet vagari,
Iam laeti studio pedes vigescunt.

Catullus.

The Call to Pilgrimage

WHAN that April with his shoures sote
  The droghte of Marche hath perced to the rote,
And bathed every veyne in swich licour,
Of which vertu engendred is the flour ;
Whan Zephirus eek with his swete breeth
Inspired hath in every holt and heeth
The tendre croppes, and the yonge sonne
Hath in the Ram his halfe cours y-ronne,
And smale fowles maken melodye,
That slepen al the night with open yë,
(So priketh hem nature in hir corages) :
Than longen folk to goon on pilgrimages.

Geoffrey Chaucer.

Why in one place tarry we?

COME, come away ! the spring,
  By every bird that can but sing
Or chirp a note, doth now invite
Us forth to taste of his delight,
In field, in grove, on hill, in dale ;
But above all the nightingale,
Who in her sweetness strives t' outdo
The loudness of the hoarse cuckoo.

'Cuckoo,' cries he; 'Jug, jug,' sings she;
From bush to bush, from tree to tree:
Why in one place then tarry we?

Come away! why do we stay?
We have no debt or rent to pay;
No bargains or accounts to make,
Nor land or lease to let or take:
Or if we had, should that remore us
When all the world's our own before us,
And where we pass and make resort,
It is our kingdom and our court?
 'Cuckoo,' cries he; 'Jug, jug,' sings she;
 From bush to bush, from tree to tree:
 Why in one place then tarry we?
         Richard Brome.

The Butterfly Wanderer

WHAT more felicitie can fall to creature
 Than to enjoy delight with libertie,
And to be Lord of all the workes of Nature,
To raine in th' aire from earth to highest skie,
To feed on flowres, and weeds of glorious feature,
To take what ever thing doth please the eie?
Who rests not pleased with such happines,
Well worthie he to taste of wretchednes.
         Edmund Spenser.

Longing to be off

WITH the first spring sunshine comes the old longing
to be off; and soon is seen, issuing from his winter
quarters, a little cavalcade, tilted cart, bag and baggage,
donkey and dogs, 'rom, romni, and tickni chavis,' and the
happy family is once more under weigh for the open
country. With dark restless eye and coarse black hair
fluttered by the fresh breeze, he slouches along, singing
as he goes. . . . No carpet can please him like the soft
green turf, and no curtains compare with the snow-white
blossoming hedgerow thorn. A child of Nature, he loves
to repose on the bare breast of the great mother. As the

smoke of his evening fire goes up to heaven, and the savoury odour of roast 'hotchi-witchi' or of 'canengri' soup salutes his nostrils, he sits in the deepening twilight drinking in with unconscious delight all the sights and sounds which the country affords. With his keen senses alive to every external impression, he feels that

> ' 'Tis sweet to see the evening star appear ;
> 'Tis sweet to listen as the night winds creep
> From leaf to leaf ' ;

he dreamily hears the distant bark of the prowling fox and the melancholy hootings of the wood-owls ; he marks the shriek of the ' night-wandering weasel,' and the rustle of the bushes, as some startled wood-creature plunges into deeper coverts ; or perchance the faint sounds from a sequestered hamlet reach his ears, or the still more remote hum of a great city. Cradled from his infancy in such haunts as these, ' places of nestling green for poets made,' and surely for Gypsies too, no wonder if, after the fitful fever of his town-life, he sleeps well. . . . Gypsies are the Arabs of pastoral England—the Bedouins of our commons and woodlands. . . . They are not the outcasts of society ; they voluntarily hold aloof from its crushing organisation, and refuse to wear the bonds it imposes. The sameness and restraints of civil life ; the routine of business and labour ; ' the dull mechanic pacings to and fro '; the dim skies, confined air, and circumscribed space of towns ; the want of freshness and natural beauty ;—these conditions of existence are for them intolerable.

Henry T. Crofton.

From Sunrise to Sunset

THE Gypsies, too, came out of the East, though no one knew from whence ; and they would not say, nor, if persuaded to speak, could their words be believed.

They were the outlaws of the human race, driven by their own will from place to place, and never staying in one spot after the ashes of their first fire had grown cold. The contemptuous trickery of their thefts, and the ironic sport of the deceit they practised on all they met, bound them to this strange life they loved. Their wanderings took them away from the sunrise into the sunset, as if they were flying from a fate that threatened there.

No sooner did the rays of the rising sun shine on the dew, and fall in little fiery tongues upon their eyelids, than instinct made them strike camp and move away. All day they would journey, until the setting sun made the air to glow like a damp fire, burning the eyes while it chilled the body. The moon, like a disk of copper, hung behind them, and the plain seemed dead. All life had fled from it, and there was nothing but thick brushwood. It lay against the horizon like the back of a huge rhinoceros, or the hide of an elephant asleep. Here, almost touching that monstrous thing, they lit their fire, and the serpent with its cold and slimy coils climbed over their naked legs as they slept.

They stretched themselves to sleep upon low branches that made a hammock for their bodies, while every leaf seemed to have a nightingale's voice. The horizon was bounded by great sheets of water, and the rays of the early sun played and glittered upon these as though they were mirrors in which diamonds were reflected. Climbing down from the boughs, an elder-tree blossom, or a branch of briar or hawthorn, caught their fancy, if it was not the dropped feather of a bird that made a ready plume for a cap. . . .

When night came they sat round their fires, and music sounded in the empty plain. In the very act of passing the bow across the violin-strings a natural inspiration suggested itself, and, without any search for them, there came forth rhythms, cadences, modulations, melodies, and tonal discourses. Their needy camp and patched garments learned in this way all the luxuries of the senses, and soon they moved to the music and ended with a frenzied dance in the forest glades.

Sacheverell Sitwell.

The Nature of the Hawk

IT is the nature of the oak to be still, it is the nature of the hawk to roam with the wind. . . . The swart gipsy, like the hawk, for ever travels on, but, like the hawk, that seems

to have no road, and yet returns to the same trees, so he,
winding in circles of which we civilised people do not
understand the map, comes, in his own times and seasons,
home to the same waste spot, and cooks his savoury *bouillon*
by the same beech. They have camped here for so many
years that it is impossible to trace when they did not ; it
is wild still, like themselves. Nor has their nature changed
any more than the nature of the trees.

Richard Jefferies.

The Gypsy's Home

ALL things journey : sun and moon,
Morning, noon, and afternoon,
Night and all her stars :
'Twixt the east and western bars
Round they journey,
Come and go !
We go with them !
For to roam and ever roam
Is the Zincali's loved home.

George Eliot.

The Charred Earth

IT was a sign and symbol that gypsy fire. Sign and
symbol of the shifting tent, the fresh morning journey
into the blue unknown, the free wild wandering, the heath
with the breeze brisk upon it, whispering bough, bramble-
berried hedgerows, dapple of shadowy leaves on the floor
of the silent lane ; partridge eggs in the furze clump beside
the by-way ; the snare, the stealthy shot, the bivouac ;
fiddle, dance, and song. Alack ! that the blood should chill,
the sap run down, the flame flicker low ; Alack ! that the
rain should hiss on the embers of life's gypsy fire.

Sir James Yoxall.

Man must move about

I SEIZED the opportunity of addressing a few words to
a Kirghiz woman, asking her if she did not weary of this
roving gypsy life of hers.   ' We cannot be so indolent,' she
replied, ' as you mollahs are, and spend the entire day in
one place.   Man must move about ; the sun, the moon, the
stars, the water, animals, birds, fish, all are moving ; only
the dead and the earth lie motionless.'

Armin Vambéry.

Jog on

JOG on, Jog on, the foot-path way,
And merrily hent the stile-a ;
A merry heart goes all the day,
Your sad tires in a mile-a.

William Shakespeare.

The Soul of a Journey

THE soul of a journey is liberty, perfect liberty, to think,
feel, do, just as one pleases.   We go a journey chiefly
to be free of all impediments and of all inconveniences ;   to
leave ourselves behind, much more to get rid of others.   It
is because I want a little breathing-space to muse on indifferent matters, where Contemplation

' May plume her feathers and let grow her wings,
That in the various bustle of resort
Were all too ruffled, and sometimes impair'd '

that I absent myself from the town for a while, without
feeling at a loss the moment I am left by myself.   Instead
of a friend in a postchaise or in a Tilbury, to exchange good
things with, and vary the same stale topics over again, for
once let me have a truce with impertinence.   Give me the
clear blue sky over my head, and the green turf beneath my
feet, a winding road before me, and a three hours' march to
dinner—and then to thinking !   It is hard if I cannot start
some game on these lone heaths.   I laugh, I run, I leap, I
sing for joy.

William Hazlitt.

The Vagabond

GIVE to me the life I love,
  Let the lave go by me,
Give the jolly heaven above
  And the byway nigh me.
Bed in the bush with stars to see,
  Bread I dip in the river—
There 's the life for a man like me,
  There 's the life for ever.

Let the blow fall soon or late,
  Let what will be o'er me ;
Give the face of earth around
  And the road before me.
Wealth I seek not, hope nor love,
  Nor a friend to know me ;
All I seek, the heaven above
  And the road below me.

Or let autumn fall on me
  Where afield I linger,
Silencing the bird on tree,
  Biting the blue finger.
White as meal the frosty field—
  Warm the fireside haven—
Not to autumn will I yield,
  Not to winter even !

Let the blow fall soon or late,
  Let what will be o'er me ;
Give the face of earth around,
  And the road before me.
Wealth I ask not, hope nor love,
  Nor a friend to know me.
All I ask, the heaven above
  And the road below me.

                    Robert Louis Stevenson.

The Colt and the Filly

'THIS is a ripping place,' said Val from under the oak-tree, where they had paused to allow the dog Balthasar to come up.

'Yes,' said Holly, and sighed. 'Of course I want to go everywhere. I wish I were a gipsy.'

'Yes, gipsies are jolly,' replied Val, with a conviction which had just come to him ; 'you 're rather like one, you know.'

Holly's face shone suddenly and deeply, like dark leaves gilded by the sun,

'To go mad-rabbiting everywhere and see everything, and live in the open—oh ! wouldn't it be fun ? '

'Let 's do it,' said Val.

'Oh yes, let 's ! '   *John Galsworthy.*

Gipsy June

OH ! could I walk round the earth
With a heart to share my mirth,
With a look to love me ever,
Thoughtful much, but sullen never,
I could be content to see
June and no variety . . .
With a finer gipsy time,
And a cuckoo in the clime,
Work at morn and mirth at noon,
And sleep beneath the sacred moon.

No offence, nevertheless, as John Buncle would have said, to the ' stationary domesticities.' For fancy takes old habits along with it in new shapes ; domesticity itself can travel ; and I never desired any better heaven, in this world or the next, than the old earth of my acquaintance put in its finest condition, my own nature being improved, of course, along with it. I have often envied the household waggon that one meets with in sequestered lanes—a cottage on wheels—moving whithersoever it pleases, and halting for as long a time as may suit it. So, at least, one fancies.

Leigh Hunt.

Wayfaring Men

IT happens to us, as it happeneth to Wayfaring men; sometimes our way is clean, sometimes foul; sometimes up hill, sometimes down hill; we are seldom at a Certainty. The Wind is not always on our Backs, nor is every one a Friend that we meet with in the Way.

John Bunyan.

Tramping in Wales

THERE were already, even in those days of 1802, numerous inns, erected at reasonable distances from each other, for the accommodation of tourists : and no sort of disgrace attached in Wales, as too generally upon the great roads of England, to the pedestrian style of travelling. Indeed, the majority of those whom I met as fellow-tourists in the quiet little cottage-parlours of the Welsh posting-houses were pedestrian travellers. All the way from Shrewsbury through Llangollen, Llanrwst, Conway, Bangor, then turning to the left at right angles through Carnarvon, and so on to Dolgelly, Tan-y-Bwlch, Harlech, Barmouth, and through the sweet solitudes of Cardiganshire, or turning back sharply towards the English border through the gorgeous wood scenery of Montgomeryshire —everywhere at interesting distances of twelve to sixteen miles, I found the most comfortable inns. . . . No huge Babylonian centres of commerce towered into the clouds on these sweet sylvan routes : no hurricanes of haste, or fever-stricken armies of horses and flying chariots, tormented the echoes of these mountain recesses. And it has often struck me that a world-wearied man, who sought for the peace of monasteries separated from their gloomy captivity—peace and silence such as theirs combined with the large liberty of nature—could not do better than revolve amongst these modest inns in the five northern Welsh counties. . . . This, upon actual experiment, and for week after week, I found the most delightful of lives. Here was the eternal motion of winds and rivers, or of the Wandering Jew liberated from the persecution which compelled him to

move, and turned his breezy freedom into a killing captivity. Happier life I cannot imagine than this vagrancy,
if the weather were but tolerable, through endless succes-
sions of changing beauty, and towards evening a courteous
welcome in a pretty rustic home.

Thomas De Quincey.

Camping on Snowdon

UP a thousand feet, Tom,
Round the lion's head,
Find soft stones to leeward
And make up our bed.
Eat our bread and bacon,
Smoke the pipe of peace,
And, ere we be drowsy,
Give our boots a grease.
Homer's heroes did so,
Why not such as we ?
What are sheets and servants ?
Superfluity.

.   .   .   .

Down, and bathe at day-dawn,
Tramp from lake to lake,
Washing brain and heart clean
Every step we take.

Charles Kingsley.

A Journey by Coach

THE coach was none of your steady-going, yokel
coaches, but a swaggering, rakish, dissipated, London
coach ; up all night, and lying by all day, and leading a
devil of a life. It cared no more for Salisbury than if it had
been a hamlet. It rattled noisily through the best streets,
defied the Cathedral, took the worst corners sharpest, went
cutting in everywhere, making everything get out of its
way ; and spun along the open country-road, blowing a
lively defiance out of its key-bugle, as its last glad parting
legacy.

It was a charming evening. Mild and bright. And even with the weight upon his mind which arose out of the immensity and uncertainty of London, Tom could not resist the captivating sense of rapid motion through the pleasant air. The four grays skimmed along, as if they liked it quite as well as Tom did ; the bugle was in as high spirits as the grays ; the coachman chimed in sometimes with his voice ; the wheels hummed cheerfully in unison ; the brass-work on the harness was an orchestra of little bells ; and thus, as they went clinking, jingling, rattling, smoothly on, the whole concern, from the buckles of the leaders' coupling-reins, to the handle of the hind boot, was one great instrument of music.

Yoho, past hedges, gates, and trees ; past cottages and barns, and people going home from work. Yoho, past donkey-chaises, drawn aside into the ditch, and empty carts with rampant horses, whipped up at a bound upon the little watercourse, and held up by struggling carters close to the five-barred gate, until the coach had passed the narrow turning in the road. Yoho, by churches dropped down by themselves in quiet nooks, with rustic burial-grounds about them, where the graves are green, and daisies sleep— for it is evening—on the bosoms of the dead. Yoho, past streams, in which the cattle cool their feet, and where the rushes grow ; past paddock-fences, farms, and rick-yards ; past last year's stacks, cut, slice by slice, away, and showing, in the waning light, like ruined gables, old and brown. Yoho, down the pebbly dip, and through the merry water-splash, and up at a canter to the level road again. Yoho ! Yoho !

Charles Dickens.

Highway and Packway

O WANDERING Road, stranger and instant friend,—
For Youth a gipsy ever was at heart,—
Highway and packway, path with many a bend
That keeps your mystery a thing of art ;
O pools of friendly water ; little lins ;
O sudden views of country ; wayside inns.

Victoria Sackville-West.

Roads

I LOVE roads :
  The goddesses that dwell
Far along invisible
Are my favourite gods.

Roads go on
While we forget, and are
Forgotten like a star
That shoots and is gone.

On this earth 'tis sure
We men have not made
Anything that doth fade
So soon, so long endure :

The hill road wet with rain
In the sun would not gleam
Like a winging stream
If we trod it not again.

They are lonely
While we sleep, lonelier
For lack of the traveller
Who is now a dream only.

From dawn's twilight
And all the clouds like sheep
On the mountains of sleep
They wind into the night.

The next turn may reveal
Heaven : upon the crest
The close pine clump, at rest
And black, may Hell conceal.

Often footsore, never
Yet of the road I weary,
Though long and steep and dreary,
As it winds on for ever.

Helen of the roads,
The mountain ways of Wales
And the Mabinogion tales,
Is one of the true gods,

Abiding in the trees,
The threes and fours so wise,
The larger companies,
That by the roadside be,

And beneath the rafter
Else uninhabited
Excepting by the dead ;
And it is her laughter

At morn and night I hear
When the thrush cock sings
Bright irrelevant things,
And when the chanticleer

Calls back to their own night
Troops that make loneliness
With their light footsteps' press,
As Helen's own are light.

Now all roads lead to France
And heavy is the tread
Of the living ; but the dead
Returning lightly dance :

Whatever the road bring
To me or take from me,
They keep me company
With their pattering,

Crowding the solitude
Of the loops over the downs,
Hushing the roar of towns
And their brief multitude.

Edward Thomas.

Joys

AND there low lying, as hour on hour
Fled, all his life in all its flower
Came back as in a sunlit shower
Of dreams, when sweet-souled sleep has power
    On life less sweet and glad to be.
He drank the draught of life's first wine
Again : he saw the moorland shine,
The rioting rapids of the Tyne,
    The woods, the cliffs, the sea.

The joy that lives at heart and home,
The joy to rest, the joy to roam,
The joy of crags and scaurs he clomb,
The rapture of the encountering foam
    Embraced and breasted of the boy,
The first good steed his knees bestrode,
The first wild sound of songs that flowed
Through ears that thrilled and heart that glowed,
    Fulfilled his death with joy.
                    Algernon Charles Swinburne.

In the Time of the Barmecides

THROUGH city and desert my mates and I
    Were free to rove and roam,
Our diapered canopy the deep of the sky,
    Or the roof of the palace dome—
O ! ours was that vivid life to and fro
    Which only sloth derides—
Men spent Life so, long, long ago,
    In the time of the Barmecides ;
Men spent Life so, long, long ago,
    In the time of the Barmecides.

I see rich Bagdad once again,
    With its turrets of Moorish mould,
And the Khalif's twice five hundred men,
    Whose binishes flamed with gold ;

I call up many a gorgeous show—
  Which the Pall of Oblivion hides—
All passed like snow, long, long ago,
  With the time of the Barmecides ;
All passed like snow, long, long ago,
  With the time of the Barmecides.

But mine eye is dim, and my beard is grey,
  And I bend with the weight of years—
May I soon go down to the House of Clay
  Where slumber my Youth's compeers !
For with them and the Past, though the thought
    wakes woe,
  My memory ever abides ;
I mourn for the Times gone long ago,
  For the Times of the Barmecides !
I mourn for the Times gone long ago,
  For the Times of the Barmecides !

James Clarence Mangan.

Time, you old Gipsy Man

TIME, you old gipsy man,
  Will you not stay,
Put up your caravan
  Just for one day ?

All things I 'll give you
Will you be my guest,
Bells for your jennet
Of silver the best,
Goldsmiths shall beat you
A great golden ring,
Peacocks shall bow to you,
Little boys sing,
Oh, and sweet girls will
Festoon you with may ;
Time, you old gipsy,
Why hasten away ?

D

Last week in Babylon,
Last night in Rome,
Morning, and in the crush
Under Paul's dome ;
Under Paul's dial
You tighten your rein—
Only a moment,
And off once again ;
Off to some city
Now blind in the womb,
Off to another
Ere that 's in the tomb.

Time, you old gipsy man,
    Will you not stay,
Put up your caravan
    Just for one day ?

Ralph Hodgson.

Wanderers in Romance

THE best part of our lives we are wanderers in
    Romance :
our fathers travel'd Eastward to revel in wonders
of pyramid and pagoda and picturesque attire,
the outlandish reliquaries of nebulous time,
as they dug Mammoths out, and Ichthyosaurian bones
from cliff or frozen scarp ; but now will the Orientals
make westward pilgrimage, like the Magi of old,
and flock to gape at our unsightly novelties,
factories, machines, and scientific tricks—they have seen
the electric light in the West, and come to worship.

Robert Bridges.

Bohémiens en Voyage

LA tribu prophétique aux prunelles ardentes
    Hier s'est mise en route, emportant ses petits
Sur son dos, ou livrant à leurs fiers appétits
Le trésor toujours prêt des mamelles pendantes.

Les hommes vont à pied sous leurs armes luisantes
Le long des chariots où les leurs sont blottis,
Promenant sur le ciel des yeux appesantis
Par le morne regret des chimères absentes.

Du fond de son réduit sablonneux, le grillon,
Les regardant passer, redouble sa chanson ;
Cybèle, qui les aime, augmente ses verdures,

Fait couler le rocher et fleurir le désert
Devant ces voyageurs, pour lesquels est ouvert
L'empire familier des ténèbres futures.
                                        Baudelaire.

Birds of Passage

NOW, in your land, Gypsies reach you, only
    After reaching all lands beside ;
North they go, South they go, trooping or lonely,
And still, as they travel far and wide,
Catch they and keep now a trace here, a trace there,
That puts you in mind of a place here, a place there:
But with us, I believe they rise out of the ground,
And nowhere else, I take it, are found
With the earth-tint yet so freshly embrowned ;
Born, no doubt, like insects which breed on
The very fruit they are meant to feed on.
                                    Robert Browning.

Gypsies of the Steppe

THE Gypsies in their clamorous throng
    Through Bessarabia range and wander ;
Their ragged tents are pitched along
The rise above the streamlet yonder.
How gay, how free, that night-camp lies !
What peaceful dreams beneath the skies !
Amid the waggon-wheels, half-hung
With rug and carpet overslung,
The meal is set, the fire is blazing ;
The horses in the plain are grazing ;
And, rearward of the tent, the bear,
Tame and unfettered, sprawls at ease ;

The steppe is all alive ; and there
The household, busy and at peace,
Labour, against the morning's ray
And the brief march ; the women sing,
The children shout ; the anvil's ring
Sounds, their companion on the way.
But now upon the gypsy camp
A drowsy silence is descending ;
With bay of dogs, and neigh and stamp,
The silence of the steppe is blending ;
And everywhere the fires are slack.
All is at rest ; the lonely moon
Upon the tranquil bivouac
Pours lustre from her highest noon.
An old man sits, alone, awake,
Within, before the coals, to take
The warmth, till the last flicker dies ;
And through the screen the night-fogs make
On the far plain he bends his eyes. . . .
    Then folk flood out tumultuously ;
The tents are struck ; each cart and load
Is trim and ready for the road.
Now all are off at once ! and see,
On the blank plain the moving masses
Throng forth ; in panniers on the asses
The children play ; and, near behind,
Damsels and dames, and old and young,
Brothers and sires, together wind.
—The shouts, the gypsy chorus sung,
The shrieks, the roar of Bruin prowling
With restive chain that clatters loud,
The gaudy rags of motley grain,
Ancients and babes, a naked crowd,
The barking of the dogs and howling,
The chattering pipes, the creaking wain,
—All 's mean and wild, all 's out of gear,
Yet all 's alive,—no rest is here !
Remote the lives *we* spend in vain,
Remote our dead faint joys, that drone
Like a serf's chant in monotone !

                                        Pushkin.

Les Rois de l'Aventure

VOUS dont les rêves sont les miens,
Vers quelle terre plus clémente,
Par la pluie et par la tourmente,
Marchez-vous, doux Bohémiens ?

Hélas ! dans vos froides prunelles
Où donc le rayon de soleil
Qui vous chantera le réveil
Des espérances éternelles ?

Le pas grave, le front courbé,
A travers la grande nature
Allez, ô rois de l'aventure !
Votre diadème est tombé !

Pour vous, jusqu'à la source claire
Que Juillet tarira demain,
Jusqu'à la mousse du chemin,
Tout se montre plein de colère.

On ne voit plus sur les coteaux,
Au milieu des vignes fleuries,
Se dérouler les draperies
Lumineuses de vos manteaux !

L'ennui profond, l'ennui sans bornes,
Vous guide, ô mes frères errants !
Et les cieux les plus transparents
Semblent sur vous devenir mornes.

Quelquefois, par les tendres soirs,
Lorsque la nuit paisible tombe,
Vous voyez sortir de la tombe
Les spectres vains de vos espoirs.

Et la Bohème poétique,
Par qui nous nous émerveillons,
Avec ses radieux haillons
Surgit, vivante et fantastique.

Et, dans un rapide galop,
Vous voyez tournoyer la ronde
Ou peuple noblement immonde
Que nous légua le grand Callot.

Ainsi, dans ma noire tristesse,
Je revois, joyeux et charmants,
Passer tous les enivrements
De qui mon âme fut l'hôtesse :

Les poëmes inachevés,
Les chansons aux rimes hautaines,
Les haltes aux bords des fontaines,
Les chants et les bonheurs rêvés ;

Tout prend une voix et m'invite
A recommencer le chemin,
Tout me paraît tendre la main . . .
Mais la vision passe vite.

Et, par les temps mauvais ou bons,
Je reprends, sans nulle pensée,
Ma route, la tête baissée,
Pareil à mes chers vagabonds !

Albert Glatigny.

Yesterday and Tomorrow

THE Gipsies, whom we met below,
They too have long roam'd to and fro ;
They ramble, leaving, where they pass,
Their fragments on the cumber'd grass.
And often to some kindly place
Chance guides the migratory race,
Where, though long wanderings intervene,
They recognise a former scene.
The dingy tents are pitch'd ; the fires
Give to the wind their wavering spires ;
In dark knots crouch round the wild flame
Their children, as when first they came ;

They see their shackled beasts again
Move, browsing, up the gray-wall'd lane.
Signs are not wanting, which might raise
The ghost in them of former days—
Signs are not wanting, if they would ;
Suggestions to disquietude.
For them, for all, Time's busy touch,
While it mends little, troubles much.
Their joints grow stiffer—but the year
Runs his old round of dubious cheer ;
Chilly they grow—yet winds in March
Still, sharp as ever, freeze and parch ;
They must live still—and yet, God knows,
Crowded and keen the country grows ;
It seems as if, in their decay,
The Law grew stronger every day.
So might they reason, so compare,
Fausta, times past with times that are.
But no !—they rubb'd through yesterday
In their hereditary way,
And they will rub through, if they can,
Tomorrow on the self-same plan,
Till death arrive to supersede,
For them, vicissitude and need.

Matthew Arnold.

Life

DUNNO a heap about the what an' why,
   Can't say 's I ever knowed.
Heaven to me 's a fair blue stretch of sky,
   Earth 's jest a dusty road.

Dunno the names o' things, nor what they are,
   Can't say 's I ever will.
Dunno about God—He 's jest the noddin' star
   Atop the windy hill.

Dunno about Life—it 's jest a tramp alone
   From wakin'-time to doss.
Dunno about Death—it 's jest a quiet stone
   All over-grey wi' moss.

An' why I live, an' why the old world spins,
    Are things I never knowed ;
My mark 's the gypsy fires, the lonely inns,
    An' jest the dusty road.

John Masefield.

Pilgrims

TELL them that they have left their House and Home,
    Are turned Pilgrims, seek a World to come :
That they have met with hardships in the way,
That they do meet with troubles night and day ;
That they have trod on Serpents, fought with Devils,
Have also overcome a many evils.
Yea tell them also of the next, who have
Of love to *Pilgrimage* been stout and brave
Defenders of that way, and how they still
Refuse this World, to do their Father's will.
    Go, tell them also of those dainty things,
That *Pilgrimage* unto the *Pilgrim* brings.
Let them acquainted be, too, how they are
Beloved of their King, under his care ;
What goodly *Mansions* for them he provides,
Tho' they meet with rough Winds, and swelling Tides
How brave a calm they will enjoy at last,
Who to their Lord, and by his ways hold fast.

John Bunyan.

III
FIELD AND SKY

III

Field and Sky

Amiens' Song

UNDER the greenwood tree
  Who loves to lie with me,
And turn his merry note
Unto the sweet bird's throat,
Come hither, come hither, come hither :
  Here shall he see
  No enemy
But winter and rough weather.

Who doth ambition shun,
And loves to lie i' the sun,
Seeking the food he eats,
And pleas'd with what he gets,
Come hither, come hither, come hither :
  Here shall he see
  No enemy
But winter and rough weather.

JAQUES. I 'll give you a verse to this note, that I made
yesterday in despite of my invention. . . . Thus it goes :

If it do come to pass
That any man turn ass,
Leaving his wealth and ease,
A stubborn will to please,
Ducdame, ducdame, ducdame :
  Here shall he see
  Gross fools as he,
An if he will come to me.

AMIENS. What 's that ' *ducdame* ' ?
JAQUES. 'Tis a Greek invocation to call fools into a
circle. I 'll go sleep if I can ; if I cannot, I 'll rail against
all the first-born of Egypt.

Shakespeare.
59

Old Meg

OLD Meg she was a Gipsy ;
  And liv'd upon the Moors :
Her bed it was the brown heath turf,
  And her house was out of doors.

Her apples were swart blackberries,
  Her currants pods o' broom ;
Her wine was dew of the wild white rose,
  Her book a churchyard tomb.

Her Brothers were the craggy hills,
  Her Sisters larchen trees—
Alone with her great family
  She liv'd as she did please.

No breakfast had she many a morn,
  No dinner many a noon,
And, 'stead of supper, she would stare
  Full hard against the Moon.

But every morn, of woodbine fresh
  She made her garlanding,
And every night, the dark glen Yew
  She wove, and she would sing.

And with her fingers old and brown,
  She plaited Mats o' Rushes,
And gave them to the Cottagers
  She met among the Bushes.

Old Meg was brave as Margaret Queen,
  And tall as Amazon ;
An old red blanket cloak she wore,
  A chip hat had she on :
God rest her aged bones somewhere—
  She died full long agone !

John Keats.

A Wayside Halt

I HAVE my eye upon a piece of Kentish road, bordered
on either side by a wood, and having on one hand, between the road-dust and the trees, a skirting patch of grass.
Wild flowers grow in abundance on this spot, and it lies
high and airy, with a distant river stealing steadily away to
the ocean, like a man's life. To gain the milestone here,
which the moss, primroses, violets, bluebells and wild
roses would soon render illegible but for peering travellers
pushing them aside with their sticks, you must come up a
steep hill, come which way you may. So, all the tramps
with carts or caravans—the gipsy-tramp, the show-tramp,
the cheapjack—find it impossible to resist the temptations
of the place ; and all turn the horse loose when they come
to it, and boil the pot. Bless the place, I love the ashes of
the vagabond fires that have scorched its grass !

Charles Dickens.

An Ideal Camping Spot

SOMETIMES, indeed, we used to see a gypsy procession
passing along the common like an eastern caravan, men,
women, and children, donkeys and dogs ; and sometimes
a patch of bare earth, strewed with ashes and surrounded
with scathed turf, on the broad green margin of some cross
road, would give token of a gypsy halt ; but a regular
gypsy encampment has always been so rare an event that I
was equally surprised and delighted to meet with one in the
course of my walks last autumn, particularly as the party
was of the most innocent description, quite free from those
tall, dark, lean, Spanish-looking men, who it must be confessed, with all my predilection for the caste, are rather
startling to meet when alone in an unfrequented path : and
a path more solitary than that into which the beauty of a
bright October morning had tempted me could not well
be imagined.

Branching off from the highroad, a little below our
village, runs a wide green lane, bordered on either side by

a row of young oaks and beeches just within the hedge,
forming an avenue, in which on a summer afternoon you
may see the squirrels disporting from tree to tree, while the
rooks, their fellow denizens, are wheeling in noisy circles
over their heads. The fields sink gently down on each side,
so that, being the bottom of a natural winding valley, and
crossed by many little hills and rivulets, the turf exhibits
even in the dryest summers an emerald verdure. Scarcely
any one passes the end of that lane without wishing to turn
into it ; but the way is in some sort dangerous and difficult
for foot passengers ; because the brooklets which intersect
it are in many instances bridgeless, and in others bestridden
by planks so decayed that it were rashness to pass them ;
and the nature of the ground treacherous and boggy, and in
many places as unstable as water, renders it for carriages
wholly impracticable.

I however who do not dislike a little difficulty where
there is no absolute danger, and who am moreover almost
as familiar with the one only safe track as the heifers who
graze there, sometimes venture along this seldom trodden
path, which terminates at the end of a mile and a half in a
spot of singular beauty. The hills become abrupt and
woody, the cultivated enclosures cease, and the long narrow
valley ends in a little green, bordered on one side by a fine
old park, whose mossy paling, overhung with thorns and
hollies, comes sweeping round it to meet the rich coppices
which clothe the opposite acclivity. Just under the high
and irregular paling, shaded by the birches and sycamores
of the park, is a dark deep pool, whose broken banks
crowned with fern and wreathed with brier and bramble
have an air of wildness and grandeur that might have suited
the pencil of Salvator Rosa.

In this lonely place (for the mansion to which the park
belongs has long been uninhabited) I first saw our gypsies.
They had pitched their tents under one of the oaktrees,
perhaps from a certain dim sense of natural beauty which
those who live with nature in the fields are seldom totally
without ; perhaps because the neighbourhood of the
coppices and of the deserted hall was favourable to the
acquisition of game, and of the little fuel which their hardy
habits required. The party consisted only of four—an old

crone in a tattered red cloak and black bonnet, who was
stooping over a kettle of which the contents were probably
as savoury as that of Meg Merrilies renowned in story ; a
pretty black-eyed girl at work under the trees ; a sun-burnt
urchin of eight or nine collecting sticks and dead leaves to
feed their out-of-door fire, and a slender lad two or three
years older, who lay basking in the sun with a couple of
shabby dogs of the sort called mongrel in all the joy of
idleness, whilst a grave patient donkey stood grazing hard-
by. It was a pretty picture with its soft autumnal sky, its
rich woodiness, its sunshine, its verdure, the light smoke
curling from the fire, and the group disposed around it so
harmless, poor outcasts ! and so happy.

Mary Russell Mitford.

The Dell of Kinnaird

THIS was a little, lean, and fiery man, with the eyes of
a dog and the face of a gipsy, whom I found one
morning encamped with his wife and children and his
grinder's wheel, beside .the burn of Kinnaird. To this
beloved dell I went, at that time, daily ; and daily the knife-
grinder and I (for as long as his tent continued pleasantly
to interrupt my little wilderness) sat on two stones, and
smoked, and plucked grass and talked to the tune of the
brown water. . . . The grinder himself had the fine self-
sufficiency and grave politeness of the hunter and the
savage ; he did me the honours of this dell, which had been
mine but the day before, took me far into the secrets of his
life, and used me (I am proud to remember) as a friend. . . .
You should have heard him speak of what he loved ; of
the tent pitched beside the talking water ; of the stars overhead at night ; of the blest return of morning, the peep of
day over the moors, the awaking birds among the birches ;
how he abhorred the long winter shut in cities ; and with
what delight, at the return of spring, he once more pitched
his camp in the living out-of-doors. But we were a pair
of tramps ; and to you, who are doubtless sedentary and a
consistent first-class passenger in life, he would scarce have
laid himself so open.

Robert Louis Stevenson.

A Romany Idyll

THE whole family camping out with horses, donkeys, and dogs. On the first wakening in the morning.

MOTHER (*speaking to my Father in the tent*). 'Now, man, wake dem boys up, to go and gether some sticks to light de fire, and to see to where dem hosses and donkeys are. I think I heared some men coming up de road, and driving de things out of de field. Now, boy, go and get some water to put in de ole kettle for breakfast.'

THE BOY. '*I dawda!* I must go and do every bit o' thing. Why don't you send dat gal to do something? Her does nothing at all, only sitting down all de blessed time.'

MOTHER. 'I am going to send her to de farmhouse for milk, Dog's Face'—when a brand of fire is flung after him, and he falls over a big piece of wood, and hurts his knee. The girl goes for the milk, and she has a river to go through, when presently a bull is heard a-roaring.

MOTHER. 'Dere now, boy, go and meet your sister. Dere 's de bull a-roaring after her. She will fall down in a faint in de middle of de ribber.'

BOY. 'How can I go to her, when I 've hurt my leg, and am quite lame?'

THE OLD WOMAN. 'Go, man; go, man, and see how dat poor gal is a-coming. Dey do say dat dat is a very bad bull after women.'

Strange men brings the horses and donkeys up to the tents, and begins to scold very much. The little girl comes with the milk, and begins to scold her brother for not going to meet her, when they both have a scuffle over the fire, and very near knocks the tea-kettle down, when the boy hops away upon one leg, and hops upon one of the dog's paws unseen, and the dog runs away barking, and runs himself near one of the donkeys, and the donkey gives him a kick until he is whining in the hedge.

THE OLD WOMAN. 'Dere now, dere now! here 's my poor dog killed.'

Breakfast is over, with a deal of bother and a little laughing and cursing and swearing. They strike the tents.

THE OLD WOMAN. 'Now, children, I 'm off. I 'm

a-going another road to-day, and you will meet me near the town. Be sure and leave a patrin by de side ob de cross-road, if you should be dere before me.' . . .

The old man and the boys pitches the tents, and gets himself ready to go to the town. The old woman comes up, and one of the girls with her, both very tired, and heavy loaded with victuals behind her back, enough to frighten waggons and carts off the road with her humpy back. They intend to stay in this delightful camping-place for a good many days. . . .

To-day is supposed to be a very hot day, and a fair-day in a town about three miles and a half from there. The old woman and one of the daughters goes out as usual. The old man takes a couple of horses to the fair to try and sell. The boys go a-fishing. The day is very bright and hot. The old man soon comes home.

One of the prettiest girls takes a stroll by herself down to a beautiful stream of water, to have herself a wash, and she begins singing to the sound of a waterfall close by her.
· When all of a sudden a very nice-looking young gentleman, who got tired fishing in the morning, and, the day being very hot, took a bit of a loll on his face, his basket on his back, and fishing-rod by his side,—the girl did not see him, nor him her, until he was attracted by some strange sound. When all of an instant he sprang upon his heels, and to his surprise seen a most beautiful creature, with her bare bosom and her long black hair, and beautiful black eyes, white teeth, and a beautiful figure.   He stared with all the eyes he had, and made an advance towards her ; and when she seen him, she stared also at him.   And approaching slowly towards her, and saying, ' From whence comest thou here, my beautiful maid ? ' and staring at her beautiful figure, thinking that she was some angel as dropped down ; when she with a pleasant smile, by showing her ivory teeth and her sparkling eyes : ' Oh ! my father's tents are not very far off ; and seeing the day very warm, I thought to have a little wash.'

GENTLEMAN.   ' Well, indeed ! I have been fishing to-day, and caught a few this morning ; but the day turned

E

out so excessively hot, I was obliged to go into a shade and
have a sleep, but was alarmed at your sweet voice mingling
with the murmuring waters.'

They both steer up to the camp, when now and then as
he is speaking to her on the road going up, a loud and shrill
laugh is heard many times. The same time he does not
show the least sign of vulgarity, by taking any sort of
liberty with her whatever. They arrive at the tents when
one of the little boys says to his daddy, ' Daddy, daddy,
there is a gentleman a-coming up.'

The gentleman sets himself down, and pulls out a big
flask very nigh full of brandy, and tobacco, and offers to the
old man. By this time that young girl goes in her tent and
pulls down the front, and presently out she comes beautifully dressed, which bewitched the young gentleman ; and
he said they were welcome to come there to stop as long as
they had a mind, so as they would not tear the hedges.
He goes and leaves them highly delighted towards home,
and he should pay them another visit.

The camping-ground belonged to the young gentleman's
father, and is situated in a beautiful part of Denbighshire.

One of the girls sees two young ladies coming a little
sideways across the common from a gentleman's house
which is very near, which turns out to be the gentleman's
two sisters.

THE LITTLE GIRL. ' Mammy, mammy, dere is two
ladies a-coming here. Get up.'

The young ladies comes to the tents and smiles ; when
the old woman says to one of them, ' Good-day, me-am ;
it 's a very fine day, me-am ; shall I tell you a few words,
me-am ? ' The old woman takes them on one side, and
tells them something just to please them, now and then a
word of truth, the rest a good lot of lies.

John Roberts, a Gypsy.

Sleep in a Meadow

ON either side of the River was also a Meadow, curiously beautified with Lilies ; and it was green all the
year long. In this Meadow they lay down and slept, for
here they might lie down safely. When they awoke, they

gathered again of the Fruit of the Trees, and drank again
of the Water of the River, and then lay down again to sleep.
Thus they did several days and nights. Then they sang :

> ' Behold ye how these Crystal streams do glide
> (To comfort Pilgrims) by the Highway side ;
> The Meadows green, besides their fragrant smell,
> Yield dainties for them : And he that can tell
> What pleasant Fruit, yea Leaves, these Trees do yield,
> Will soon sell all, that he may buy this Field.'

So when they were disposed to go on (for they were not,
as yet, at their Journey's end) they eat and drank, and
departed.   *John Bunyan.*

The Wide World

GIPSIES, she said, were a different sort : gipsies camped
in gentlemen's parks ; gipsies, horses, fiddles, and the
wide world—that was what she liked. The wide world
she described as a heath, where you looked and never saw
the end of it.   *George Meredith.*

Camping in the Sun

LINES of bluish smoke ascend from among the bracken
of the wild open ground, where a tribe of gipsies have
pitched their camp. Three of the vans are time-stained and
travel-worn, with dull red roofs ; the fourth is brightly
picked out with fresh yellow paint, and stands a marked
object at the side. Orange-red beeches rise beyond them
on the slope ; two hoop-tents, or kibitkas, just large enough
to creep into, are near the fires, where the women are cooking the gipsy's *bouillon*, that savoury stew of all things good :
vegetables, meat, and scraps, and savouries, collected as it
were in the stock-pot from twenty miles round. . . . The
gipsy is a cook. The man with a gold ring in his ear ; the
woman with a silver ring on her finger, coarse black snaky
hair like a horse's mane ; the boy with naked olive feet ;
dark eyes all of them, and an Oriental, sidelong look, and
a strange inflection of tone that turns our common English
words into a foreign language—there they camp in the
fern, in the sun, their Eastern donkeys of Syria scattered

round them, their children rolling about like foals in the grass, a bit out of the distant Orient under our Western oaks.

Richard Jefferies.

' *Here today and there tomorrow* '

BY day I saw his van in the lane,
　Where the moorland rises high,
His little brood watched his ponies move,
As they cropped the grass close by.
Whilst he went hunting, heron-like,
Upstream, from bend to mere,
Sending his mongrel through the sedge
And his whistle carrying clear.

At night I saw his van in the copse
That out of the village lies ;
His fire was on the dewy ground,
His hearth beneath bare skies.
And he amongst his chattering brood
Like a gentle chieftain stood ;
His fingers danced on his fiddle strings,
His laughter filled the wood.

And who tonight can say where he is ?
He has left behind on the green
Two blackened stones and some bluish dust
And a smell of smoke where he 's been.
He is not tied to a house in a street,
And his life is sweet as may be.
He can please himself where he goes to roam
And die where God may decree.

Eifion Wyn.

The Haunted Camp

I CAN just about remember the old times when our old folk spoke hardly any Gaujines.　They were timid folk. You might hear them say :—
　' Who is that, father ? '

' I do not know. Did you see anything ? '

' No. I heard something. And what I heard went like a cow.'

' Go up the road and see what it is.'

' I went just now. I saw and I heard nothing. It is the devil, sure enough.'

' Don't be afraid ! '

' I am afraid.'

' Cheer up ! Wait ! I heard it again. Some one was killed here. Is it he ? '

' In the morning I shall go from here. Such places as these near great woods are not good. Murdering places they look.'

' Ei, dordi ! It is an evil-looking place. It is a true ghost's place, I believe.'

' The night is dark. Every evil thing is upon us. One evil thing makes many other evil things.'

Sylvester Boswell, a Gypsy.

The Idlers

THE gipsies lit their fires by the chalk-pit gate anew,
And the hoppled horses supped in the further dusk and dew ;
The gnats flocked round the smoke like idlers as they were
And through the goss and bushes the owls began to churr.

An ell above the woods the last of sunset glowed
With a dusky gold that filled the pond beside the road ;
The cricketers had done, the leas all silent lay,
And the carrier's clattering wheels went past and died away.

The gipsies lolled and gossiped, and ate their stolen swedes,
Made merry with mouth-organs, worked toys with piths of reeds :
The old wives puffed their pipes, nigh as black as their hair,
And not one of them all seemed to know the name of care.

Edmund Blunden.

Mr. Wordsworth on the Gipsies

YET are they here the same unbroken knot
  Of human Beings, in the self-same spot !
    Men, women, children, yea the frame
    Of the whole spectacle the same !

Only their fire seems bolder, yielding light,
Now deep and red, the colouring of night ;
  That on their Gipsy-faces falls,
  Their bed of straw and blanket-walls.

—Twelve hours, twelve bounteous hours are gone,
    while I
Have been a traveller under open sky,
  Much witnessing of change and cheer,
  Yet as I left I find them here !

The weary Sun betook himself to rest ;—
Then issued Vesper from the fulgent west,
  Outshining like a visible God
  The glorious path in which he trod.

And now, ascending, after one dark hour
And one night's diminution of her power,
  Behold the mighty Moon ! this way
  She looks as if at them—but they

Regard not her :—oh, better wrong and strife
(By nature transient) than this torpid life ;
  Life which the very stars reprove
  As on their silent tasks they move !

Yet, witness all that stirs in heaven or earth !
In scorn I speak not ;—they are what their birth
  And breeding suffer them to be ;
  Wild outcasts of society !
                                William Wordsworth.

Hazlitt on Mr. Wordsworth

MR. WORDSWORTH, who has written a sonnet to the King on the good that he has done in the last fifty years, has made an attack on a set of gipsies for having done nothing in four and twenty hours. ' The stars had gone their rounds, but they had not stirred from their place.' And why should they, if they were comfortable where they were ? We did not expect this turn from Mr. Wordsworth, whom we had considered as the prince of poetical idlers, and patron of the philosophy of indolence, who formerly insisted on our spending our time ' in a wise passiveness.' Mr. W. will excuse us if we are not converts to his recantation of his original doctrine ; for he who changes his opinion loses his authority. We did not look for this Sunday-school philosophy from him. What had he himself been doing in these four and twenty hours ? Had he been admiring a flower, or writing a sonnet ? We hate the doctrine of utility, even in a philosopher, and much more in a poet ; for the only real utility is that which leads to enjoyment, and the end is, in all cases, better than the means. A friend of ours from the North of England proposed to make Stonehenge of some use, by building houses with it. Mr. W.'s quarrel with the gipsies is an improvement on this extravagance, for the gipsies are the only living monuments of the first ages of society. They are an everlasting source of thought and reflection on the advantages and disadvantages of the progress of civilisation : they are a better answer to the cotton manufactories than Mr W. has given in the *Excursion*. ' They are a grotesque ornament to the civil order.' We should be sorry to part with Mr. Wordsworth's poetry, because it amuses and interests us : we should be still sorrier to part with the tents of our old friends, the Bohemian philosophers, because they amuse and interest us more. If any one goes a journey, the principal event in it is his meeting with a party of gipsies. The pleasantest trait in the character of Sir Roger de Coverley is his interview with the gipsy fortune-teller. This is enough.

William Hazlitt.

At Heaven's Gate

THEN down the hill to gipsies' pitch
By where the brook clucks in the ditch.
A gipsy's camp was in the copse,
Three felted tents, with beehive tops,
And round black marks where fires had been,
And one old waggon painted green,
And three ribbed horses wrenching grass,
And three wild boys to watch me pass,
And one old woman by the fire
Hulking a rabbit warm from wire.
I loved to see the horses bait.
I felt I walked at Heaven's gate,
That Heaven's gate was opened wide
Yet still the gipsies camped outside.
The waste souls will prefer the wild,
Long after life is meek and mild.
Perhaps when man has entered in
His perfect city free from sin,
The campers will come past the walls
With old lame horses full of galls,
And waggons hung about with withies,
And burning coke in tinkers' stithies,
And see the golden town, and choose,
And think the wild too good to lose,
And camp outside, as these camped then,
With wonder at the entering men.

John Masefield.

A Shieling in the Wood

I HAVE a shieling in the wood,
None knows it save my God :
An ashtree on the hither side, a hazelbush beyond,
A huge old tree encompasses it.

Two heath-clad doorposts for support,
And a lintel of honeysuckle :
The forest around its narrowness sheds
Its mast upon fat swine.

The size of my shieling tiny, not too tiny,
Many are its familiar paths :
From its gable a sweet strain sings
My lady in her cloak of the ousel's hue.

A hiding mane of green-barked yew-tree
Supports the sky :
Beautiful spot ! the large green of an oak
Fronting the storm.

A tree of apples—great its bounty !
Like a hostel vast :
A pretty bush, thick as a fist, of tiny hazelnuts,
Branching, green.

A choice pure spring and princely water
To drink :
There spring watercresses, yew-berries,
Ivy-bushes of a man's thickness.

Around it tame swine lie down,
Goats, pigs,
Wild swine, grazing deer,
A badger's brood.

A peaceful troop, a heavy host of denizens of the soil,
Atrysting at my house :
To meet them foxes come,
How delightful !

Fairest princes come to my house,
A ready gathering !
Pure water, perennial bushes,
Salmon, trout.

A bush of rowan, black sloes,
Dusky blackthorns,
Plenty of food, acorns, pure berries,
Bare flags.

A clutch of eggs, honey, delicious maſt,
God has sent it :
Sweet apples, red whortle-berries,
Berries of the heath.

Ale with herbs, a dish of ſtrawberries,
Of good taſte and colour,
Haws, berries of the yew,
Sloes, nuts.

A cup with mead of hazelnut, blue-bells,
Quick-growing rushes,
Dun oaklets, manes of briar,
Goodly sweet tangle.

When pleasant summertime spreads its coloured mantle,
Sweet-taſting fragrance !
Pignuts, wild marjoram, green leeks,
Verdant pureness.

The music of the bright redbreaſted men,
A lovely movement !
The ſtrain of the thrush, familiar cuckoos
Above my house.

Swarms of bees and chafers, the little musicians of the world,
A gentle chorus :
Wild geese and ducks, shortly before summer's end,
The music of the dark torrent.

An aᶜtive songſter, a lively wren
From the hazelbough,
Beautiful hooded birds, woodpeckers,
A vaſt multitude !

Fair white birds come, herons, seagulls,
The cuckoo sings in between,—
No mournful music !—dun heathpoults
Out of the russet heath.

Old Irish Song (X Cent.)

Musicians of the Air

THESE I will pass by, but not those little nimble
Musicians of the air, that warble forth their curious
ditties, with which nature hath furnished them to the shame
of art.

As first the Lark, when she means to rejoice, to cheer
herself and those that hear her, she then quits the earth,
and sings as she ascends higher into the air, and having
ended her heavenly employment, grows then mute and
sad, to think she must descend to the dull earth, which she
would not touch, but for necessity.

How do the Blackbird and Thrassel with their melodious
voices bid welcome to the cheerful Spring, and in their
fixed months warble forth such ditties as no art or instrument can reach to !

Nay, the smaller birds also do the like in their particular
seasons, as namely the Leverock, the Titlark, the little
Linnet, and the honest Robin, that loves mankind both
alive and dead.

But the Nightingale, another of my airy creatures,
breathes such sweet loud music out of her little instrumental
throat, that it might make mankind to think miracles are
not ceased.   He that at midnight, when the very labourer
sleeps securely, should hear, as I have very often, the clear
airs, the sweet descants, the natural rising and falling, the
doubling and redoubling of her voice, might well be lifted
above earth, and say, Lord, what music hast thou provided
for the Saints in Heaven, when thou affordest bad men
such music on Earth !

Izaak Walton.

Folk-songs of the Birds

. . . LOV'ST thou in the blithe hour
of April dawns—nay marvelest thou not—to hear
the ravishing music that the small birdës make
in garden or woodland, rapturously heralding
the break of day ; when the first lark on high hath warn'd

the vigilant robin already of the sun's approach,
and he on slender pipe calleth the nesting tribes
to awake and fill and thrill their myriad-warbling throats
praising life's God, untill the blisful revel grow
in wild profusion unfeign'd to such a hymn as man
hath never in temple or grove pour'd to the Lord of
    heav'n?
  Hast thou then thought that all this ravishing music,
that stirreth so thy heart, making thee dream of things
illimitable unsearchable and of heavenly import,
is but a light disturbance of the atoms of air,
whose jostling ripples, gather'd within the ear, are tuned
to resonant scale, and thence by the enthron'd mind
    received
on the spiral stairway of her audience chamber
as heralds of high spiritual significance?
and that without thine ear, sound would hav no report,
Nature hav no music ; nor would ther be for thee
any better melody in the April woods at dawn
than what an old stone-deaf labourer, lying awake
o'night in his comfortless attic, might perchance
be aware of, when the rats run amok in his thatch?
  Now since the thoughtless birds not only act and enjoy
this music, but to their offspring teach it with care,
handing on those small folk-songs from father to son
in such faithful tradition that they are familiar
unchanging to the changeful generations of men—
and year by year, listening to himself the nightingale
as amorous of his art as of his brooding mate
practiseth every phrase of his espousal lay,
and still provoketh envy of the lesser songsters
with the same notes that woke poetic eloquence
alike in Sophocles and the sick heart of Keats—
see then how deeply seated is the urgence whereto
Bach and Mozart obey'd, or those other minstrels
who pioneer'd for us on the marches of heav'n
and paid no heed to wars that swept the world around,
nor in their homes were more troubled by cannon-roar
than late the small birds wer, that nested and carol'd
upon the devastated battlefields of France.

Robert Bridges.

The Nightingale

WHAT bird so sings, yet so does wail ?
O 'tis the ravished nightingale.
' Jug, jug, jug, jug, tereu,' she cries,
And still her woes at midnight rise.
Brave prick-song ! who is 't now we hear ?
None but the lark so shrill and clear ;
Now at heaven's gates she claps her wings,
The morn not waking till she sings.
Hark, hark, with what a pretty throat,
Poor robin redbreast tunes his note ;
Hark how the jolly cuckoos sing,
Cuckoo to welcome in the spring !
Cuckoo to welcome in the spring !

John Lyly.

Surpassing Summertime

THE corncrake, a strenuous bard, discourses,
The lofty virgin waterfall sings
A welcome to the warm pool,
The talk of the rushes is come.

Light swallows dart aloft,
Loud melody encircles the hill,
The soft rich mast buds,
The stuttering quagmire rehearses.

The peat-bog is as the raven's coat,
The loud cuckoo bids welcome,
The speckled fish leaps,
Strong is the bound of the swift warrior.

Man flourishes, the maiden buds
In her fair strong pride.
Perfect each forest from top to ground,
Perfect each great stately plain.

Delightful is the season's splendour,
Rough winter has gone,
White is every fruitful wood,
A joyous peace is summer.

A flock of birds settles
In the midst of meadows,
The green field rustles,
Wherein is a brawling white stream.

May-day, season surpassing !
Splendid is colour then.
Blackbirds sing a full lay,
If there be a slender shaft of day.

The dust-coloured cuckoo calls aloud :
Welcome, splendid summer !
The bitter bad weather is past,
The boughs of the wood are a thicket.

Summer cuts the river down,
The swift herd of horses seeks the pool,
The long hair of the heather is outspread,
The soft white wild-cotton blows.

Panic startles the heart of the deer,
The smooth sea runs apace,
Season when ocean sinks asleep,
Blossom covers the world.

Bees with puny strength carry
A goodly burden, the harvest of blossoms ;
Up the mountain-side kine take with them mud,
The ant makes a rich meal.

The harp of the forest sounds music,
The sail gathers—perfect peace.
Colour has settled on every height,
Haze on the lake of full waters.

A wild longing is on you to race horses,
The ranked host is ranged around :
A bright shaft has been shot into the land,
So that the water-flag is gold beneath it.

A timorous tiny persistent little fellow
Sings at the top of his voice,
The lark sings clear tidings :—
Surpassing May-day of delicate colours !

Old Irish Song (IX Cent.).

The Grasshopper and Cricket

THE poetry of earth is never dead :
  When all the birds are faint with the hot sun,
  And hide in cooling trees, a voice will run
From hedge to hedge about the new-mown mead ;
That is the Grasshopper's—he takes the lead
  In summer luxury—he has never done
  With his delights ; for when tired out with fun
He rests at ease beneath some pleasant weed.
The poetry of earth is ceasing never :
  On a lone winter evening, when the frost
  Has wrought a silence, from the stove there shrills
The Cricket's song, in warmth increasing ever,
  And seems to one in drowsiness half lost
  The Grasshopper's among some grassy hills.

John Keats.

To Autumn

PITCH camp, dark Romany, within our wood ;
  On twig and thorn hang now thy cloak of gold,
With nut and briar trim thy ruby hood,
Look to thy patchwork, that thy quilting hold,
And to thy pillow, that it hath not prick
Nor burr nor awn to mock thy calm at night ;
And to thy lamp, that it hath oil and wick,
Or bid a glow-worm rim thy path with light.

On hawthorn hook hang up thy ruby gown,
Box up thy brooch in walnut pith or cob,
And wrap thy ladyhood in airy down,
And guard thy fruit-hoard from the prying hob.

But charm not thou my ploughman, who would borrow
Romany luck to cut our crop to-morrow.

Gwen Clear.

The Sun has long been set

THE sun has long been set,
  The stars are out by twos and threes,
The little birds are piping yet
  Among the bushes and trees ;
There 's a cuckoo and one or two thrushes
And a far-off wind that rushes,
And a sound of water that gushes,
And the cuckoo's sovereign cry
Fills all the hollow of the sky.
  Who would go ' parading '
In London, ' and masquerading,'
On such a night of June
With that beautiful soft half-moon
And all these innocent blisses ?
On such a night as this is !

William Wordsworth.

The Friendly Stars

DA eu gwedd, baderau Duw gwyn,
  Yn alanastr heb linyn.

Goodly are they to behold, the unstrung and scattered
rosary of Holy God.

Dafydd ab Gwilym.

Sun and Wind and Rain

THE sun went down, and though the distressed birds had cried till they were weary of crying, I did not go away. Something on this occasion kept me, in spite of the gathering gloom and a cold wind which blew over the wide heath. . . . The blue sky, the brown soil beneath, the grass, the trees, the animals, the wind, and rain, and sun, and stars are never strange to me ; for I am in and of and am one with them ; and my flesh and the soil are one, and the heat in my blood and in the sunshine are one, and the winds and tempests and my passions are one. I feel the ' strangeness ' only with regard to my fellow-men, especially in towns, where they exist in conditions un-natural to me but congenial to them ; where they are seen in numbers and in crowds, in streets and houses, and in all places where they gather together ; when I look at them, their pale civilised faces, their clothes, and hear them eagerly talking about things that do not concern me. They are out of my world—the real world. All that they value, and seek and strain after all their lives long, their works and sports and pleasures, are the merest baubles and childish things ; and their ideals are all false, and nothing but by-products, or growths, of the artificial life—little funguses cultivated in heated cellars.

In such moments we sometimes feel a kinship with, and are strangely drawn to, the dead, who were not as these ; the long, long dead, the men who knew not life in towns, and felt no strangeness in sun and wind and rain.

W. H. Hudson.

Night

NIGHT is a dead monotonous period under a roof : but in the open world it passes lightly, with its stars and dews and perfumes, and the hours are marked by changes in the face of Nature. What seems a kind of temporal death to people choked between walls and cur-tains, is only a light and living slumber to the man who sleeps afield. All night long he can hear Nature breathing

F

deeply and freely ; even as she takes her rest, she turns and smiles ; and there is one stirring hour unknown to those who dwell in houses, when a wakeful influence goes abroad over the sleeping hemisphere, and all the outdoor world are on their feet. It is then that the cock first crows, not this time to announce the dawn, but like a cheerful watchman speeding the course of night. Cattle awake on the meadows ; sheep break their fast on dewy hillsides, and change to a new lair among the ferns ; and houseless men, who have lain down with the fowls, open their dim eyes and behold the beauty of the night.

At what inaudible summons, at what gentle touch of Nature, are all these sleepers thus recalled in the same hour to life ? Do the stars rain down an influence, or do we share some thrill of mother earth below our resting bodies ? Even shepherds and old country-folk, who are the deepest read in these arcana, have not a guess as to the means or purpose of this nightly resurrection. Towards two in the morning they declare the thing takes place, and neither know nor inquire further. And at least it is a pleasant incident. We are disturbed in our slumber, only, like the luxurious Montaigne, 'that we may the better and more sensibly relish it.' We have a moment to look up on the stars. And there is a special pleasure for some minds in the reflection that we share the impulse with all outdoor creatures in our neighbourhood, that we have escaped out of the Bastille of civilisation, and are become, for the time being, a mere kindly animal and a sheep of Nature's flock.

Robert Louis Stevenson.

Peace

O'ER all the hill-tops
Is quiet now,
In all the tree-tops
Hearest thou
Hardly a breath ;
The birds are asleep in the trees.
Wait ; soon like these
Thou too shalt rest.

Goethe.

IV

GYPSIES AND GENTILES

IV

Gypsies and Gentiles

Oppression

ONE Law for the Lion and Ox is Oppression.

William Blake.

Gypsy Philosophy

THE house is good for the housedweller.

Romani Saying.

East and West

WHEN the Gentile way of living and the Gypsy way of living come together, it is anything but a good way of living.

George Borrow.

The Law of the Calé

MYSELF. ' What do you mean by the Gypsy law ? '

FIRST GYPSY. 'Wherefore do you ask, brother? You know what is meant by the law of the Calés better even than ourselves.'

MYSELF. ' I know what it is in England and in Hungary, but I can only give a guess as to what it is in Spain.'

BOTH GYPSIES. 'What do you consider it to be in Spain ? '

MYSELF. ' Cheating and choring the Busné on all occasions, and being true to the erráte in life and death.'

At these words both the Gitános sprang simultaneously from their seats, and exclaimed with a boisterous shout :—
' Chachipé.'

George Borrow.

85

The Boy of Calo Blood

MYSELF.   ' How came your mother, being a good Calli, to marry one of a different blood ? '

STRANGER.   ' It was no fault of hers ; there was no remedy.   In her infancy, she loſt her parents, who were executed ; and she was abandoned by all, till my father, taking compassion on her, brought her up and educated her : at laſt he made her his wife, though three times her age.   She, however, remembered her blood, and hated my father, and taught me to hate him likewise, and avoid him. When a boy, I used to ſtroll about the plains, that I might not see my father ; and my father would follow me and beg me to look upon him, and would ask me what I wanted; and I would reply, Father, the only thing I want is to see you dead.'

MYSELF.   ' That was ſtrange language from a child to its parent.'

STRANGER.   ' It was,—but you know the couplet, which says, " I do not wish to be a lord—I am by birth a Gypsy ; —I do not wish to be a gentleman—I am content with being a Caló ! " '   *George Borrow.*

Scorn

THEY roll, clan by clan, kin by kin, on wide orderly
          roads,
Burghers and citizens all, in a ſtately procession,
Driving before them the wealth of their worldly possession,
Cattle, and horses, and pack-mules with sumptuous loads.

In velvet and fur and fat pearls,—rich luſtre and sheen,
Paunches and plenty, and fatuous voices contented
Counting their gain, and their women all jewelled and
          scented
Smiling false smiles with the little sharp word in between.

But those in the by-paths of vagrancy, ſtar-gazers, they,
Ragged and feckless and young, with no thought but their
          singing,
Derisive of gain, and light as the bird in its winging,
Stopping to kiss or to frolic, the simple and gay.

God's fools—the beloved of God who made them and the
    wind,
Gipsies and wastrels of life, the heedless of warning,
Chasing the butterfly now on the breeze of the morning,
Laugh at the passing procession that leaves them behind.

                           Victoria Sackville-West.

The Laws of God and Man

THE laws of God, the laws of man,
   He may keep that will and can ;
Not I : let God and man decree
Laws for themselves and not for me ;
And if my ways are not as theirs
Let them mind their own affairs.
Their deeds I judge and much condemn,
Yet when did I make laws for them ?
Please yourselves, say I, and they
Need only look the other way.
But no, they will not ; they must still
Wrest their neighbour to their will,
And make me dance as they desire
With jail and gallows and hell-fire. . . .

                           A. E. Housman.

Enemies of Nature

INCOMPREHENSION, ignorance, the incapacity of
that almost forgotten virtue of live and let live, are the
far more essential faults and errors of those who call themselves civilised races. From the first entry of the Gypsies
into Europe, the hand of every man has been against them.
Once they were burned and hanged ; now we would
shuffle them off the very earth to which they have the
universal human right. How many Gypsies have said to
me quietly and as a matter of course, that they would die if
they had to live always under a roof. An unnatural desire,
say the magistrates and reformers, as they sit in their un-
wholesome city cages, closed in behind the bars of their
shut windows. But it is they who are living an unnatural

life, desiring only the levelling of a multiform and irresponsible universe. They are the enemies of nature. They are the enemies of the natural man. The desire of the natural man is to go his own way, a friend among friends, without choice among roads, as all roads lead somewhere, and everywhere there is sun and wind. He has no desire to work for the sake of work, an odious modern creed from which only the Gypsy is traditionally and persistently exempt. He turns his back on great cities, once beautiful and human, now filled with smoke, noise, unnatural speed, degraded into the likeness of a vast machine, creating and devastating soulless bodies for useless tasks. To the natural man the freedom of the Gypsy is like a lesson against civilisation ; it shows him that it is still possible to live, do as one likes, thrive, be healthy, and take for one's pattern the instinctive, untamable life of the animals, which all our whips, leashes, and traces have not beaten out of their souls.

Arthur Symons.

Law of the Gentiles

. . . WE therefore, the s'd Justices, willing to keep this lewde company to conform them accordinge to lawe in that case provided, did therefore cause the whole number of them to be apprehended and committed to her Highness gaols in the said countie of Yorke ; whereof so many of them of full age, one hundred and six persons, were arraigned the Tuesdaie being the viii day of May last past, at a quarter Sessions holden at Yorke aforesaid, at which Sessions . . . those offenders were by lawful inquest, though not *per medietatem linguae,* condemned. Whereupon judgement being given that the said offenders should receive pains of death, according to the provisions of the said Statute ; whereupon issued execution, and nine of the most valiant persons having least charge of children, and found by the said inquest to be strangers, aliens born in foreign parts beyond the seas, and none of the Queene Majesty natural born subjects, suffered accordingly. The terror whereof so much appalled the residue of the condemned persons, and their children, which stood to behold the miserable end of their parents, did then cry out so piteously as had been seldom seen or heard, to the great sorrow and grief of all the beholders ; lamentably beseeching reprieves for their parents, then ready to suffer death, alledging that they being sixty infants and young children, which could not help themselves, should perish through the loss of their parents ; wherefore being moved with compassion upon so doleful cry of such infants, we, the foresaid justices, reprieved the residue of their condemned parents, and sent them back to the gaols from whence they came, where they continued till the vii of July last past.

Deed of 1596.

The Notice-Board

HIGH up and facing every one who enters a village there still remains an old notice-board with the following inscription :—' *All persons found wandering abroad, lying, lodging, or being in any barn, outhouse, or in the open air, and not giving a good account of themselves, will be apprehended as rogues and vagabonds, and be either publicly whipt or sent to the house of correction, and afterwards disposed of according to law, by order of the magistrates. Any person who shall apprehend any rogue or vagabond will be entitled to a reward of ten shillings.*' It very often happens that we cannot see the times in which we actually live. A thing must be gone by before you can see it, just as it must be printed before it is read. This little bit of weather-stained board may serve, perhaps, to throw up the present into a picture so that it may be visible. For this inhuman law still holds good, and is not obsolete or a mere relic of barbarism. The whipping, indeed, is abrogated for very shame's sake ; so is the reward to the informer ; but the magistrate and the imprisonment and the offence remain. You must not sleep in the open, either in a barn or a cart-house or in a shed, in the country, or on a door-step in a town, or in a boat on the beach ; and if you have no coin in your pocket you are still more diabolically wicked—you are a vagrom man, and the cold cell is your proper place. . . . Something in this weather-beaten board to be very proud of, is it not ? Something human and comforting and assuring to the mind that we have made so much progress. . . .

In the gathering dusk of the afternoon I saw a mouse rush to a wall—a thick stone wall,—run up it a few inches, and disappear in a chink under some grey lichen. The poor little biter, as the gipsies call the mouse, had a stronghold wherein to shelter himself, and close by there was a corn-rick from which he drew free supplies of food. A few minutes afterwards I was interested in the movements of a pair of wrens that were playing round the great trunk of an elm, flying from one to another of the little twigs standing out from the rough bark. First one said something in wren language, and then the other answered; they were husband and wife, and after a long consultation they flew to the corn-rick and crept into a warm hole under the thatch. So both these, the least of animals and the least of birds, have a resource, and man is the only creature that punishes his fellow for daring to lie down and sleep.

Richard Jefferies.

A Hardship

WHEN one's pitched up one's little tent, made one's little fire before the door, and hung one's kettle by the kettle-iron over it, one doesn't like that an inspector or constable should come and say : What are you doing here ? Take yourself off, you Gypsy dog.

George Borrow.

Move on

BY the ragged hedge and straggling fence,
　　Beneath the broken willow-tree,
I sat, while Gipsies pitched their tents
　　Around, and chaffed in Rommany.

The children, who could hardly walk,
　　Were sent to pick a bit of wood ;
Old Liz, so fierce in all her talk,
　　Spoke as a little infant should.

Ah! when age grows young again—
   And such old age—it 's strange to see ;
And stranger still to think there should
   Be baby-talk in Rommany.

But, as the horses went to graze,
   And as the fire began to burn,
Out of the lane, among the strays,
   Came our Inspector, grim and stern.

' You know that this won't do,' he cried.
   ' Be off, or I shall lock you up ! '
' If you do that,' old Liz replied,
   ' Please lock me in a cookin' shop.'

' Pack and be out of this forthwith !
   You know you have no business here ! '
' No ; we hain't got,' said Samuel Smith,
   ' No business to be Anywhere.'

So wearily they went away,
   Yet soon were camped in t'other lane,
And soon they laughed as wild and gay,
   And soon the kettle boiled again.

And as they settled down below,
   I could but think upon the bliss
'Twould be to many men I know
   To move as lightly ' out of this ' :—

     .   .   .   .   .

Oh, what a blessing it would be
   To hear some angel cry, ' Be gone ! '
Some heavenly Inspector C.,
   Who 'd say, ' Now none of this—Move on ! '

                              Charles Godfrey Leland.

Gentility

'DO you think,' said Alice, as they crossed the orchard, 'that that man is a gentleman?'

'How can I possibly tell? We hardly know him.'

'But what do you think? There is always a certain something about a gentleman that one recognizes by instinct.'

'Is there? I have never observed it.'

'Have you not?' said Alice, surprised, and beginning uneasily to fear that her superior perception of gentility was in some way the effect of her social inferiority to Miss Carew. 'I thought one could always tell.'

'Perhaps so,' said Lydia. 'For my part I have found the same varieties of address in every class. Some people enjoy a native distinction and grace of manner——'

'That is what I mean,' said Alice.

'—but they are seldom ladies and gentlemen; often actors, Gipsies, and Celtic or foreign peasants.'

George Bernard Shaw.

The House-Dweller

YOU passed me by this werry way,
   An' ' *Sarishan?* ' you said to me.
I 've often wondered, since that day,
What sort of person you might be?

Says I, ' Them 's Gypsy words he spoke,
But where could he ha' learnt, and how? '
I don't see much o' Romm'ny folk,
I 'm livin' in a house, sir, now.

I hate this sort o' life, I do !
I 'm Rommany, and want to roam.—
Just fancy ! ' *Sarishan?* ' from *you*,
And only English talk at home !

Edward Henry Palmer.

Dull-Eyed Gorgios

TO those who are deprived of every other advantage, even nature is a *book sealed*. I have made this capital mistake all my life, in imagining that those objects which lay open to all, and excited an interest merely from the *idea* of them, spoke a common language to all ; and that nature was a kind of universal home, where all ages, sexes, classes meet. Not so. The vital air, the sky, the woods, the streams—all these go for nothing, except with a favoured few. The poor are taken up with their bodily wants—the rich with external acquisitions : the one, with the sense of property—the other, of its privation. Both have the same distaste for *sentiment*. The *genteel* are the slaves of appearances—the vulgar, of necessity ; and neither has the smallest regard to true worth, refinement, generosity. All savages are irreclaimable. I can understand the Irish character better than the Scotch. I hate the formal crust of circumstances and the mechanism of society.

William Hazlitt.

Suum Cuique

IN a talk I had with a gipsy a short time ago, he said to me : ' You know what the books say, and we don't. But we know other things that are not in the books, and that 's what we have. It 's ours, our own, and you can't know it.' . . .

W. H. Hudson.

The Roving Line

' I AM glad to see you all,' said I ; ' and particularly you, madam,' said I, making a bow to Mrs. Petulengro ; ' and you also, madam,' taking off my hat to Mrs. Chikno.

' Good day to you, sir,' said Mrs. Petulengro ; ' you look as usual, charmingly, and speak so, too ; you have not forgot your manners.'

' It is not all gold that glitters,' said Mrs. Chikno. ' However, good-morrow to you, young rye.'

' I do not see Tawno,' said I, looking around ; ' where is he ? '

' Where, indeed ! ' said Mrs. Chikno ; ' I don't know ; he who countenances him in the roving line can best answer.'

' He will be here anon,' said Mr. Petulengro ; ' he has merely ridden down a by-road to show a farmer a two-year-old colt ; she heard me give him directions, but she can't be satisfied.'

' I can't, indeed,' said Mrs. Chikno.

' And why not, sister ? '

' Because I place no confidence in your words, brother ; as I said before, you countenances him.'

' Well,' said I, ' I know nothing of your private concerns ; I am come on an errand. Isobel Berners, down in the dell there, requests the pleasure of Mr. and Mrs. Petulengro's company at breakfast. She will be happy also to see you, madam,' said I, addressing Mrs. Chikno.

' Is that young female your wife, young man ? ' said Mrs. Chikno.

' My wife ? ' said I.

' Yes, young man, your wife, your lawful certificated wife.'

' No,' said I, ' she is not my wife.'

' Then I will not visit with her,' said Mrs. Chikno ; ' I countenance nothing in the roving line.'

' What do you mean by the roving line ? ' I demanded.

' What do I mean by the roving line ? Why, by it I mean such conduct as is not tatcheno. When ryes and rawnies lives together in dingles, without being certificated, I calls such behaviour being tolerably deep in the roving line, everything savouring of which I am determined not to sanctify. I have suffered too much by my own certificated husband's outbreaks in that line to afford anything of the kind the slightest shadow of countenance.'

' It is hard that people may not live in dingles together without being suspected of doing wrong,' said I.

' So it is,' said Mrs. Petulengro, interposing ; ' and, to tell you the truth, I am altogether surprised at the illiberality of my sister's remarks. I have often heard say, that is in good company—and I have kept good company in my

time—that suspicion is king's evidence of a narrow and
uncultivated mind ; on which account I am suspicious of
nobody, not even of my own husband, whom some people
would think I have a right to be suspicious of, seeing that
on his account I once refused a lord ; but ask him whether
I am suspicious of him, and whether I seeks to keep him
close tied to my apron-strings ; he will tell you nothing of
the kind ; but that, on the contrary, I always allows him
an agreeable latitude, permitting him to go where he
pleases, and to converse with anyone to whose manner of
speaking he may take a fancy. But I have had the advantage of keeping good company, and therefore . . .'

'Meklis,' said Mrs. Chikno, 'pray drop all that, sister ;
I believe I have kept as good company as yourself ; and
with respect to that offer with which you frequently fatigue
those who keeps company with you, I believe, after all, it
was something in the roving and uncertificated line.'

'In whatever line it was,' said Mrs. Petulengro, 'the
offer was a good one.'

George Borrow.

Tom Jones and His Gypseian Majesty

AT length they arrived at the place whence the lights
and different noises had issued. This Jones perceived
to be no other than a barn, where a great number of men
and women were assembled, and diverting themselves with
much apparent jollity.

Jones no sooner appeared before the great doors of the
barn, which were open, than a masculine and very rough
voice from within demanded, who was there ?—To which
Jones gently answered, a friend ; and immediately asked
the road to Coventry.

'If you are a friend,' cries another of the men in the barn,
'you had better alight till the storm is over' (for indeed it
was now more violent than ever) ; 'you are very welcome
to put up your horse, for there is sufficient room for him
at one end of the barn.'

'You are very obliging,' returned Jones ; 'and I will
accept your offer for a few minutes, whilst the rain con-

tinues; and here are two more who will be glad of the same favour.'

.   .   .   .   .   .

The people then assembled in this barn were no other than a company of Egyptians, or, as they are vulgarly called, Gypsies, and they were now celebrating the wedding of one of their society.

It is impossible to conceive a happier set of people than appeared to be here met together. The utmost mirth indeed showed itself in every countenance; nor was their ball totally void of all order and decorum. Perhaps it had more than a country assembly is sometimes conducted with : for these people are subject to a formal government and laws of their own, and all pay obedience to one great magistrate, whom they call their king.

Greater plenty likewise was nowhere to be seen, than what flourished in this barn. Here was indeed no nicety nor elegance, nor did the keen appetite of the guests require any. Here was good store of bacon, fowls, and mutton, to which every one present provided better sauce himself, than the best and dearest French cook can prepare.

Aeneas is not described under more consternation in the temple of Juno,

' Dum stupet obtutuque haeret defixus in uno,'

than was our hero at what he saw in this barn. While he was looking everywhere round him with astonishment, a venerable person approached him with many friendly salutations, rather of too hearty a kind to be called courtly. This was no other than the king of the Gypsies himself. He was very little distinguished in dress from his subjects, nor had he any regalia of majesty to support his dignity; and yet there seemed (as Mr. Jones said) to be somewhat in his air which denoted authority, and inspired the beholders with an idea of awe and respect; though all this was perhaps imaginary in Jones; and the truth may be, that such ideas are incident to power, and almost inseparable from it.

There was somewhat in the open countenance and courteous behaviour of Jones, which, being accompanied with much comeliness of person, greatly recommended him at first sight to every beholder. These were perhaps a little heightened in the present instance, but that profound respect which he paid to the king of the Gypsies, the moment he was acquainted with his dignity, and which was the sweeter to his Gypseian majesty, as he was not used to receive such homage from any but his own subjects.

The king ordered a table to be spread with the choicest of their provisions for his accommodation ; and having placed himself at his right hand, his majesty began to discourse with our hero in the following manner :

' Me doubt not, Sir, but you have often seen some of my people, who are what you call de parties detache : for dey go about every where ; but me fancy you imagine not we be so considerable body as we be ; and may be you will be surprise more, when you hear de Gypsy be as orderly and well govern people as any upon face of de earth.'

Henry Fielding.

La Roulotte

LES beaux spectacles de misère
Roulant carosse à prix réduits
Par les champs baignés de lumière
Et la splendeur des belles nuits !

Là-bas, superbe et théorique,
Apparaît la troupe, estompant
Une silhouette héroïque
Sous l'auréole du couchant—

A la roulotte, hésitante, ivre
De soleil, aux profils hautains
Le ciel met des reflets de cuivre
Et le mirage des lointains.

Ils vont, errant à l'aventure
La tête haute et les yeux clairs,
Libres amants de la Nature
Qui, jamais, n'asservit leurs chairs.

G

Ils vont, lentement, vers l'espace
Dans leur rêve de liberté
Sans qu'un but illusoire trace
Une limite à leur fierté.

Sans un repli que les feuillages
Ornent de festons capricieux
Et de tentures à ramages
Sous le lampadaire des cieux.

Ils s'arrêtent vivante fresque,
Ajoutant aux graves décors
La note de leur pittoresque
Et la noblesse de leurs corps.

Car nulle facile contrainte
N'abaissa leurs fronts orgueilleux
Et leur cœur ignore la crainte
Et la servilité des gueux.

Dans leurs larges prunelles claires
Resplendit l'éternel mépris
Que les libertés séculaires,
Dès le berceau, leur ont appris.

Ils ont l'âpre et morne conscience
D'être les monarques errants
Des grands chemins où leur patience
Cherche à reconquérir leurs rangs !

Ils savent qu'ils sont craints, qu'on veille
Sur leur passage et que parmi
Les gens en qui la peur s'éveille,
Ils sont l'éternel ennemi.

Mais, ils passent fiers et superbes
Dans leur misère et leur beauté,
Foulant du pied les hautes herbes
Allant toujours vers la clarté !

Henri S. Simoni.

The Philanthropist

AGAIN, the country was enclosed, a wide
   And sandy road has banks on either side ;
Where, lo ! a hollow on the left appear'd,
And there a Gypsy-tribe their tent had rear'd ;
'Twas open spread, to catch the morning sun,
And they had now their early meal begun,
When two brown boys just left their grassy seat,
The early Trav'ller with their prayers to greet :
While yet Orlando held his pence in hand,
He saw their sister on her duty stand ;
Some twelve years old, demure, affected, sly,
Prepared the force of early powers to try ;
Sudden a look of languor he descries,
And well-feign'd apprehension in her eyes ;
Train'd but yet savage, in her speaking face
He mark'd the features of her vagrant race ;
When a light laugh and roguish leer express'd
The vice implanted in her youthful breast :
Forth from the tent her elder brother came,
Who seem'd offended, yet forbore to blame
The young designer, but could only trace
The looks of pity in the Trav'ller's face. . . .

But this Orlando felt not ; ' Rogues,' said he,
' Doubtless they are, but merry rogues they be ;
' They wander round the land, and be it true,
' They break the laws—then let the laws pursue
' The wanton idlers ; for the life they live,
' Acquit I cannot, but I can forgive.'
This said, a portion from his purse was thrown,
And every heart seem'd happy like his own.

George Crabbe.

The Three Gypsies

I SAW three gypsy men, one day,
   Camped in a field together,
As my wagon went its weary way,
   All over the sand and heather.

And one of the three whom I saw there
Had his fiddle just before him,
And played for himself a stormy air,
While the evening-red shone o'er him.

And the second puffed his pipe again
Serenely and undaunted,
As if he at least of earthly men
Had all the luck that he wanted.

In sleep and comfort the last was laid,
In a tree his cymbal lying,
Over its strings the breezes played,
O'er his heart a dream went flying.

Ragged enough were all the three,
Their garments in holes and tatters ;
But they seemed to defy right sturdily
The world and all worldly matters.

Thrice to the soul they seemed to say,
When earthly trouble tries it,
How to fiddle, sleep it, and smoke it away,
And so in three ways despise it.

And ever anon I look around,
As my wagon onward presses,
At the gypsy faces darkly browned,
And the long black flying tresses.

Lenau.

The Gypsies leave Ellangowan

IT was in a hollow way, near the top of a steep ascent,
upon the verge of the Ellangowan estate, that Mr.
Bertram met the gipsy procession.   Four or five men
formed the advanced guard, wrapped in long, loose great-
coats that hid their tall slender figures, as the large slouched
hats, drawn over their brows, concealed their wild features,
dark eyes, and swarthy faces.   Two of them carried long
fowling-pieces, one wore a broadsword without a sheath,

and all had the Highland dirk, though they did not wear
that weapon openly or oﬅentatiously. Behind them followed the train of laden asses, and small carts, or *tumblers*,
as they were called in that country, on which were laid the
decrepit and the helpless, the aged and infant part of the
exiled community. The women in their red cloaks and
ﬅraw hats, the elder children with bare heads and bare feet,
and almoﬅ naked bodies, had the immediate care of the
little caravan. The road was narrow, running between
two broken banks of sand, and Mr. Bertram's servant rode
forward, smacking his whip with an air of authority, and
motioning to the drivers to allow free passage to their
betters. His signal was unattended to. He then called
to the men who lounged idly on before, ' Stand to your
beaﬅs' heads, and make room for the Laird to pass.'
    ' He shall have his share of the road,' answered a male
gipsy from under his slouched and large brimmed hat,
and without raising his face, ' and he shall have nae mair ;
the highway is as free to our cuddies as to his gelding.'
    The tone of the man being sulky, and even menacing,
Mr. Bertram thought it beﬅ to put his dignity in his pocket,
and pass by the procession quietly, on such space as they
chose to leave for his accommodation, which was narrow
enough. To cover with an appearance of indifference his
feeling of the want of respeﬅ with which he was treated,
he addressed one of the men, as he passed without any
show of greeting, salute, or recognition, ' Giles Baillie,'
he said, ' have you heard that your son Gabriel is well ? '
(The queﬅion respeﬅed the young man who had been
pressed.)
    ' If I had heard otherwise,' said the old man, looking up
with a ﬅern and menacing countenance, ' you should have
heard of it too.' And he plodded on his way, tarrying no
farther queﬅions. When the Laird had pressed on with
difficulty among a crowd of familiar faces, which had on
all former occasions marked his approach with the reverence due to that of a superior being, but in which he now
only read hatred or contempt, and had got clear of the
throng, he could not help turning his horse, and looking
back to mark the progress of their march. The group
would have been an excellent subjeﬅ for the pencil of

Callot. The van had already reached a small and stunted thicket, which was at the bottom of the hill, and which gradually hid the line of march until the last stragglers disappeared.

Sir Walter Scott.

Freedom

THIS unconquerable love of freedom, and of the country, is not felt in the same degree by any other people on the face of the globe, as it is by the Gypsies, universally, and has been so, through all the ages since they were first known. It seems inseparable from their nature and must have been impressed upon it, for some good purpose, by the Almighty power.

Samuel Roberts.

The Bohemian

'WHAT countryman, then, are you?' demanded Quentin.

'I am of no country,' answered the guide.

'How! of no country,' repeated the Scot.

'No,' answered the Bohemian, 'of none. I am a Zingaro, a Bohemian, an Egyptian, or whatever the Europeans, in their different languages, may choose to call our people; but I have no country.'

'Are you a Christian?' asked the Scotchman.

The Bohemian shook his head.

'Dog,' said Quentin (for there was little toleration in the spirit of Catholicism in those days), 'dost thou worship Mahoun?'

'No,' was the indifferent and concise answer of the guide, who neither seemed offended nor surprised at the young man's violence of manner.

'Are you a Pagan, then, or what are you?'

'I have no religion,' answered the Bohemian.

Durward started back; for though he had heard of Saracens and Idolaters, it had never entered into his idea or belief, that any body of men could exist who practised no

mode of worship whatever. He recovered from his
astonishment, to ask his guide where he usually dwelt.
' Wherever I chance to be for the time,' replied the
Bohemian. ' I have no home.'
' How do you guard your property ? '
' Excepting the clothes which I wear, and the horse I
ride on, I have no property.'
' Yet you dress gaily, and ride gallantly,' said Durward.
' What are your means of subsistence ? '
' I eat when I am hungry, drink when I am thirsty, and
have no other means of subsistence than chance throws in
my way,' replied the vagabond.
' Under whose laws do you live ? '
' I acknowledge obedience to none, but as it suits my
pleasure or my necessities,' said the Bohemian.
' Who is your leader, and commands you ? '
' The father of our tribe—if I choose to obey him,' said
the guide—' otherwise I have no commander.'
' You are then,' said the wondering querist, ' destitute of
all that other men are combined by—you have no law, no
leader, no settled means of subsistence, no house or home.
You have, may Heaven compassionate you, no country—
and, may Heaven enlighten and forgive you, you have no
God ! What is it that remains to you, deprived of government, domestic happiness, and religion ? '
' I have liberty,' said the Bohemian—' I crouch to no
one—obey no one—respect no one. I go where I will—
live as I can—and die when my day comes.'
' But you are subject to instant execution, at the pleasure
of the Judge ? '
' Be it so,' returned the Bohemian ; ' I can but die so
much the sooner.'
' And to imprisonment also,' said the Scot ; ' and where,
then, is your boasted freedom ? '
' In my thoughts,' said the Bohemian, ' which no chains
can bind ; while yours, even while your limbs are free,
remain fettered by your laws and your superstitions, your
dreams of local attachment, and your fantastic visions of
civil policy. Such as I are free in spirit when our limbs
are chained—you are imprisoned in mind, even when
your limbs are most at freedom.'

'Yet the freedom of your thoughts,' said the Scot,
'relieves not the pressure of the gyves on your limbs.'

'For a brief time that may be endured,' answered the
vagrant; 'and if within that period I cannot extricate
myself, and fail of relief from my comrades, I can always
die, and death is the most perfect freedom of all.'

Sir Walter Scott.

The Lasso of Civilisation

IF a man, and an Englishman, be not born of his mother
with a Chiffney-bit in his mouth, there comes to him a
time for loathing the wearisome ways of society—a time for
not liking tame people—a time for not sitting in pews—a
time for impugning the foregone opinions of men, and
haughtily dividing truth from falsehood—a time, in short,
for questioning, scoffing, and railing. . . . It is from nine-
teen to two- or three-and-twenty, perhaps, that this war of
the man against men is like to be waged most sullenly.
You are yet in this smiling England, but you find yourself
bending your way to the dark sides of her mountains—
climbing the dizzy crags—exulting in the fellowship of
mists and clouds, and watching the storms how they gather,
or proving the mettle of your mare upon the broad and
dreary downs because that you feel congenially with the
yet unparcelled earth. A little while you are free and un-
labelled, like the ground that you compass; but Civilisation is watching to throw her lasso; you will be surely
enclosed, and sooner or later brought down to a state of
mere usefulness—your grey hills will be curiously sliced
into acres, and roods and perches, and you, for all you sit
so wilful in your saddle will be caught—you will be taken
up from travel, as a colt from grass, to be trained, and tried,
and matched, and run. This in time; but first come
Continental tours, and the moody longing for Eastern
travel : the downs and the moors of England can hold you
no longer; with larger stride you burst away from these
slips and patches of free land—you thread your path
through the crowds of Europe, and at last on the banks of
Jordan, you joyfully know that you are upon the very

frontier of all accustomed respectabilities.   There, on the other side of the river (you can swim it with one arm), there reigns the people that will be like to put you to death for *not* being a vagrant, for *not* being a robber, for *not* being armed and houseless.

A. W. Kinglake.

A Wild Man in a Tame Land

ON the very next day I was out on the down with a gipsy, and we got talking about wild animals.   He was a middle-aged man and a very perfect specimen of his race—not one of the blue-eyed and red or light-haired bastard gipsies, but dark as a Red Indian, with eyes like a hawk, and altogether a hawk-like being, lean, wiry, alert, a perfectly wild man in a tame, civilized land.   The lean, mouse-coloured lurcher that followed at his heels was perfect, too, in his way—man and dog appeared made for one another.   When this man spoke of his life, spent in roaming about the country, of his very perfect health, and of his hatred of houses, the very atmosphere of any indoor place producing a suffocating and sickening effect on him, I envied him as I envy birds their wings and as I can never envy men who live in mansions !   His was the real life, and it seemed to me that there was no other worth living.

W. H. Hudson.

Peter Bell

THOUGH Nature could not touch his heart
   By lovely forms, and silent weather,
And tender sounds, yet you might see
At once, that Peter Bell and she
Had often been together.

A savage wildness round him hung
As of a dweller out of doors ;
In his whole figure and his mien
A savage character was seen
Of mountains and of dreary moors. . . .

His face was keen as is the wind
That cuts along the hawthorn-fence ;—
Of courage you saw little there,
But, in its stead, a medley air
Of cunning and of impudence.

He had a dark and sidelong walk,
And long and slouching was his gait ;
Beneath his looks so bare and bold,
You might perceive, his spirit cold
Was playing with some inward bait.

His forehead wrinkled was and furred ;
A work, one half of which was done
By thinking of his ' *whens* ' and ' *hows* ' ;
And half, by knitting of his brows
Beneath the glaring sun.

There was a hardness in his cheek,
There was a hardness in his eye,
As if the man had fixed his face,
In many a solitary place,
Against the wind and open sky !

William Wordsworth.

A Gypsy Fiddler

THE sun was shining, the sky was blue, the air was sweet with the fragrance of the fresh-turned earth, but men and women were too busy at their endless labours to know or care. The mountains of Fogaras were still shadowy on the horizon, when, by the roadside, in the middle of the plain, we came upon an old Gypsy in the white shirt and trousers of the Wallach, sitting in the grass, playing on his violin. There was no one near : he was playing to the sun and to the birds and to himself. When he heard us, he stood up and went on fiddling in the dusty road, his eyes dancing, his feet keeping time. We stopped to listen to his poor crazy tune, expecting every minute that he would beg. But presently he pulled off his hat, made a low bow, turned, and walked away with the graceful swing

of the race, an erect white figure in the white road, fiddling
as he went. A wagon passed us, and the peasants in it
overtaking him, made him jump in at their side. When we
rode on again, he was sitting by the driver still fiddling, the
only man, in all that broad plain dotted with its Millet-like
toilers, who was idle and heedless of to-day and the
morrow !

Elizabeth Robins Pennell.

Lawless Music

IN art as in life Gypsies recognize no dogma, law, rule or
discipline. Everything is good, everything permissible
so long as it pleases them. They shy at no audacity in music
so long as it corresponds to their own bold instinct, and
reflects a true image of their inmost being. Art is for them
no science to be learned, no business run for a profit, no
trick of skill to be acquired like jugglery, no feat of witchcraft that requires only a formula. Art is to them an
inspired language, a mystic song only to be understood by
the initiated ; they embrace it solely from the need of com-
municating their innermost feelings ; and in their compositions they allow themselves to be influenced by no
external considerations whatever. They discovered their
music, and discovered it for their own delight, to enable
their soul to talk and sing to itself, in deep thrilling mono-
logues of self-revelation. Wherefore then admit law and
restraints in this province, which they would tolerate
nowhere else ?

   .   .   .   .   .   .

The chief characteristic of this music is the freedom,
richness, variety and versatility of its rhythms, found nowhere else in a like degree. They change ceaselessly, inter-
twine, intersect, supersede one another, and lend themselves to the most varied shades of expression, ranging
from the wildest impetuosity to the most lulling of Dol-
cezzas, the gentlest Smorzando, from a martial movement
to a dance, from a triumphal march to a funeral procession,
from a winding elfin-dance in the meadows to a bacchanalian chant. Through their sequence, combination, separ-
ation and coalescence these rhythms are peculiarly fitted to

arouse poetic visions in the mind. They are one and all
characteristic, full of fire, flexibility, force and undulation,
full of imagination and weirdly strange phantasies. Now
they burst forth boldly with defiant charm, now are
breathed sighingly like a plaintive confession of love ; now
they advance to the attack like a thoroughbred charger ;
now they hop delicately to and fro as birds in the broad
sunshine ; now they resemble the frenzied rush of the stag
escaping from the pack, or the dull roaring of the panic-
stricken boar returning for shelter to his thicket ; ardently
plaintive like a love-sick swain, or vaunting and dashing
like a conqueror hastening to fresh victories ; now babbling
and fleet like a bevy of giggling maidens, and now spurred
and champing like a troop of cavalry galloping to the
charge.

Franz Liszt.

Evangelisation

I HAVE counted seventeen Gitánas assembled at one
time in my apartment in the Calle de Santiágo in Madrid;
for the first quarter of an hour we generally discoursed upon
indifferent matters, when, by degrees, I guided the subject
to religion and the state of souls. I finally became so bold
that I ventured to speak against their inveterate practices,
thieving and lying, telling fortunes, and stealing *á pastésas* ;
this was touching upon delicate ground, and I experienced
much opposition and much feminine clamour. I perse-
vered, however, and they finally assented to all I said, not
that I believe my words made much impression upon their
hearts. . . .

One day they arrived, attended by a Gypsy jockey, whom
I had never previously seen. We had scarcely been seated
a minute, when this fellow, rising, took me to the window,
and without any preamble or circumlocution, said,—' Don
Jorge, you shall lend me two barias ' (ounces of gold).
' Not to your whole race, my excellent friend,' said I ; ' are
you frantic ? Sit down and be discreet.' He obeyed me
literally, sat down, and when the rest departed, followed
with them. We did not invariably meet at my own house,
but occasionally at one in a street inhabited by Gypsies.

On the appointed day I went to this house, where I found the women assembled ; the jockey was also present. On seeing me he advanced, again took me aside, and again said, ' Don Jorge, you shall lend me two barias.' I made him no answer, but at once entered on the subject which brought me thither. I spoke for some time in Spanish ; I chose for the theme of my discourse the situation of the Hebrews in Egypt, and pointed out its similarity to that of the Gitános in Spain. I spoke of the power of God, manifested in preserving both as separate and distinct people amongst the nations until the present day. I warmed with my subject. I subsequently produced a manuscript book, from which I read a portion of Scripture, and the Lord's Prayer and Apostle's Creed in Rommany. When I had concluded, I looked around me.

The features of the assembly were twisted, and the eyes of all turned upon me with a frightful squint ; not an individual present but squinted,—the genteel Pépa, the good-humoured Chicharóna, the Cadasmí, etc., etc., all squinted. The Gypsy fellow, the contriver of the jest, squinted worst of all. Such are Gypsies.

George Borrow.

A Fifteenth Century Tapestry

THE repute and rumour of the Egyptians had gone before them and the Knights and Ladies had heard of their sorcery and the spell of their music. It was decided to put the powers of the Egyptians to the test, and they were summoned to come forward to the castle-walls.

It is this moment that was chosen by the tapestry designer. A Gypsy woman comes in front of her companions to tell the fortune of one of the ladies of the castle. The whole Gypsy caravan is just behind her, some on horseback and some on foot ; with nine children, five of whom are perfectly naked after the usual Gypsy custom. The Gypsy king is in the midst of his followers armed with club and sword. His queen sits on the ground near by, feeding a baby with a wooden spoon from a bowl held by another child, while the purse of a lady who is looking at her is being stolen by one of the Gypsy children.

A young knight is speaking to this unsuspecting victim, and at the back of them stand the lord and lady of the castle, dressed very richly, and talking to the head-huntsman, who shows them a quarter of deer, and to another young nobleman who holds up a rabbit for which a dog is reaching. A peacock with spread tail is perched on the wall of the castle, and, behind this, the background of the tapestry is filled with castles, with hills, and with hunting scenes, as though these latter were in perpetual activity. . . .

The visit of these Gypsies was a sorcery come from the interminable vast, and its strangeness entered straight into the soul of all who saw it. . . . Chivalry was called out of its own borders into the whole of the huge, hollow orbit lit by the sun's dying and reviving fire, and the apotheosis of the white man took him to the four quarters of the winds. His isolation was broken, the present was extended and the past came back again.   *Sacheverell Sitwell.*

Antique Apparel

THE old men wore knee breeches, made out of cashmere, when they couldn't get buckskin or sheepskin; they used to make them themselves, and they had leggings buttoned behind. They had two waistcoats, one inside, and one sleeved waistcoat of plush, with two rows of pearl buttons down it, and flaps on the pockets, with three buttons on each flap. And him they called Julius Caesar had silver buttons to the coat he had in his chest, and some had two rows of gold pieces down the coat for buttons. They had boots with the tongues hanging out of them, and very short toe-caps, with round toes and four rows of nails with ' palantines ' in the top.

And they had coral beads for *roringeras* round their necks in the old style that they had from some place abroad, and great watches with close on half a pound of silver in the case, but few of them could tell the time properly by them. And the kind of purse they used to carry in them days had beads at each end worked into about six stars and a half moon each side, about ten inches long, with a slit in the middle, one side for gold and one for silver, screwed up with bone rings that they used to carve out for themselves,

and some of them would take days over it, for they had
nothing else to do. They were made of horse hair, knitted
with a needle made out of the handle of an old razor, and
they only worked with one of them. And they were
coloured with ' tarmic ' or else ' feather-flue,' that comes
out of some tree, that the old people knew all about abroad,
and remembered about.

They used to dye their clothes themselves. They had
yellow waistcoats, and some of the old men had green coats
as they set a mortal store by. The kind of cloaks the old
men used to wear, they were made of nothing but skins
riveted together with fine little nails made of copper pieces,
old ' card ' pennies. They 're tied by a knot on both
shoulders, made in a curious position. Some of them
wears them brought up like a bunch of ribbons on one
shoulder, for grandeur, with copper hooks to them in front.

They always had white hats.   Any one of them would go
fifty miles for a white hat with a small brought-up-sloped
crown and broad leaf. The men wore earrings made of
copper and rings on both hands, one on the little finger and
three on each of the others. Some had bracelets on the
wrist, and old Golias Gezias, the oldest man out of the
whole generation of them, had them on his ankles as well,
and he was buried in them.

In winter they wore them things they called *bizemblis*
round their necks, like you see on ladies in the street, made
out of fur or rabbit skins with silk inside, but another class
got up in this last hundred years took to wearing a kind of
posnakos they called ' grinders.'

For the last three hundred years I seen their *idza* in a
makta, what goes from one generation to another till they 're
nearly melted away, and then they have them with wire
round them, for fear they fall to pieces. Old Sam Fiansi
showed me a chest that had his great-grandfather's clothes
in it, and he cried like a *tikno* when he thought of the old
people and the *purro divesses*, and he was close on eighty-six.
' Look there, Phil,' he says, ' that 's close on a hundred and
fifty, and the box is over three hundred ; but it 's made of
the right thing. I 've been offered a hundred and twenty
bar for it, but I wouldn't take it ' ; and why should he ?
He had plenty of money.

Their shirts were made of lambskin. They used to kill them for it when they were passing by a farmer's field, and put them by for winter; but they wore calico in summer. And the oldest of them wore their hair in three plaits, one plait down the back, reaching to the shoulder, and two tails coming down each side; hair on the top lip and clean chin, with narrow whiskers coming down each side, and their hair clipped close in front. But the new race for the last hundred years wore black curls, coming down each side, with a crooked split in front.

The women's dress was buttoned up close round the neck, with the body very short, coming down straight to near the ankles, with sleeves just above the elbow, and striped like the old style abroad, one *boro yuk* and one *bitti yuk*, and in the middle of the back, the tops of two rams' horns for buttons. They had low-sized shoes, with big buckles polished up every morning with brick-dust. The men made these buckles for them. There's a pair of them this day that the Lees have, that belonged to Shuggurn Lee's great-grandmother, the handsomest young Gypsy that was ever knowed on this God's world. She had hair the colour of a raven, and features like waxwork; and she killed Johnny Smith, my wife's first cousin. She took a liking to a *vover ghora*, and she made him throw her man over a bridge. She was the handsomest and *vasavest* young woman that ever saw the face of the sun.

They had cloaks with hoods to them, with a drawing-string, so you could put them up or down, coming right down to their heels, and made out of this grey wool; they'd go miles and miles to get it. They wore them both red and grey; but the most of them were red, and they coloured them themselves. Their hats were like the old Welsh hats, brought up very small and tall. And sometimes they'd have a band of fine cloth going round and round the head with these rosettes on it—one each side of the front part of the head, and three at the back. And more too! you'd see an old woman with as many stars on her head as there be in the sky. And as many rings and beads and earrings as they could carry on them; and the bigger they were, the better they were pleased.

Philip Murray, a Tinker.

A Singular Personage

WHILE passing through Marseilles in the early part of February, 1910, I took a seat one afternoon on the *terrasse* of the ' Bar Auzas.' . . . Opposite me, at the foot of the Porte d'Aix, lounged a group of Gitanos of Almeria, with bright *diklos* knotted over the shoulder, their jetty black hair brushed rigidly forward over the ears and there snipped abruptly, their staves in their hands, and the instruments of the craft of the *tondeur de chiens* hanging at their sides in little satchels. From time to time young *Romis* crossed the Place in couples, aloof and enigmatic, like nuns of some unknown and brilliant order.

I was to make the acquaintance of these folk later. What presently riveted my attention was an even more remarkable figure which hove in sight. It belonged to a tall and bulky man of middle age, attired in voluminous high-boots, baggy trousers, decorated at the sides with insertions of green and red, a short braided coat garnished with huge silver pendants and chains, and a hat of less magnificence if of greater antiquity upon his shaggy head. This singular personage was making his way slowly across the Place, looking this way and that, while puffing at his great German pipe, and acknowledging with dignity, as he passed, the salutations of the loungers. I rose, confronted him, and ' entered into conversation ' with an unceremonious *Sar san, Kako* ?

Augustus John.

An Egyptian

HER kyrtel Brystow red ;
With clothes vpon her hed
That wey a sowe of led,
Wrythen in wonder wyse,
After the Sarasyns gyse,
With a whym wham
Knyt with a trym tram,
Vpon her brayne pan,
Lyke an Egyptian
Capped about,
Whan she goeth out.

John Skelton.

H

A Gypsy Amazon

SHE had a tall man's height or more;
Her face from summer's noontide heat
No bonnet shaded, but she wore
A mantle, to her very feet
Descending with a graceful flow,
And on her head a cap as white as new-fallen snow.

Her skin was of Egyptian brown:
Haughty, as if her eye had seen
Its own light to a distance thrown,
She towered, fit person for a Queen
To lead those ancient Amazonian files;
Or ruling Bandit's wife among the Grecian isles.

Advancing, forth she stretched her hand
And begged an alms with doleful plea
That ceased not; on our English land
Such woes, I knew, could never be;
And yet a boon I gave her, for the creature
Was beautiful to see—a weed of glorious feature. . . .

William Wordsworth.

Beg on, Brother

ABOUT half a mile beyond Highbury, making a sudden
turn, and deeply shaded by elms on each side, it [the
Richmond Road] became for a considerable stretch very
retired; and when the young ladies had advanced some
way into it, they had suddenly perceived, at a small distance
before them, on a broader patch of greensward by the side,
a party of gipsies. A child on the watch, came towards
them to beg; and Miss Bickerton, excessively frightened,
gave a great scream, and calling on Harriet to follow her,
ran up a steep bank, cleared a slight hedge at the top, and
made the best of her way by a short cut back to Highbury.
But poor Harriet could not follow. She had suffered very
much from cramp after dancing, and her first attempt to
mount the bank brought on such a return of it as made

her absolutely powerless ; and in this state, and exceedingly terrified, she had been obliged to remain.

How the trampers might have behaved, had the young ladies been more courageous, must be doubtful ; but such an invitation for attack could not be resisted ; and Harriet was soon assailed by half a dozen children, headed by a stout woman and a great boy, all clamorous, and impertinent in look, though not absolutely in word. More and more frightened, she immediately promised them money, and taking out her purse, gave them a shilling, and begged them not to want more, or to use her ill. She was then able to walk, though but slowly, and was moving away— but her terror and her purse were too tempting, and she was followed, or rather surrounded, by the whole gang, demanding more.

In this state Frank Churchill had found her, she trembling and conditioning, they loud and insolent. . . .

The terror which the woman and boy had been creating in Harriet was then their own portion. He left them completely frightened ; and Harriet eagerly clinging to him, and hardly able to speak, had just strength enough to reach Hartfield, before her spirits were quite overcome. . . .

The gipsies did not wait for the operations of justice ; they took themselves off in a hurry.

Jane Austen.

A Masterful Beggar

WHENEVER Mizeli spoke of her Aunt Rodi it was with righteous indignation, and even on this occasion, when she was relating how Rodi fleeced the ancient enemy, she never once lapsed into laughing approval. It was not that she disagreed in theory, or refrained in practice from similar extortions ; nor was she slow as a rule to see the humorous side of the Gypsy woman's traditional calling. But there are methods and methods, and to put the matter briefly Mizeli drew the line at her Aunt Rodi's. Whether she had cause the reader must judge for himself, and that he may not be prejudiced I will strip from Mizeli's narrative the frequent outbursts of feeling with which it was interspersed.

' My Aunt Rodi,' she said, ' was calling to a house the
tother day, and the woman said that she didn't want nothing ;
but she kep' on at her and kep' on at her till at last the
woman says as she 'd take a bit o' comb or summat, just
on purpose for to get rid 'n her.   Well, she pays her the
money, the woman does, and then she makes for to shut
the dooar.   But my Aunt Rodi puts her basket in the road.
" Stop a minute, misses," she says, " I think Is 'll come in
and have a cup o' tea wid yous.   I 's fair fagged out," she
says, " wid standing here haggling wid yous, and all for the
sake 'n a sixpence, which ain't neither here nor there when
yous has a fambly o' roaring lions to feed.   And being as
yous has kep' I all this time it 's the littlest yous can do,
misses, is to give I a cup o' tea."   And she walks right in
afore the woman could stop her, and sets down her basket,
and takes her shawl off, and settles hersel' down comfortable, the same as if the place belonged to her.
' " And don't gid it I *ratvali* cowld," she says, " I likes
my tea fresh brewed, and plenty o' milk and sugar into it,
and a nice plate o' bread and butter to ate wid it."   The
woman pokes the fire up and puts the kettle on.   " That 's
a noo bread cake as yous has got there," she says—that 's
my Aunt Rodi.   " Is 'll have som 'n that," she says, " and
plenty o' butter to it, misses."   So the woman cuts her a
plate o' noo bread and butter and gi'es her her tea.   " I
know'd as yous wouldn't refuse I," says my Aunt Rodi.
" The Lord Jesus Christ 'll deward yous, misses ; He never
forgets hanybody what is kind to we.   We 'm His children, misses ; and that 's what it says into the Bible, don't
it now ? "   She has two cups o' tea, my Aunt Rodi has,
and three or fower slices o' bread and butter.   " Nice noo
bread this, misses," she says.   " I should like for a loaf for
to take home to my children.   It 's not once in five years
as they tastes noo bread, and it 'd be a treat for they."   The
woman gi'es her a loaf.   " Thank yous, misses ; thank
yous kindly," she says.   " Yous was born under a lucky
star I can see.   And Is 'll have a bit o' butter to go wid it,
misses.   No," she says, " I don't want a *ratvali* small bit
like that 'n "—the woman was cutting her a slice—" It 'd
melt," she says, " afore I get home.   About half a pound,
misses, 'll do me nicely.   Yous can well spare it, and

never know the miss'n it." The woman, soft-like, gid
it her.

'"And now," she says—that's the woman—"I mun be
gittin' on wi' mi wark." (You know the funny way o'
talking these *gorgios* has.) "And quite right, misses,"
says my Aunt Rodi; "I won't keep yous, not above five
or ten minutes. Just let I smoke a pipe first, and then Is 'll
be going. You know, misses, it looks bad for we to smoke
in the street, and let me tell yous we 'm a very partic'lar
class o' people." So she lights her pipe and takes a look
round. "I wants a piece o' soap, misses," she says, "for
to wash my babies." "Here thoo is, then," says the
woman, and she gi'es her the bit off'n the sink. "I can't
do wid that, woman," says my Aunt Rodi; "it puts I in
mind o' the soap they lays into coffins wid the corpse. I
must have a noo piece." She 'd sin a noo pound bar.
"Is 'll have half o' that'n," she says. "I wouldn't rob
yous, misses, but a piece o' soap ain't to say nothing to
yous, is it now?" She gets that as well, and puts it in her
basket.

'The poor woman thought she was going to get rid'n
her this time, but she didn't know my Aunt Rodi. "Yous
has got a howld white diaper tablecloth into that chest o'
drawers there," she says, "and it 's got a big hole into it.
Yous might as well to gid I that." "Nay, I can't," says
the woman; "I 's gaen to mend it up, and then it 'll deu
nicely except when we 've company." "Better gid it I,"
says my Aunt Rodi, "else yous 'll have nothing but bad
luck to it. I 's a-warning of yous now." "Here then,"
says the woman, "tak it and begone, thoo ald witch "; and
she throw'd it in her face. "No cause to angrify yoursel',
woman," says my Aunt Rodi, "for I 's a-going in a minute,
and it wouldn't never do for me to leave a curse behind."
She folded up the cloth and put it into her basket. "Now,
into that cupboard, misses," she says, "the 's a big coloured
cup what I ta'en a fancy to. My eyes can't see it," she says,
"but I knows as it 's there. Gid I that, misses, and Is 'll
bid you a civil good morning." The woman 's a bit
frightened at this : she couldn't think as however my Aunt
Rodi know'd about that cup, as it was put away wrapped
up into a howld napkin. She must have powers, she

thinks. So she shows her all the cups as she has into the cupboard, all saving this one. " Here," she says, " tak' thi pick, and then let 's be done wi' tha." " I wouldn't thank yous for non 'n they," says my Aunt Rodi ; " they 's a poverty lot. It 's the big coloured cup as I wants, and if yous don't gid it I, woman, I tell yous as it 'll be broke afore the week is out." " That 's as may be," says the woman, " but anyway thoo shan't hev it. It belengs ta my lile lass, and she thinks t' world 'n it. It 'd brek her lile heart if I was ta part wi' it." " Mark my words," says my Aunt Rodi, " if yous don't gid it I . . ." But the woman's monkey was up now. " Here," she says, " git thisel' oot o' my hoose, and leuk sharp aboot it, or I 'll fetch t' bobby ta tha." My Aunt Rodi picks up her shawl. " My curse is onto it," she says, " and there 's them in this town knows as when I curses a thing . . ." " I da'say," says the woman, " but Stop a minute. That 's oor fella's hankisher thoo 's juSt picked up. I saa tha put thi shawl on t' top'n it when thoo cam in, and I 've hed mi eye on it ivver sen." " That 's all right, misses," says my Aunt Rodi ; " I was only juSt a-going to take it to show it to my grandmother. I don't know as I ever sin a nicer," she says, " and I thought as my grandmother 'd be sure to like to see it. You see, misses, our people 's got a fancy for such things." " Aye," says the woman, " and for aw maks o' things as doesn't beleng 'em. Give it here noo, or off thoo gaes ta t' lock-up." " Take it then, you rotten monkey," says my Aunt Rodi, and she called her all the names she could think of. " Take it," she says, " but your husband 'll never make no use of it, for by this day week," she says, " he 'll be rotting in his grave. And them," she says, " is my last words."

' I was to the poor woman's house laSt night, and she was fair out 'n her mind, poor thing. The cup got broke the same as my Aunt Rodi said it would—she 's a *tachi chovakanon* you *jin*—and now the poor woman 's *trash*'d to death as it 'll come true about her husband as well. She axed me should she send my Aunt Rodi the handkerchief, but I towld her no. " She 'll ax for more and more if yous do," I said, " and the firSt time as yous defuse she 'll call down the curse again." " But isn't ther nowt I can deu ? "

she axes. " No," I says, " ther isn't, but put your confidence in me," I says, " and Is 'll see as no harm comes to
your husband. Ther 's things as is known to we," I says,
" as we can't tell, not to nobody." I had to put the poor
woman's mind to rest, and besides, there 's no knowing
what I can do when I sets myself to it.'

Thomas William Thompson.

An Answered Prayer

IT was Charley Wood of Dyffryn, near Barmouth, who
was talking about his uncle, John Roberts, the harper.
' In the olden times as we was going about from place
to place, we used to stop at farms and sleep in the barns
or *atch* outside quite close to them. And when we went
in to supper, you *jin*, my uncle used to say " grace," and
would cover his eyes with his hand, and begin with *Diolch
iddo*, endsettras. Then when we was outside, it would be
my turn to tell the tale, or yours—and now it is yours, my
dear *pen* ; go on.'
Here Charley turned round and demanded a story from
me, but after a little persuasion, he continued as follows :—
' So my uncle began, and he had a big, deep voice, and he
was the best one to tell a story that ever I knew. In the
middle of the story he would say, " You listening, boy ? "
—" Yes, my *kokko*."—" Dat 's right, my *chavo*." We was
rokkering till past three o'clock that time. Next morning
the farmer came out. " Come you up now, all of you, to
my house at once, if you please," he says to the old man.
' My uncle looks round at us all. " Have any of you
boys been up to your games with the fowl ? " Of course
he was *rokkering Romanes*, but we 'd never touched so much
as an egg ; we dursen't, the old man was so particular.
" Come you up now, at once," says the farmer, so up we
all went.
' When we came into the kitchen, the table was all put
out for breakfast, and the farmer says very pious : " We
are wanting to thank you for your beautiful praying last
night. Oh, it did go to our hearts ; indeed yes, it was a
very powerful prayer, and we are hoping that you will be

excusing us for listening outside the tent, but we *must* listen
when we hear the beautiful praying! And you shall all
sit down right now and have a good breakfast, and I will
be begging of you, sir, to ask a blessing."

'It was a sight to see my uncle's face. He made him a
grand bow, like as if he was the Prince of Wales. There
we were, all standing round the table, and the old man
saying " grace " : but, instead of saying grace, he was
thanking God for the *dinilo gorgios*.'

Fanny Marston.

A Religious Spirit

THOUGH to the Mosque I come with pious air,
By Allah! think not I have come for prayer;
I stole a mat once from a worshipper—
That sin worn out, again I here repair.

Omar Khayyam.

V

THE ROMANY CHYE

V

The Romany Chye

A Supernatural Look

IT has long struck me that in the countenances of those who are young and handsome among that people, whether male or female, there is a look of somewhat approaching to superhuman. A little of this I thought perceptible in this young Gypsy girl.

Samuel Roberts.

The Chi and the Chal

THE Gypsy women are by far more remarkable beings than the men. It is the Chi and not the Chal who has caused the name of Gypsy to be a sound-awaking wonder, awe, and curiosity in every part of the civilised world. Not that there have never been remarkable men of the Gypsy race both abroad and at home. Duke Michael, as he was called, the leader of the great Gypsy horde which suddenly made its appearance in Germany at the beginning of the fifteenth century, was no doubt a remarkable man ; the Gitano Conde, whom Martin del Rio met at Toledo a hundred years afterwards, who seemed to speak all languages, and to be perfectly acquainted with the politics of all the Courts of Europe, must certainly have been a remarkable man ; so, no doubt, here at home was Boswell ; so undoubtedly was Cooper, called by the gentlemen of the Fives Court—poor fellows ! they are all gone now—the ' wonderful little Gypsy ' ;—but upon the whole the poetry, the sorcery, the devilry, if you please to call it so, are vastly on the side of the women. How blank and inanimate is the countenance of the Gypsy man, even when trying to pass off a foundered donkey as a flying dromedary, in com-

123

parison with that of the female Romany, peering over the
wall of a par-yard at a jolly hog !

> ' Sar shin Sinfye ?
> Koshto divvus Romany Chi !
> So shan tute kairing acoi ?

> ' Sinfye, Sinfye ! how do you do ?
> Daughter of Rome, good day to you !
> What are you thinking here to do ? '

George Borrow.

The Indian Gipsy

IN tattered robes that hoard a glittering trace
Of bygone colours, broidered to the knee,
Behold her, daughter of a wandering race,
Tameless, with the bold falcon's agile grace,
And the lithe tiger's sinuous majesty.

With frugal skill her simple wants she tends,
She folds her tawny heifers and her sheep
On lonely meadows when the daylight ends,
Ere the quick night upon her flock descends
Like a black panther from the caves of sleep.

Time's river winds in foaming centuries
Its changing, swift, irrevocable course
To far off and incalculable seas ;
She is twin-born with primal mysteries,
And drinks in life at Time's forgotten source.

Sarojini Naidu.

Preciosa

'AND whence do you know so much ? ' said one of the
cavaliers.
' Are you not aware,' said Preciosa, ' that there are men
who do not learn, yet know all ? I am of their number ;
so are all the gypsies, men and women. Our mind is
different from yours ; our understanding makes us older
than our years. We sail over strange seas, and turn to a

pole-star unknown to you ; for since it is by our skill and our industry that we live, we are proficient in them from the cradle. Frankly confess, have you in your life seen a silly Gypsy man or a simple Gypsy woman ? Cast your eyes on these young girls, my companions ; they do not speak, and from their silence you would take them for statues ; but they are artful damsels, and farseeing, whose wit might outmatch your wisdom. Of a truth there is no Gypsy girl twelve years old who does not know more than a Spanish lady of twenty-five. A little dexterity,' she added smiling, ' and a little of the black art teach us in a year what the rest of the world do not learn in half a century.'

Cervantes.

The Child of a Sun-favoured Clime

PASSING I saw her as she stood beside
A lonely stream between two barren wolds ;
Her loose vest hung in rudely-gathered folds
On her swart bosom, which in maiden pride
Pillowcd a string of pearls ; among her hair
Twined the light bluebell and the stonecrop gay ;
And not far thence the small encampment lay,
Curling its wreathéd smoke into the air.
She seemed a child of some sun-favoured clime ;
So still, so habited to warmth and rest :
And in my wayward musings on past time,
When my thought fills with treasured memories,
That image nearest borders on the blest.

Dean Alford.

Sinfi Lovell

A GYPSY girl, dressed in fine Gypsy costume, very dark but very handsome, was sitting on a settle drinking from a pot of ale, and nursing an instrument of the violin kind, which she was fondling as though it were a baby. She was quite young, not above eighteen years of age, slender, graceful—remarkably so, even for a Gypsy girl. Her hair, which was not so much coal-black as blue-black, was plaited in the old-fashioned Gypsy way, in little plaits that looked almost as close as plaited straw, and as it was of an unusually soft and fine texture for a Gypsy, the plaits gave it a lustre quite unlike that which unguents can give. As she sat there, one leg thrown over the other, displaying a foot which, even in the heavy nailed boots, would have put to shame the finest foot of the finest English lady I have ever seen, I could discern that she was powerful and tall ; her bosom, gently rising and falling beneath the layers of scarlet and yellow and blue handkerchiefs, which filled up the space the loose-fitting gown of bright merino left open, was of a breadth fully worthy of her height. A silk handkerchief of deep blood-red colour was bound round her head, not in the modern Gypsy fashion, but more like an Oriental turban. From each ear was suspended a massive ring of red gold. Round her beautiful, towering, tanned neck was a thrice-twisted necklace of half-sovereigns and amber and red coral. She looked me full in the face. Then came a something in the girl's eyes the like of which I had seen in no other Gypsy's eyes. . . . It was not exactly an uncanny expression, yet it suggested a world quite other than this. It was an expression such as one might expect to see in a ' budding spae-wife,' or in a Roman Sibyl.

Theodore Watts-Dunton.

Father Hedgehog describes Sybil Stanley

SHE was very beautiful. Her skin was like a trout pool —clear and yet brown. I never saw any eyes like her eyes, though our neighbour's—the Water Rat—at times recalls them. Her hair was the colour of ripe blackberries in a hot hedge—very ripe ones, with the bloom on. She moved like a snake. I have seen my father chase a snake more than once, and I have seen a good many men and women in my time. Some of them walk like my father, they bustle along and kick up the leaves as he does ; and some of them move quickly and yet softly, as snakes go. The gypsy girl moved so, and wherever she went the gypsy man's eyes went after her.

Juliana Horatia Ewing.

Rhona Boswell's Love Letter

Gypsy Dell, Wensdy.

THIS ere comes hoppen, leaven me the same
And lykwise all our breed in Gypsy Dell,
Barrin the spotted gry, wot 's turned up lame ;
A crick have made his orfside fetlock swell.
The Scollard 's larnen me to rite and spel,
It 's 'ard, but then I longed to rite your name :
Then squrrels in the Dell have grow'd that tame !
    How sweet the haycocks smel !

Dordi ! how I should like you just to see
The Scollard when he 's larnen me to rite,
A buzzin like a chafer or a bee,
Else cussen you wi' bloodshot yockers bright
And moey girnin, danniers gleamin white.
He 's wuss nor ever follerin arter me,
Peepin roun' every bush an every tree
    Mornin and noon and night.

When I wur standin by the river's brim,
Hearin the chirikels in Rington wood,
And seein the moorhens larn their chicks to swim,
Thinks I, ' I hears the Scollard's heavy thud ' ;
And when I turned, behold ye, there he stood !
He says I promised as I 'd marry him,
And if I di'n't he 'd tear me limb from limb.
    Sez I, ' That 's if you could.'

But when I thinks o' you, a choon aglall,
Dray mendys tan a-study in Romany—
Nock, danniers, moey, yockers, canners, bal—
It make me sometime larf and sometime cry ;
And that makes Granny's crinkles crinkle sly ;
' Dabla ! ' my daddy says, ' de blessed gal
Shall lel herself a tarnow Rye she shall—
    A tarnow Romany Rye.'

I lets em larf, but well I knows—too well—
The ondly tarnow Rye, and ondly man,
That in my dreams I sometime seem to lel
Ain't for the lyks o' mee in this 'ere tan,
The Rye wot sat by mee where Dell-brook ran,
And larnt my Romany words and used to tell
Sich sweet, strange things all day, till shadders fell
And light o' stars began.

Mose nights I lays awake, but when the cock
Begin to crow and rooks begin to fly
And chimes come livelier out o' Rington clock,
It 's then I sees your pictur in the sky
(So plane, it seems to bring the mornin nigh,)
Bal, danniers, canners, yockers moey, nock.
My dady's bort me sich a nicet new frock.
      Your comly korly chy.
                                        Theodore Watts-Dunton.

Sagul

A GIRL darted in and dropped down cross-legged,
motionless. She was a girl of sixteen, but looked
more like twenty. Her eyes, which, except on occasion,
were all one saw of her, were of the first magnitude, with
blues, not whites, and with brown-black, dark-lantern
pupils—one moment blank and expressionless, the next
positively blazing. Only when they were blank, could you
see besides that she was tall and lithe and strong, that she
had a wealth of wavy black hair, that her face was an
exquisite oval, that her teeth were even whiter than they
were regular, that—Of a sudden her eyes blazed again, and
you were solely conscious of a beautiful wild creature.
                                        Francis Hindes Groome.

Kiomi

THE women grinned, and the men yawned. The business of the men appeared to be to set to work about
everything as if they had a fire inside them, and then to
stretch out their legs and lie on their backs, exactly as if the

fire had gone out. Excepting Osric's practice on the
fiddle, and the father's bringing in and leading away of
horses, they did little work in my sight but brown themselves in the sun. One morning Osric's brother came to
our camp with their cousin the prizefighter—a young man
of lighter complexion, upon whom I gazed, remembering
John Thresher's reverence for the heroical profession.
Kiomi whispered some story concerning her brother having
met the tramp. I did not listen ; I was full of a tempest,
owing to two causes : a studious admiration of the smart
young prizefighter's person, and wrathful disgust at him
for calling Kiomi his wife, and telling her he was prepared
to marry her as soon as she played her harp like King David.
The intense folly of his asking a girl to play like David
made me despise him, but he was splendidly handsome and
strong, and to see him put on the gloves for a spar with big
William, Kiomi's brother, and evade and ward the huge
blows, would have been a treat to others besides old John
of Dipwell Farm. He had the agile grace of a leopard ;
his waistcoat reminded me of one ; he was like a piece of
machinery in free action. Pleased by my enthusiasm, he
gave me a lesson, promising me more.

' He 'll be champion some day.' said Kiomi, at gnaw
upon an apple he had given her.

I knocked the apple on the ground, and stamped on it.
She slapped my cheek. In a minute we stood in a ring. I
beheld the girl actually squaring at me.

' Fight away,' I said, to conceal my shame, and imagining
I could slip from her hits as easily as the prizefighter did
from big William's. I was mistaken.

' Oh ! you think I can't defend myself,' said Kiomi ; and
rushed in with one, two, quick as a cat, and cool as a statue.

' Fight, my merry one ; she takes punishment,' the
prizefighter sang out. ' First blood to you, Kiomi ; un-
cork his claret, my duck ; straight at the nozzle, he sees
more lamps than shine in London, I warrant. Make him
lively, cook him ; tell him who taught you ; a downer to
him, and I 'll marry you to-morrow ! '

I conceived a fury against her as though she had injured
me by appearing the man's property—and I was getting
the worst of it ; her little fists shot straight and hard as bars

I

of iron ; she liked fighting ; she was at least my match.
To avoid the disgrace of seriously striking her, or of being
beaten at an open exchange of blows, I made a feint, and
caught her by the waist and threw her, not very neatly, for
I fell myself in her grip.   They had to pluck her from me
by force.
    ' And you 've gone a course of tuition in wrestling,
squire ? ' the prizefighter said to me rather savagely.
    The others were cordial, and did not snarl at me for
going to the ropes, as he called it.   Kiomi desired to renew
the conflict.   I said aloud :
    ' I never fight girls, and I tell you I don't like their
licking me.'
    ' Then you come down to the river and wash your face,'
said she, and pulled me by the fingers, and when she had
washed my face clear of blood, kissed me.   I thought she
tasted of the prizefighter.

George Meredith.

Sub Dio

WITH regard to those peculiar people, the gypsies, one
thing is very remarkable, and especially as they came
from warmer climates ;   and that is, that while other
beggars lodge in barns, stables, and cow-houses, these
sturdy savages seem to pride themselves in braving the
severities of winter, and in living *sub dio* the whole year
round.   Last September was as wet a month as ever was
known ;   and yet, during those deluges, did a young gypsy
girl lie-in in the midst of one of our hop-gardens, on the
cold ground, with nothing over her but a piece of blanket,
extended on a few hazel-rods bent hoop-fashion, and stuck
into the earth at each end, in circumstances too trying for a
cow in the same condition :   yet within this garden there
was a large hop-kiln, into the chambers of which she might
have retired, had she thought shelter an object worthy her
attention.

Gilbert White, of Selborne.

The Romany Girl

THE sun goes down, and with him takes
The coarseness of my poor attire ;
The fair moon mounts, and aye the flame
Of Gypsy beauty blazes higher.

Pale Northern girls ! you scorn our race ;
You captives of your air-tight halls,
Wear out in-doors your sickly days,
But leave us the horizon walls.

And if I take you, dames, to task,
And say it frankly without guile,
Then you are Gypsies in a mask,
And I the lady all the while.

If, on the heath, below the moon,
I court and play with paler blood,
Me false to mine dare whisper none,—
One sallow horseman knows me good.

Go, keep your cheek's rose from the rain,
For teeth and hair with shopmen deal ;
My swarthy tint is in the grain,
The rocks and forest know it real.

The wild air bloweth in our lungs,
The keen stars twinkle in our eyes,
The birds gave us our wily tongues,
The panther in our dances flies.

You doubt we read the stars on high,
Nathless we read your fortunes true ;
The stars may hide in the upper sky,
But without glass we fathom you.

Ralph Waldo Emerson.

Lila

IT was quite dark when we stopped before some house where the sound of music led us to suppose we had found an inn. We were mistaken, however, and while the servant was making inquiries, and receiving answers which he could not understand, as to the whereabouts of the hostelry, a gipsy girl came out of the house, and hearing the nature of our difficulty, at once took the arrangement of the matter on herself. At a single bound she threw herself into H—'s waggon, seated herself beside him, and giving her orders to the peasant, desired him to drive through the river up the steep bank and along the deep road—we being left to follow them to the inn as best we could. Before we arrived, our gipsy guide had roused the whole house, got the keys of the chambers, unlocked the rooms, and while we were yet joking H— on his adventure, the heroine of it had already lit the fires, mended the cracked stoves, got the carriage unloaded, laid the cloth, and was cooking the supper, ere it was yet ordered. Everything was so quickly done, that it had an air of conjuration about it. It was strange to find one who, five minutes before, we had never even seen, already our guide, our hostess, our cook, our factotum. Nor was the interest lessened when we had time to observe our mysterious friend. Lila was a pretty gipsy girl of about sixteen, with features more regular than those of her tribe commonly are, but with all a gipsy's cunning flattery on her tongue. She was rather fancifully dressed, for over the Wallach shirt she had a bodice of scarlet cloth, embroidered with black. The coloured fillet over her forehead was ornamented with a gay bow in front, and behind each ear was a nosegay of the brightest flowers. Her rich brown hair, parted in front, fell, in a profusion of clustering curls, on her neck, and hung down the back in the long-braided band of maidenhood. She spoke alternately Wallach, Magyar, and German, as she in turns scolded, directed, and coaxed. Before we ceased wondering at so pleasant an apparition, a good supper was smoking on the table, and the pretty gipsy by her laughing and talking almost persuaded us that we were

supping on ambrosia, while she played the gentle Hebe to
our godships.

John Paget.

Carmencita

' VOILÀ la gitanilla ! ' Je levai les yeux, et je la vis.
C'était un vendredi, et je n'oublierai jamais. Je vis
cette Carmen que vous connaissez, chez qui je vous ai
rencontré il y a quelques mois.

Elle avait un jupon rouge fort court qui laissait voir
des bas de soie blancs avec plus d'un trou, et des souliers
mignons de maroquin rouge attachés avec des rubans
couleur de feu. Elle écartait sa mantille afin de montrer
ses épaules et un gros bouquet de cassie qui sortait de sa
chemise. Elle avait encore une fleur de cassie dans le
coin de la bouche, et elle s'avançait en se balançant sur ses
hanches comme une pouliche du haras de Cordoue. Dans
mon pays, une femme en ce costume aurait obligé le monde
à se signer. A Séville, chacun lui adressait que.que compli-
ment gaillard sur sa tournure ; elle répondait à chacun,
faisant les yeux en coulisse, le poing sur la hanche, effrontée
comme une vraie bohémienne qu'elle était. D'abord elle
ne me plut pas, et je repris mon ouvrage ; mais elle, suivant
l'usage des femmes et des chats qui ne viennent pas quand
on les appelle et qui viennent quand on ne les appelle pas,
s'arrêta devant moi et m'adressa la parole :

' Compère, me dit-elle à la façon andalouse, veux-tu me
donner ta chaîne pour tenir les clefs de mon coffre-fort.'

' C'est pour attacher mon épinglette,' lui répondis-je.

' Ton épinglette ! ' s'écria-t-elle en riant. 'Ah ! monsieur
fait de la dentelle, puisqu'il a besoin d'épingles ! '

Tout le monde qui était là se mit à rire, et moi je me
sentais rougir, et je ne pouvais trouver rien à lui répondre.

' Allons, mon cœur,' reprit-elle, ' fais-moi sept aunes
de dentelle noire pour une mantille, épinglier de mon
âme ! '

Et prenant la fleur de cassie qu'elle avait à la bouche, elle
me la lança, d'un mouvement du pouce, juste entre les deux
yeux.

Prosper Mérimée.

Esmeralda

'ESMERALDA ! Esmeralda is in the square ! '
This cry had a magical effect. Every one in the hall
rushed to the windows, climbing up the walls to get a
glimpse, and repeating ' Esmeralda ! Esmeralda ! '

' What do they mean by their Esmeralda ? ' said Gringoire, clasping his hands in despair. . . . ' May the devil flay
me if I know what they mean by their Esmeralda. What
kind of a word is that, anyhow ? It must be Egyptian. . . .'

In the vast spaces left free between the crowd and the
fire a young girl was dancing.

Whether this young girl was a human being, or a fairy
or an angel, was more than Gringoire, cynic, philosopher
and sarcastic poet though he was, could for a moment
decide, so greatly was he fascinated by the dazzling vision.

She was not tall, but seemed to be, so proudly erect did
she hold her slender figure. She was brown, but it was
evident that by daylight her skin must have that lovely
golden gleam peculiar to Spanish and Roman beauties.
Her tiny foot was Andalusian, too, for it fitted both snugly
and easily into its dainty shoe. She danced, she turned,
she twirled upon an antique Persian carpet thrown carelessly beneath her feet ; and every time her radiant figure
passed, as she turned, her great black eyes sent forth lightning flashes.

Upon her every eye was riveted, every mouth gaped
wide, and in very truth, as she danced to the hum of the
tambourine which her round and graceful arms held high
above her head, slender, quick and active as any wasp,
with smoothly-fitting golden bodice, her many-coloured
full skirts, her bare shoulders, her shapely legs, from
which her skirts now and then swung away, her black hair,
her eyes of flame, she seemed more than mortal creature.

' Indeed,' thought Gringoire, ' she is a salamander, a
nymph, a goddess, a bacchante from Mount Maenalus.'

At this moment one of the salamander's tresses was
loosened and a bit of brass which had been fastened to it
fell to the ground.

' Alas, no,' said he, ' she 's a Gypsy.'

Victor Hugo.

To a Gitana Dancing

BECAUSE you are fair as souls of the lost are fair,
And your eyelids laugh with desire, and your laughing
feet
Are winged with desire, and your hands are wanton, and
sweet
Is the promise of love in your lips, and the rose in your hair
Sweet, unfaded, a promise sweet to be sought,
And the maze you tread is old as the world is old,
Therefore you hold me, body and soul, in your hold,
And time, as you dance, is not, and the world is as nought.
You dance, and I know the desire of all flesh, and the pain
Of all longing of body for body ; you beckon, repel,
Entreat, and entice, and bewilder, and build up the spell,
Link by link, with deliberate steps, of a flower-soft chain.
You laugh, and I know the despair, and you smile, and I
know
The delight of your love, and the flower in your hair is a
star.
It brightens, I follow ; it fades, and I see it afar ;
You pause : I awake ; have I dreamt ? was it longer ago
Than a dream that I saw you smile ? for you turn, you
turn,
As a startled beast in the toils ; it is you that entreat,
Desperate, hating the coils that have fastened your feet,
The desire you desired that has come ; and your lips now
yearn,
And your hands now ache, and your feet faint for love.
Longing has taken hold even on you,
You, the witch of desire ; and you pause, and anew
Your stillness moves, and you pause, and your hands move.

Arthur Symons.

Wills of the Wisp

LUNATIC Witch-fires ! Ghosts of Light and Motion !
Fearless I see you weave your wanton dances
Near me, far off me ; you, that tempt the traveller
Onward and onward.

Wooing, retreating, till the swamp beneath him
Groans—and 'tis dark !—This woman's wile—I know it !
Learnt it from *thee*, from *thy* perfidious glances !
     Black-eyed Rebecca !

Samuel Taylor Coleridge.

Fritillaries

AND then I came to a field where the springing grass
 Was dulled by the hanging cups of fritillaries,
Sullen and foreign-looking, the snaky flower,
Scarfed in dull purple, like Egyptian girls
Camping among the furze, staining the waste
With foreign colour, sulky-dark and quaint ;
Dangerous too, as a girl might sidle up,
An Egyptian girl, with an ancient snaring spell,
Throwing a net, soft round the limbs and heart,
Captivity soft and abhorrent, a close-meshed net,
—See the square web on the murrey flesh of the flower—
Holding her captive close with her bare brown arms,
Close to her little breast beneath the silk,
A gipsy Judith, witch of a ragged tent.
And I shrank from the English field of fritillaries
Before it should be too late, before I forgot
The cherry white in the woods, and the curdled clouds,
And the lapwings crying free above the plough.

Victoria Sackville-West.

The Gipsy Girl

'COME, try your skill, kind gentlemen,
 A penny for three tries ! '
Some threw and lost, some threw and won
A ten-a-penny prize.

She was a tawny gipsy girl,
A girl of twenty years,
I liked her for the lumps of gold
That jingled from her ears ;

I liked the flaring yellow scarf
Bound loose about her throat,
I liked her showy purple gown
And flashy velvet coat.

A man came up, too loose of tongue,
And said no good to her ;
She did not blush as Saxons do,
Or turn upon the cur ;

She fawned and whined ' Sweet gentleman,
A penny for three tries ! '
—But oh, the den of wild things in
The darkness of her eyes !

Ralph Hodgson.

Ursula and Lavengro

' I THINK I will sit down with you, Ursula ; for after
all, reading godly books in dingles at eve is rather
sombre work. Yes, I think I will sit down with you ' ;
and I sat down by her side.

' Well, brother, now you have sat down with me under
the hedge, what have you to say to me ? '

' Why, I hardly know, Ursula.'

' Not know, brother ; a pretty fellow you to ask young
women to come and sit with you under hedges, and, when
they come, not know what to say to them.'

'Oh ! ah ! I remember ; do you know, Ursula, that I
take a great interest in you ? '

' Thank ye, brother ; kind of you, at any rate.'

' You must be exposed to a great many temptations,
Ursula ? '

' A great many indeed, brother. It is hard to see fine
things, such as shawls, gold watches and chains in the
shops, behind the big glasses, and to know that they are
not intended for one. Many 's the time I have been
tempted to make a dash at them ; but I bethought myself
that by so doing I should cut my hands, besides being
almost certain of being grabbed and sent across the gull's
bath to the foreign country.'

'Then you think gold and fine things temptations, Ursula?'

'Of course, brother, very great temptations; don't you think them so?'

'Can't say I do, Ursula.'

'Then more fool you, brother.' . . .

'Then money and fine clothes would induce you to do anything, Ursula?'

'Ay, ay, brother, anything.'

'To chore, Ursula?'

'Like enough, brother; gypsies have been transported before now for choring.'

'To hokkawar?'

'Ay, ay; I was telling dukkerin only yesterday, brother.'

'In fact, to break the law in everything?'

'Who knows, brother, who knows? As I said before, gold and fine clothes are great temptations.'

'Well, Ursula, I am sorry for it, I should never have thought you so depraved.'

'Indeed, brother.'

'To think that I am seated by one who is willing to--to——'

'Go on, brother.'

'To play the thief.'

'Go on, brother.'

'The liar.'

'Go on, brother.'

'The—the——'

'Go on, brother.'

'The—the lubbeny.'

'The what, brother?' said Ursula, starting from her seat.

'Why, the lubbeny; don't you——'

'I tell you what, brother,' said Ursula, looking somewhat pale, and speaking very low, 'if I had only something in my hand, I would do you a mischief.'

'Why, what is the matter, Ursula?' said I; 'how have I offended you?'

'How have you offended me? Why, didn't you insinivate just now that I was ready to play the—the——'

' Go on, Ursula.'

' The—the—I 'll not say it ; but I only wish I had something in my hand.'

' If I have offended, Ursula, I am very sorry for it ; any offence I may have given you was from want of under-standing you.   Come, pray be seated, I have much to question you about—to talk to you about.'

' Seated, not I !   It was only just now that you gave me to understand that you was ashamed to be seated by me, a thief, a liar.'

' Well, did you not give me to understand that you were both, Ursula ? '

' I don't much care being called a thief and a liar,' said Ursula ; ' a person may be a liar and a thief, and yet a very honest woman, but—— '

' Well, Ursula.'

' I tell you what, brother, if you ever sinivate again that I could be the third thing, so help me duvel !   I 'll do you a mischief.   By my God I will ! '

George Borrow.

Ursula and Lavengro again

' AND you had nothing better to say to me,' said Ursula, ' when you wanted to talk to me beneath a hedge, than that you liked me in a brotherly way !   well, I declare—— '

' You seem disappointed, Ursula.'

' Disappointed, brother !   not I.'

' You were just now saying that you disliked gorgios, so, of course, could only wish that I, who am a gorgio, should like you in a brotherly way ;   I wished to have a conversation with you beneath a hedge, but only with the view of procuring from you some information respecting the song which you sung the other day, and the conduct of Roman females, which has always struck me as being highly unaccountable, so, if you thought anything else—— '

' What else should I expect from a picker-up of old words, brother ?   Bah !   I dislike a picker-up of old words worse than a picker-up of old rags.'

George Borrow.

Song of the Broken Chastity

SAID the gypsy girl to her mother dear,
'O mother dear, a sad load I bear.'
'And who gave thee that load to bear,
My gypsy girl, my own daughter dear ? '
'O mother dear, 'twas a lord so proud,
A lord so rich of gentile blood,
That on a mettled stallion rode—
'Twas he gave me this heavy load.'
'Thou wanton young, thou wanton vile,
Begone ! my tent no more defile ;
Had gypsy seed within thee sprung,
No angry word had left my tongue,
But thou art a wanton base and lewd,
To stain thyself with gentile blood ! '

George Borrow.

Death the Lover

THERE was once a beautiful young Gypsy woman.
She had neither father nor mother, nor brothers nor
kindred—all were dead. She lived alone in a little cottage,
and no one ever came to visit her, and she never went to
visit any one. One evening a handsome stranger came
to her house, and opened the door, and cried, 'I am a way-
farer and I come from afar. Fain would I rest here. I can
go no farther ! ' The young woman said to him, 'Stay
here, then ! I will give thee a pillow to sleep upon, and
if thou desirest food and drink, I will give thee of that
which I have.' The stranger laid himself down and said,
'Now I am going to sleep once more : long is it since I
have slept ! ' The young woman asked him, 'Tell me how
long it is since thou hast slept.' Said the man, 'Sweet
woman, I sleep but once in a thousand years ! ' Then she
laughed and said, 'Thou mockest me, dost thou ? Thou
art a bad fellow ! ' But the fair stranger was already asleep.
In the morning when he rose, he said to her, 'Thou art a
beautiful young woman. If thou wilt, I will stay here a
week.'

The woman gladly had it so, for she was already in love with the stranger.

One night as they slept, the woman aroused the handsome stranger, and said to him, ' Sweet man, hearken ! I have had an evil dream. Methought thou wert very cold and white, and we were journeying together in a fine wagon. Thou blewest a great horn. Then all the dead arose and followed thee, for thou wert their king, and wert clad in a splendid mantle of fine cloth.' Then said the beautiful stranger, ' This is an ill dream.' And he arose and said, ' Sweetheart, I must begone, for in the world no one now has died for a long while. I must needs go. Loose me ! ' The woman wept and said, ' Go not away ! tarry yet a little ! ' Then said the man, ' I must needs begone. God have thee in his care ! ' But the woman sobbed as he pressed her hand, and she said to him, ' Tell me then who thou art.' Then the man cried, ' Who learns that, dies. Thou askest me in vain ; I will not tell thee who I am.' Then wept the woman saying, ' Let me suffer all things, only tell me who thou art.' Then said the stranger, ' It is well, for so thou comest with me ; I am Death.'

A great fear fell upon the young woman and she died.

Transylvanian Gypsy Folk-Tale.

The Daughter to her Mother

SWEET mother, sweet, would that thou hadst not borne me. Would rather that thou hadst borne a stone ! The stone knows not when its mother is dead, But I, poor lark, sing in the breeze, Sing in the sunshine the death of my sweet little mother.

No one now will warm me, When I am cold ; No one will shade me, When I am oppressed by the heat ! And who will prepare my couch, When I am sleepy ? The wind blows not ever, The sun shines not ever, But I, poor one, shall ever weep.

Into the wood will I go, When the wind blows, And to thee will I call, oh sweet mother ; But thou comest not. Thou

doſt not wipe away my tears, My heart thou doſt not heal.
Lonely shall I wander, A poor *Keshalyi* ; Henceforth will
I sit me down, On barren rocks, Where sings no bird,
Where grows no grass, There will I sit and sorrow.

Transylvanian Gypsy Lament.

Flamenca of Egyptian Race

UNLESS within a fortnight's space
  Thy face, O maid, I see,
Flamenca of Egyptian race
  My lady love shall be.

Flamenca of Egyptian race,
  If thou wert only mine,
Within a bonny cryſtal case
  For life I 'd thee enshrine.

Extend to me the hand so small,
  Wherein I see thee weep,
For O thy balmy tear-drops all
  I would colleſt and keep.

George Borrow.

Fragments of Tchinghiané Love-Songs

AWAKE thee ! and all the flowers in the garden will
  open.

*   *   *

Thy two hands I caught them
And thou haſt caught my heart.

*   *   *

When thou lookeſt at me and laugheſt,
The ſtars in heaven laugh also.

*   *   *

I would fain become a swallow to perch upon thy neck,
And kiss the olive that neſtles on thy cheek.

*   *   *

Pity, pity ! Frasha,
Because of the red cherries that pout forth from thee.

*   *   *

And when the birds sing
I think upon thy breasts,
And all night long I cannot sleep.

*   *   *

Thou wearest a fine chemisette, and thou sayest I am
distraught,
But thou dost not see thy feet, which are like unto instruments of music.

*   *   *

Thy navel is like a goblet,
Thy little breasts are like the coral.

*   *   *

I behold thy bosom opened to my view, and I say ' Lo ! it
is day.'

*   *   *

Thy bosom is like the sea, and thy breasts like the waves,
And if I fall therein and be drowned, thine will be the sin.

*   *   *

My little bird, come to me,
Take me at night into thy nest.

*   *   *

O my woman come, and let us twain become one.

From the Turkish Gypsy text of Paspati.

O my World !

SHE hath a gay silken gown,
And a kerchief soft as down,
And her coats make mad the town—
—Farthings upon farthings there,
  Halfpence upon halfpence there—
Stand thee still, girl, while I stare
  At my world !
Would her father gave her me,
Would that gown my smock might be,
  O my world !

Stand thee still, girl, while I stare ;
When I for the dance declare,
Whirl around with flying hair,
   O my world !

How the little prickly swine
Groweth fat while others pine,
Would to God such hap were mine,
   O my world !
Always in the taverns going
Where the wine is bravely flowing,
In the dance with maids delighting,
Candle after candle lighting—
   Yon small bird upon the tree,
     O my world !
   Twitters no good luck for me,
     O my world !

—Ah, my God, two fishes fine
Once were mine, once were mine,
But, alas ! one summer's day
They flew away, flew away
In the meadow grass to play ;
   Then, sweetheart say me sooth—
Let me perish, let me die
If I tell my dear a lie.
With thee, thine alone am I :
Absent, for another sigh :
   Fie on fickle youth !

For her eyes of wondrous shape
Black and sweet as fruit of grape,
And for her twin breasts so fair
Carven like two goblets rare,
For her eyes and for her breast
I have lost my rest, my rest,
   O my world !
For her breast and for her eyes
I my mother's love despise,
   O my world !

South Hungarian Gypsy Song.

Give to me a Mantle fine

OH, my God, to still my longing,
  Give to me a mantle fine,
Garnished all with buttons bright,
  In the golden light to shine.

Grant to me a goodly wife,
  In her jacket pure and neat,
With willow-like arms,
  And flower-like feet.

Her two shoulders
  Like white bread ;
Her eyes in shape
  Like seed of grape ;
And her two lips
  Like blossoms red.

Transylvanian Gypsy Song.

The Fine Chemise

Ma činger man, ma mar man, Ma činger mro sano gat,

Mer man nane   pir-a - no, Ko man tyinel   sa-no gat.

Ah, beat me not ! Ah, hurt me not !
  Tear not my fine chemise ;
For no true lover have I got
  To buy a new chemise.

Hungarian Gypsy Song.

K

Splendide Mendax

ON Tuesday last, as two Gentlemen were riding over Hounslow Heath, they observed a number of people assembled under two trees which grow by themselves, and, curiosity leading them to see what could be the matter, found that they were a gang of Gypsies, about twelve in number, who were boiling and roasting in the modern taste *al fresco*, on account of a conversion, as they called it : this conversion consisted of rubbing or dyeing a fine young girl about seventeen with walnut shell, it being the first day of her entering into the society.

The Annual Register, 1769.

A Procession of Dark Beauties

ALABAINA. Alamina. Alethea. Amoretta. Anselina. Aquilla. Athalaia. Barina. Begonia. Bellamarina. Berthenni. Bethorina. Canairis. Carnation. Cinderella. Celidonia. Clevansi. Concubina. Coralina. Dalitha. Damaris. Darklis. Delaia. Deleta. Deloraifi. Delorenni. Dorelia. Drusilla. Eldorai. Elvaina. Elvaira. Esmeralda. Ethelenda. Everilda. Fenella. Florentia. Fuchsia. Gentilla. Gerania. Kadilia. Kensilia. Kunsaletti. Kurlenda. Lavinia. Lementina. Lepronia. Liberina. Lucretia. Lurenni. Madona. Mairenni. Malindi. Mandra. Marbelenni. Marianna. Melita. Melvinia. Memberensi. Merenda. Milbora. Mirella. Mizelli. Modi. Morgiana. Narcissa. Nastasia. Orlenda. Penelli. Perella. Perpinia. Prunella. Repronia. Richenda. Rhoda. Rosaina. Rubaina. Saibirenni. Saieri. Saiforella. Sandra. Sanspirella. Savaina. Scorsafilia. Shurensi. Siani. Sibella. Silvaina. Sinaminta. Sinetta. Sinfai. Smaranda. Starlina. Sairenda. Theodosia. Trainit. Truffenni. Urania. Vashti. Venselina. Virginta.

VI
GYPSY CHILDREN

VI

Gypsy Children

Birth

I a Gypsy child was born,
  Of a mother all forlorn ;
In the long grass I was lain,
None baptized me but the rain.

Transylvanian Gypsy Song.

Small Deer

NO one is fond of Gipsies, but is fonder of Gipsy
children— odd compounds of pluck and shyness, of
cheek and courtesy, of thoughtlessness and meditation,
of quicksilver gaiety and quaint old-fashionedness.

Francis Hindes Groome.

Hearts-ease

I WILL dare to say that this Boy lives a merrier Life, and
wears more of that herb called *Hearts-ease* in his Bosom,
than he that is clad in Silk and Velvet.

John Bunyan.

Youth and Age

THE race of the Rommany is by nature perhaps the
most beautiful in the world ; and amongst the children
of the Russian Zigáni are frequently to be found countenances, to do justice to which would require the pencil
of a second Murillo ; but exposure to the rays of the
burning sun, the biting of the frost, and the pelting of the
pitiless sleet and snow, destroys their beauty at a very early
age. . . . A hundred years, could I live so long, would not
efface from my mind the appearance of an aged Ziganskie
Attaman, or Captain of Zigáni, and his grandson, who

149

approached me on the meadow before Novo Gorod, where stood the encampment of a numerous horde. The boy was of a form and face which might have entitled him to represent Astyanax, and Hector of Troy might have pressed him to his bosom, and called him his pride ; but the old man wanted but the dart and kingly crown to have been mistaken for the monster who opposed the progress of Lucifer.

George Borrow.

Arcady in England

I MET some children in a wood,
A happy and tumultuous rout
That came with many a wanton shout
And darted hither and about
(As in a stream the fickle trout),
To ease their pagan lustihood.

And in their midst they led along
A goat with wreaths about his neck
That they had taken pains to deck
To join the bacchanalian throng.

And one of them was garlanded
With strands of wild convolvulus
About his ringlets riotous,
And carried rowan-berries red.

And one, the eldest of the band,
Whose life was seven summers glad,
Was all in flowered muslin clad,
And naked dancing feet she had
To lead the sylvan saraband.
With hazel skin and coral bead
A gypsy dryad of the mead
She seemed ; she led the gay stampede
With fruited branches in her hand.

For all were bearing autumn fruit ;
Some, apples on the loaded bough,
And pears that on the orchard's brow
With damask-plums are hanging now ;
And much they had of woodland loot,
Of berries black and berries blue,
Of fircones and of medlars too ;
And one, who bore no plunder, blew
On reeds like an Arcadian flute.

They passed and still I stood knee-deep
In thymy grass to watch their train.
They wound along the wooded lane
And crossed a streamlet with a leap,
And as I saw them once again
They passed a shepherd and his sheep.

And you might think, I made this song
For joy of song as I strode along
One day between the Kentish shaws,
Slashing at scarlet hips and haws.
But thinking so, you nothing know
Of children taken unawares,
Of tinkers' tents among the gorse,
The poor lean goat, the hobbled horse,
And painted vans for country fairs.

Victoria Sackville-West.

In Bohemia

ONE most picturesque sight, however, was a group of gypsy children on the way. These had issued out of some of the distant woods to beg from the passengers on the highway. Bohemia is so old a haunt of this singular race, that in France they even still bear the name of Bohemians ; and truly these were of the wildest. There were three or four of them from ten to twelve years of age. They had nothing on them but a coarse shirt of hemp nearly black, and yet their skins were still more tawny. They were really handsome in their wildness. Their features were clearly cut, and full of expression ; their eyes were like dark fires ; their jet black hair hung in rich masses down their backs ; and their limbs had a shapely elasticity about them which nothing but their life of utter nature could give. They were, in fact, in appearance just such as Murillo often paints. In elasticity they were exactly as if made of India rubber. They were lithe and supple as snakes, and seemed as light as if their bodies were not framed of the same heavy material as our own. They threw themselves on their knees on the road as the *eilwagens* slowly ascended a hill ; with gestures full of life, and rapid tongues. They sprang up, ran, cast themselves down again ; threw at us such speaking looks, and were in such constant change of figure and clamour of importunity, that in their dusky wildness they looked rather like things in a dream than actual living creatures.

William Howitt.

Dancing the Zorongo

. . . SOUS les racines de ces grandes plantes grasses qui semblent leur servir de chevaux de frise et d'artichauts, sont creusées dans le roc vif les habitations des bohémiens. L'entrée de ces cavernes est blanchie à la chaux ; une corde tendue, sur laquelle glisse un morceau de tapisserie éraillée, leur tient lieu de porte. C'est là dedans que grouille et pullule la sauvage famille ; les enfants, plus fauves de peau que des cigares de la Havane, jouent tout nus devant le seuil, sans distinction de sexe, et se roulent dans la poussière en poussant des cris aigus et gutturaux. . . . Quelques rues désertes et à moitié en ruine de l'Albaycin sont aussi habitées par des gitanos plus riches ou moins nomades. Dans une de ces ruelles, nous aperçûmes une petite fille de huit ans, entièrement nue, qui s'exerçait à danser le *zorongo* sur un pavé pointu. Sa sœur, hâve, décharnée, avec des yeux de braise dans une figure de citron, était accroupie à terre à côté d'elle, une guitare sur les genoux, dont elle faisait ronfler les cordes avec le pouce, musique assez semblable au grincement enroué des cigales. La mère, richement habillée et le cou chargé de verroteries, battait la mesure du bout d'une pantoufle de velours bleu que son œil caressait complaisamment. La sauvagerie d'attitude, l'accoutrement étrange et la couleur extraordinaire de ce groupe, en eussent fait un excellent motif de tableau pour Callot ou Salvator Rosa. *Théophile Gautier.*

A Gypsy Boy

A FORTNIGHT before Christmas Gypsies were every-
where :
Vans were drawn up on wastes, women trailed to the fair.
' My gentleman,' said one, ' You 've got a lucky face.'
' And you 've a luckier,' I thought, ' if such a grace
And impudence in rags are lucky.' ' Give a penny
For the poor baby's sake.' ' Indeed I have not any
Unless you can give change for a sovereign, my dear.'
' Then just half a pipeful of tobacco can you spare ? '
I gave it. With that much victory she laughed content.
I should have given more, but off and away she went
With her baby and her pink sham flowers to rejoin
The rest before I could translate to its proper coin
Gratitude for her grace. And I paid nothing then,
As I pay nothing now with the dipping of my pen
For her brother's music when he drummed the tambourine
And stamped his feet, which made the workmen passing
    grin,
While his mouth-organ changed to a rascally Bacchanal
    dance
' Over the hills and far away.' This and his glance
Outlasted all the fair, farmer, and auctioneer,
Cheap-jack, balloon-man, drover with crooked stick, and
    steer,
Pig, turkey, goose, and duck, Christmas corpses to be.
Not even the kneeling ox had eyes like the Romany.
That night he peopled for me the hollow wooded land,
More dark and wild than stormiest heavens, that I searched
    and scanned
Like a ghost new-arrived. The gradations of the dark
Were like an underworld of death, but for the spark
In the Gypsy boy's black eyes as he played and stamped his
    tune,
' Over the hills and far away,' and a crescent moon.
                                        Edward Thomas.

In Belgrade

I HAD seen one old woman, an animal worn to subtlety, with the cunning of her race in all her wrinkles, trudging through the streets with a kind of hostile gravity. But here it was the children who fascinated me. There were three little girls, with exactly the skin of Hindus, and exactly the same delicately shaped face, and lustrous eyes, and long dark eyelashes ; and they followed me through the market, begging in strange tongues—little catlike creatures full of humour, vivacity and bright instinctive intelligence. As we came to one end of the market, they ran up to a young girl of about fifteen, who stood leaning against a pump. She was slender with a thin perfectly shaped face, the nose rather arched, the eyes large, black, lustrous, under the black eyebrows ; thick masses of black hair ran across her forehead, under the scarlet kerchief. She leaned there, haughty, magnetic, indifferent ; a swift animal, like a strung bow, bringing the East with her, and a shy wildness which is the Gypsy's only.

Arthur Symons.

To a Gypsy Child by the Sea-shore
Douglas, Isle of Man

WHO taught this pleading to unpractis'd eyes ?
    Who hid such import in an infant's gloom ?
Who lent thee, child, this meditative guise ?
Who mass'd, round that slight brow, these clouds of
    doom ?

Lo ! sails that gleam a moment and are gone ;
The swinging waters, and the cluster'd pier.
Not idly Earth and Ocean labour on,
Nor idly do these sea-birds hover near.

But thou, whom superfluity of joy
Wafts not from thine own thoughts, nor longings vain,
Nor weariness, the full-fed soul's annoy—
Remaining in thy hunger and thy pain ;

Thou, drugging pain by patience ; half averse
From thine own mother's breaſt, that knows not thee ;
With eyes that sought thine eyes thou didſt converse,
And that soul-searching vision fell on me.

Glooms that go deep as thine I have not known :
Moods of fantaſtic sadness, nothing worth.
Thy sorrow and thy calmness are thine own :
Glooms that enhance and glorify this earth.

What mood wears like complexion to thy woe ?—
His, who in mountain glens, at noon of day,
Sits rapt, and hears the battle break below ?—
Ah ! thine was not the shelter, but the fray.

What exile's, changing bitter thoughts with glad ?
What seraph's, in some alien planet born ?—
No exile's dream was ever half so sad,
Nor any angel's sorrow so forlorn.

Is the calm thine of ſtoic souls, who weigh
Life well, and find it wanting, nor deplore :
But in disdainful silence turn away,
Stand mute, self-centred, ſtern, and dream no more ?

Or do I wait, to hear some grey-hair'd king
Unravel all his many-colour'd lore ;
Whose mind hath known all arts of governing,
Mus'd much, lov'd life a little, loath'd it more ?

Down the pale cheek long lines of shadow slope,
Which years, and curious thought, and suffering give—
Thou haſt foreknown the vanity of hope,
Foreseen thy harveſt—yet proceed'ſt to live.

O meek anticipant of that sure pain
Whose sureness grey-hair'd scholars hardly learn !
What wonder shall time breed, to swell thy ſtrain ?
What heavens, what earth, what suns shalt thou discern ?

Ere the long night, whose stillness brooks no star,
Match that funereal aspect with her pall,
I think, thou wilt have fathom'd life too far,
Have known too much—or else forgotten all.

The Guide of our dark steps a triple veil
Betwixt our senses and our sorrow keeps ;
Hath sown with cloudless passages the tale
Of grief, and eas'd us with a thousand sleeps.

Ah ! not the nectarous poppy lovers use,
Not daily labour's dull, Lethean spring,
Oblivion in lost angels can infuse
Of the soil'd glory, and the trailing wing ;

And though thou glean, what strenuous gleaners may,
In the throng'd fields where winning comes by strife ;
And though the just sun gild, as all men pray,
Some reaches of thy storm-vext stream of life ;

Though that blank sunshine blind thee ; though the cloud
That sever'd the world's march and thine, is gone ;
Though ease dulls grace, and Wisdom be too proud
To halve a lodging that was all her own :

Once, ere the day decline, thou shalt discern,
Oh once, ere night, in thy success, thy chain !
Ere the long evening close, thou shalt return,
And wear this majesty of grief again.

Matthew Arnold.

Shelley and the Gypsy Children

WE were strolling one day in the neighbourhood of
Oxford, when Shelley was attracted by a little girl :
he turned aside, and stood and observed her in silence.
She was about six years of age, small and slight, bare-
headed, bare-legged, and her apparel variegated and

tattered. She was busily employed in collecting empty snail-shells, so much occupied indeed, that some moments elapsed before she turned her face towards us. When she did so, we perceived that she was evidently a young gipsy ; and Shelley was forcibly struck by the vivid intelligence of her wild and swarthy countenance, and especially by the sharp glance of her fierce black eyes. ' How much intellect is here ! ' he exclaimed, ' in how humble a vessel, and what an unworthy occupation for a person who once knew perfectly the whole circle of the sciences; who has forgotten them all, it is true, but who could certainly recollect them, although most probably she will never do so ; will never recall a single principle of any one of them ! '

As he spoke, he turned aside a bramble with his foot, and discovered a large shell, which the alert child instantly caught up and added to her store ; at the same moment a small stone was thrown from the other side of the road ; it fell in the hedge near us. We turned round and saw on the top of a high bank a boy some three years older than the girl, and in as rude a guise ; he was looking at us over a low hedge with a smile, but plainly not without suspicion. We might be two kidnappers, he seemed to think : he was in charge of his little sister, and did not choose to have her stolen before his face. He gave the signal therefore, and she obeyed it, and had almost joined him before we missed her from our side. They both disappeared, and we continued our walk.

Shelley was charmed with the intelligence of the two children of nature, and with their marvellous wildness : he talked much about them, and compared them to birds, and to the two wild leverets, which that wild mother, the hare, produces. We sauntered about, and half an hour afterwards, on turning a corner, we suddenly met the two children again full in the face. The meeting was unlooked for, and the air of the boy showed that it was unpleasant to him : he had a large bundle of dry sticks under his arm ; these he gently dropped, and stood motionless with an apprehensive smile—a deprecatory smile. We were perhaps the lords of the soil, and his patience was prepared, for patience was his lot—an inalienable inheritance long entailed upon his line—to hear a severe reproof with heavy threats, possibly even to receive blows with a stick gathered by himself, not altogether unwittingly, for his own back ; or to find mercy and forbearance. Shelley's demeanour soon convinced him that he had nothing to fear : he laid a hand on the round, matted, knotted, bare, and black head of each, viewed their moving, mercurial countenances with renewed pleasure and admiration, and shaking his long locks, suddenly strode away. ' That little ragged fellow knows as much as the wisest philosopher,' he presently cried, clapping the wings of his soul, and crowing aloud with shrill triumph at the felicitous union of the true with the ridiculous,—' but he will not communicate any portion of his knowledge : it is not from churlishness, however, for of that his nature is plainly incapable ; but the sophisticated urchin will persist in thinking he has forgotten all that he knows so well. I was about to ask him myself to communicate some of the doctrines Plato unfolds in his *Dialogues* : but I felt that it would do no good : the rogue would have laughed at me, and so would his little sister. I wonder you did not propose to them some mathematical questions : just a few interrogations in your geometry ; for that being so plain and certain, if it be once thoroughly understood, can never be forgotten ! '

A day or two afterwards (or it might be on the morrow) as we were rambling in the favourite region at the foot of Shotover Hill, a gipsy's tent by the roadside caught Shelley's eye : men and women were seated on the ground in front of it, watching a pot suspended over a smoky fire of sticks. He cast a passing glance at the ragged group, but immediately stopped on recognising the children, who remembered us, and ran laughing into the tent. Shelley laughed also, and waved his hand, and the little girl returned the salutation. . . .

As soon as he saw the children enter the tent, he darted after them with his peculiar agility, followed them into their low, narrow, and fragile tenement, penetrated to the bottom of the tent without removing his hat, or striking against the woven edifice. He placed a hand on each round, rough head, spoke a few kind words to the skulking children, and then returned not less precipitately, and with as much ease and accuracy, as if he had been a dweller in tents from the hour when he first drew air and milk to that day—as if he had been the descendant, not of a gentle house, but of a long line of gipsies. His visit roused the jealousy of a stunted, feeble dog, which followed him and barked with helpless fury : he did not heed it, nor perhaps hear it. The company of gipsies were astonished at the first visit that had ever been made by a member of either University to their humble dwelling ; but as its object was evidently benevolent, they did not stir or interfere, but greeted him on his return with a silent and unobserved salutation. He seized my arm, and we prosecuted our speculations, as we walked briskly to our college.

The marvellous gentleness of his demeanour could conciliate the least sociable natures, and it had secretly touched the wild things which he had thus briefly noticed.

We were wandering through the roads and lanes at a short distance from the tent soon afterwards, and were pursuing our way in silence ; I turned round at a sudden sound ;—the young gipsy had stolen upon us unperceived, and with a long bramble had struck Shelley across the skirts of his coat ; he had dropped his rod, and was returning softly to the hedge. . . .

As soon as [Shelley] understood the rude but friendly welcome to the heaths and lanes, he drew an orange from his pocket, and rolled it after the retreating gipsy along the grass by the side of the wide road. The boy started with surprise as the golden fruit passed him, quickly caught it up, and joyfully bore it away, bending reverently over it, and carrying it with both his hands, as if, together with almost the size, it had also the weight of a cannon-ball.

Thomas Jefferson Hogg.

The Orchard and the Heath

I CHANCED upon an early walk to spy
A troop of children through an orchard gate :
The boughs hung low, the grass was high ;
They had but to lift hands or wait
For fruits to fill them ; fruits were all their sky

They shouted, running on from tree to tree,
And played the game the wind plays, on and round.
'T was visible invisible glee
Pursuing ; and a fountain's sound
Of laughter spouted, pattering fresh on me.

I could have watched them till the daylight fled,
Their pretty bower made such a light of day.
A small one tumbling sang ' Oh ! head ! '
The rest to comfort her straightway
Seized on a branch and thumped down apples red.

The tiny creature flashing through green grass,
And laughing with her feet and eyes among
Fresh apples, while a little lass
Over as o'er breeze-ripples hung :
That sight I saw, and passed as aliens pass.

My footpath left the pleasant farms and lanes,
Soft cottage-smoke, straight cocks a-crow, gay flowers
Beyond the wheel-ruts of the wains,
Across a heath I walked for hours,
And met its rival tenants, rays and rains.

Still in my view mile-distant firs appeared,
When, under a patched channel-bank enriched
With foxglove whose late bells drooped seared,
Behold, a family had pitched
Their camp, and labouring the low tent upreared.

Here, too, were many children, quick to scan
A new thing coming ; swarthy cheeks, white teeth :
In many-coloured rags they ran,
Like iron runlets of the heath.
Dispersed lay broth-pot, sticks, and drinking-can.

Three girls, with shoulders like a boat at sea
Tipped sideways by the wave (their clothing slid
From either ridge unequally),
Lean, swift and voluble, bestrid
A starting-point, unfrocked to the bent knee.

They raced ; their brothers yelled them on, and broke
In act to follow, but as one they snuffed
    Wood-fumes, and by the fire that spoke
    Of provender, its pale flame puffed,
And rolled athwart dwarf furzes grey-blue smoke.

Soon on the dark edge of a ruddier gleam,
The mother-pot perusing, all, stretched flat,
    Paused for its bubbling-up supreme :
    A dog upright in circle sat,
And oft his nose went with the flying steam.

I turned and looked on heaven awhile, where now
The moor-faced sunset broaden'd with red light ;
    Threw high aloft a golden bough,
    And seemed the desert of the night
Far down with mellow orchards to endow.

George Meredith.

Brother and Sister

I SHALL never forget that morning. I was only a little
fellow, but even now I can close my eyes and see the
gypsy tent and waggon in the lane. The fire is burning
outside on the ground, and the kettle is hanging over it in
true gypsy fashion, and a bucket of water is standing near
by. Some clothes that my father has been washing are
hanging on the hedge. I can see the old horse grazing
along the lane. I can see the boughs bending in the
breeze and I can almost hear the singing of the birds, and
yet when I try to call back the appearance of my dear
mother I am baffled. . . . I wandered up the lane that
morning with the hand of my sister Tilly in mine. We
two little things were inseparable. We could not go to
father, for he was too full of his grief. The others were
sick. We two had gone off together, when suddenly I
heard my name called : ' Rodney ! ' and running to see
what I was wanted for, I encountered my sister Emily.
She had got out of bed, for bed could not hold her that
morning, and she said to me : ' Rodney, mother 's
dead ! ' . . .

L

My mother's death caused a gloom indescribable to settle down upon the tent life. The day of the funeral came. My mother was to be buried at the dead of night. We were only gypsies, and the authorities would not permit the funeral to take place in the daytime. In the afternoon the coffin was placed on two chairs outside the waggon, waiting for the darkness. Sister and brother were so much better that the waggon had been emptied. My father had been trying to cleanse it, and the clothes, such as we had for wearing and sleeping in, had been put into the tent. While we were watching and weeping round the coffin—father and his five children—the tent caught fire, and all our little stock of worldly possessions was burnt to ashes. The sparks flew around us on all sides of the coffin, and we expected every moment that that too would be set on fire. We poor little things were terrified nearly to death. ' Mother will be burnt up,' we wept. ' Mother will be burnt up.' Father fell upon his face on the grass crying like a child. The flames were so strong that he could do nothing to stop their progress, and indeed he had to take great care to avoid harm to himself. Our agonies while we were witnessing this, to us, terrible conflagration, helpless to battle against it, may easily be imagined, but, strange to relate, while the sparks fell all around the coffin, the coffin itself was untouched.

And now darkness fell, and with it came to us an old farmer's cart. Mother's coffin was placed in the vehicle, and between ten and eleven o'clock my father, the only mourner, followed her to the grave by a lantern light.

Rodney Smith.

A Gypsy Child's Christmas

DEAR Sinfi rose and danced along ' The Dells,'
    Drawn by the Christmas chimes, and soon she sate
  Where 'neath the snow around the churchyard gate
The ploughmen slept in bramble-banded cells.
The gorgios passed, half fearing Gypsy spells,
  While Sinfi, gazing, seemed to meditate ;
  She laughed for joy, then wept disconsolate :
' De poor dead gorgios cannot hear de bells.'

Within the church the clouds of gorgio breath
Arose, a steam of lazy praise and prayer,
To Him who weaves the loving Christmas-stair
O'er sorrow and sin and wintry deeps of Death ;
But where stood He ? beside our Sinfi there,
Remembering childish tears in Nazareth ?

Theodore Watts-Dunton.

A Babe's Prayer

LITTLE bird of Sparadise,
Do the work of Jesu Chrise,
Go by sea, go by lan',
Go by Goddes holy han'.

God make me a branch and flower,
May the Lord send us all a happy hour.

Patience Davis, a Gypsy.

VII

STURT AND STRIFE

VII

Sturt and Strife

Gitano Rhymes

O WHEN I sit my courser bold,
　My bantling in my rear,
And in my hand my musket hold,
　O how they quake with fear.

The false Juanito, day and night,
　Had best with caution go,
The Gypsy carles of Yeira height
　Have sworn to lay him low.

I wash'd not in the limpid flood,
　The shirt which binds my frame ;
But in Juanito Ralli's blood
　I bravely wash'd the same.

I walk'd the street, and there I spied
　A goodly gallows-tree,
And in my ear methought it cried :
　Gypsy, beware of me.

I left my house and walk'd about,
　They seized me fast and bound ;
It is a Gypsy thief, they shout,
　The Spaniards here have found.

From out the prison me they led,
　Before the scribe they brought ;
It is no Gypsy thief, he said,
　The Spaniards here have caught.

Throughout the night, the dusky night,
    I prowl in silence round,
And with my eyes look left and right,
    For him, the Spanish hound,
That with my knife I him may smite,
    And to the vitals wound.

They bore me from the prison nook,
    They bade me rove at large ;
When out I 'd come a gun I took,
    And scathed them with its charge.

O, I am not of gentle clan,
    I 'm sprung from Gypsy tree ;
And I will be no gentleman,
    But an Egyptian free.

                                George Borrow.

The Messenger

' RISE, brother, and tell me whether any one is coming
    down the pass.'
    ' I see a distant object,' I replied ; ' like a speck on the
side of the hill.'
    The Gypsy started up, and we both fixed our eyes on the
object : the distance was so great that it was at first with
difficulty that we could distinguish whether it moved or
not. A quarter of an hour, however, dispelled all doubts,
for within this time it had nearly reached the bottom of
the hill, and we could descry a figure seated on an animal
of some kind.
    ' It is a woman,' said I, at length, ' mounted on a grey
donkey.'
    ' Then it is my messenger,' said Antonio, ' for it can be
no other.'
    The woman and the donkey were now upon the plain,
and for some time were concealed from us by the copse
and brushwood which intervened. They were not long,
however, in making their appearance at the distance of
about a hundred yards. The donkey was a beautiful

creature of a silver grey, and came frisking along, swinging her tail, and moving her feet so quick that they scarcely seemed to touch the ground. The animal no sooner perceived us than she ſtopped short, turned round, and attempted to escape by the way she had come ; her rider, however, detained her, whereupon the donkey kicked violently, and would probably have flung the former, had she not sprung nimbly to the ground. The form of the woman was entirely concealed by the large wrapping man's cloak which she wore. I ran to assiſt her, when she turned her face full upon me, and I inſtantly recognized the sharp clever features of Antonia, whom I had seen at Badajoz, the daughter of my guide. She said nothing to me, but advancing to her father, addressed something to him in a low voice, which I did not hear. He ſtarted back, and vociferated ' All ? ' ' Yes,' said she in a louder tone, probably repeating the words which I had not caught before, ' All are captured.'

The Gypsy remained for some time like one aſtounded, and, unwilling to liſten to their discourse, which I imagined might relate to business of Egypt, I walked away amidſt the thickets. I was absent for some time, but could occasionally hear passionate expressions and oaths. In about half an hour I returned ; they had left the road, but I found them behind the broom clump, where the animals ſtood. Both were seated on the ground ; the features of the Gypsy were peculiarly dark and grim ; he held his unsheathed knife in his hand, which he would occasionally plunge into the earth, exclaiming, ' All ! All ! '

George Borrow.

The King's Juſtice

' PALE slave of Eblis ! ' said a man in imperfeƈt French, ' are you robbing him you have murdered ? But we have you—and you shall abye it.'

There were knives drawn on every side of him, as these words were spoken, and the grim and diſtorted countenances which glared on him, were like those of wolves rushing on their prey.

Still the young Scot's courage and presence of mind bore
him out. 'What mean ye, my masters?' he said; 'if that
be your friend's body, I have just now cut him down in
pure charity, and you will do better to try to recover his
life, than to misuse an innocent stranger to whom he owes
his chance of escape.'

The women had by this time taken possession of the
dead body, and continued the attempts to recover anima-
tion which Durward had been making use of, though with
the like bad success; so that, desisting from their fruitless
efforts, they seemed to abandon themselves to all the
Oriental expressions of grief; the women making a piteous
wailing and tearing their long black hair, while the men
seemed to rend their garments, and to sprinkle dust upon
their heads. . . .

The singular assemblage, both male and female, wore
turbans and caps, more similar in general appearance to
his own bonnet than to the hats commonly worn in France.
Several of the men had curled black beards, and the complexion of all was nearly as dark as that of Africans. One
or two who seemed their chiefs, had some tawdry orna-
ments of silver about their necks and in their ears, and
wore showy scarfs of yellow, or scarlet, or light green;
but their legs and arms were bare, and the whole troop
seemed wretched and squalid in appearance. There were
no weapons among them that Durward saw, except the long
knives with which they had lately menaced him, and one
short crooked sabre, or Moorish sword, which was worn
by an active-looking young man, who often laid his hand
upon the hilt, while he surpassed the rest of the party in
his extravagant expressions of grief, and seemed to mingle
with them threats of vengeance.

The disordered and yelling group were so different in
appearance from any beings whom Quentin had yet seen,
that he was on the point of concluding them to be a party
of Saracens, of those 'heathen hounds,' who were the
opponents of gentle knights and Christian monarchs, in all
the romances which he had heard or read, and was about
to withdraw himself from a neighbourhood so perilous,
when a galloping of horse was heard, and the supposed
Saracens, who had raised by this time the body of their

comrade upon their shoulders, were at once charged by a party of French soldiers.

This sudden apparition changed the measured wailing of the mourners into irregular shrieks of terror. The body was thrown to the ground in an instant, and those who were around it showed the utmost and most dexterous activity in escaping, under the bellies as it were of the horses, from the point of the lances which were levelled at them with exclamations of ' Down with the accursed heathen thieves—take and kill—bind them like beasts— spear them like wolves ! '

These cries were accompanied with corresponding acts of violence ; but such was the alertness of the fugitives, the ground being rendered unfavourable to the horsemen by thickets and bushes, that only two were struck down and made prisoners, one of whom was the young fellow with the sword, who had previously offered some resistance. . . .

' Trois-Eschelles and Petit-André,' said the down-looking officer to two of his band, ' these same trees stand here quite convenient. I will teach these misbelieving, thieving sorcerers to interfere with the King's justice, when it has visited any of their accursed race. Dismount, my children, and do your office briskly.'

Trois-Eschelles and Petit André were in an instant on foot, and Quentin observed that they had each at the crupper and pommel of his saddle a coil or two of ropes, which they hastily undid, and shewed that in fact each coil formed a halter, with the fatal noose adjusted, ready for execution. . . .

The Provost rode on followed by his guard, excepting two or three who were left to assist in the execution. The unhappy youth cast after him an eye almost darkened by despair, and thought he heard in every tramp of his horse's retreating hoofs the last slight chance of his safety vanish. He looked around him in agony, and was surprised, even in that moment, to see the stoical indifference of his fellow-prisoners. They had previously testified every sign of fear, and made every effort to escape ; but now when secured and destined apparently to inevitable death, they awaited its arrival with the utmost composure. The scene

of fate before them gave perhaps a more yellow tinge to
their swarthy cheeks ; but it neither agitated their features,
nor quenched the stubborn haughtiness of their eye. They
seemed like foxes, which after all their wiles and artful
attempts at escape are exhausted, die with a silent and sullen
fortitude, which wolves and bears, the fiercer objects of
the chase, do not exhibit.

Sir Walter Scott.

A Sermon in Praise of Thieves and Thievery

A sermon of parson Haberdyne which he made at the
  commandment of certain thieves, after they had
  robbed him besides Hartlerow in Hampshire, in the
  fields, there standing upon a hill where as a wind mill
  had been, in the presence of the thieves that robbed
  him, as followeth.

the sermon as followeth.

I GREATLY marvel that any man will presume to dis-
praise thievery and think the doers thereof to be worthy
of death, considering it is a thing that cometh near unto
virtue being used of many in all countries and commended
and allowed of God him self. The which thing because I
cannot compendiously show unto you at so short a warning
and in so sharp a weather, I shall desire you, gentle audience
of thieves, to take in good part these things that at this time
cometh to my mind, not misdoubting but that you of your
good knowledge are able to add much more unto it then
this which I shall now utter unto you. First, fortitude and
stoutness of courage and also boldness of mind is commended of some men to be a vertue ; which, being granted,
who is it then that will not judge thieves to be vertused ?
for they be of all men most stout and hardy, and most without fear ; for thievery is a thing most usual among all men,
for not only you that be here present, but many other in
diverse places, both men and women and children, rich and
poor, are daily of this faculty as the hangman of Tyburn
can testify. And that it is allowed of God him self as it is

evident in many stories of the scriptures ; for if you look
in the whole course of the bible, you shall find that thieves
have been beloved of God ; for Jacob, when he came out
of Mesopotamia did steal his uncle Laban's kids ; the same
Jacob also did steal his brother Esau's blessing ; and yet
God said, ' I have chosen Jacob and refused Esau.' The
children of Israel, when they came out of Egypt, did steal
the Egyptians' jewels of silver and gold, as God com-
manded them so to do. David, in the days of Abiathar
the high priest, did come into the temple and did steal the
hallowed bread ; and yet God said ' David is a man even
after mine own heart.' Christ him self, when he was here
on the earth, did take an ass and a colt that was none of
his ; and you know that God said of him ' this is my
beloved son, in whom I delight.' Thus you may see that
God delighteth in thieves. But most of all I marvel that
men can despise you thieves, where as in all points almost
you be like unto Christ him self : for Christ had no dwelling place ; no more have you. Christ went from town to
town ; and so do you. Christ was hated of all men saving
of his friends ; and so are you. Christ was laid wait upon
in many places ; and so are you. Christ at the length was
caught ; and so shall you be. He was brought before the
judges ; and so shall you be. He was accused ; and so shall
you be. He was condemned ; and so shall you be. He
was hanged ; and so shall you be. He went down into hell ;
and so shall you do. Marry ! in this one thing you differ
from him, for he rose again and ascended into heaven ; and
so shall you never do without God's great mercy, which
God grant you ! To whom with the Father, and the Son,
and the Holy Ghost, be all honour and glory, for ever and
ever. Amen.

Thus his sermon being ended, they gave him his money
again that they took from him, and ij s. to drink for his
sermon.

finis.

MS. Cotton Vesp. (XVI Cent.)

Prayer of the Gypsy Modoran

SWEET little God, I beseech thee to grant me everything I ask, because thou art beautiful, high and
mighty.

If thou lettest me steal a loaf, brandy, a hen, a goose, a
sheep, a pig, or a horse I will give thee a big candle.

If I have stolen anything, and the gentiles enter my tent
to discover the stolen property and find nothing, I will
give thee two big candles.

If the officers of the law enter my tent, and having
searched it and found nothing, depart in peace, I will give
thee three big candles.

Because thou art my sweet little golden God.

Rumanian Gypsy Prayer.

The Gypsy's Malison

(? *Jan.* 29*th*, 1829.)

WHEN Miss Ouldcroft (who is now Mrs. Beddome,
and Bed-dom'd to her !) was at Enfield, which she
was in summertime, and owed her health to its sun and
genial influences, she wisited (with young lady-like impertinence) a poor man's cottage that had a pretty baby
(O the yearnling !), and gave it fine caps and sweetmeats.
On a day, broke into the parlour our two maids uproarious.
' O ma'am, who do you think Miss Ouldcroft (they pro-
nounce it Holcroft) has been working a cap for ? ' ' A
child,' answered Mary, in true Shandean female simplicity.
' It 's the man's child as was taken up for sheep-stealing.'
Miss Ouldcroft was staggered, and would have cut the
connection ; but by main force I made her go and take her
leave of her protégée (which I only spell with a g because
I can't make a pretty j). I thought, if she went no more,
the Abactor or Abactor's wife (*vide* Ainsworth) would
suppose she had heard something ; and I have delicacy
for a sheep-stealer. The overseers actually overhauled a
mutton-pie at the baker's (his first, last, and only hope of
mutton-pie), which he never came to eat, and thence in-

ferred his guilt. *Per occasionem cujus* I framed the sonnet ; observe its elaborate construction. I was four days about it.

The Gypsy's Malison

Suck, baby, suck, Mother's love grows by giving,
    Drain the sweet founts that only thrive by wasting ;
Black Manhood comes, when riotous guilty living
    Hands thee the cup that shall be death in tasting.
Kiss, baby, kiss, Mother's lips shine by kisses,
    Choke the warm breath that else would fall in blessings ;
Black Manhood comes, when turbulent guilty blisses
    Tend thee the kiss that poisons 'mid caressings.
Hang, baby, hang, mother's love loves such forces,
    Choke the forld neck that bends still to thy clinging ;
Black Manhood comes, when violent lawless courses
    Leave thee a spectacle in rude air swinging.

    So sang a wither'd Sibyl energetical,
    And bann'd the ungiving door with lips prophetical.

Barry, study that sonnet. It is curiously and perversely elaborate. 'Tis a choking subject, and therefore the reader is directed to the structure of it. See you ? and was this a fourteener to be rejected by a trumpery annual ? forsooth, 'twould shock all mothers ; and may all mothers who would so be shocked, bed dom'd ! as if mothers were such sort of logicians as to infer the future hanging of *their* child from the theoretical hangibility (or capacity of being hanged, if the judge pleases) of every infant born with a neck on. Oh B. C., my whole heart is faint, and my whole head is sick (how is it ?) at this damned, canting, unmasculine unbxwdy (I had almost said) age ! Don't show this to your child's mother or I shall be Orpheusized, scattered into Hebras. Damn the King, lords, commons, and *specially* (as I said on Muswell Hill on a Sunday when I could get no beer a quarter before one) all Bishops, Priests and Curates. Vale.

Charles Lamb.

M'Pherson's Farewell

FAREWELL, ye dungeons dark and strong,
   The wretch's destinie !
M'Pherson's time will not be long
   On yonder gallows-tree.
    Sae rantingly, sae wantonly,
      Sae dauntingly gaed he ;
    He play'd a spring and danc'd it round,
      Below the gallows-tree.

O, what is death but parting breath ?
   On many a bloody plain
I 've dared his face, and in this place
   I scorn him yet again.

Untie these bands from off my hands,
   And bring to me my sword ;
And there 's no a man in all Scotland
   But I 'll brave him at a word.

I 've liv'd a life of sturt and strife ;
   I die by treacherie :
It burns my heart I must depart,
   And not avengèd be.

Now farewell light, thou sunshine bright,
   And all beneath the sky !
May coward shame distain his name,
   The wretch that dare not die !

                 Robert Burns.

I bean't afeard

ALTHOUGH some Gypsies on the approach of death
show great fear and distress of mind, others among
them have been callous and unconcerned. Some years
since old Gypsy Buckland, who was so desperate a character that even his own people were compelled to discard
him, was sentenced to be hanged for murder. . . . Just
before his execution, having asked to have his shoe strings

untied, he threw his shoes into the crowd, and called out
in a bold, defiant manner : ' I bean't afeard.'   In a few
moments he ceased to exist.
                                              Vernon S. Morwood.

Gilderoy

GILDEROY was a bonnie boy,
     Had roses tull his shoone;
His stockings were of silken soy,
     Wi' garters hanging doune.
It was, I weene, a comelie sight,
     To see sae trim a boy ;
He was my jo and hearts delight,
     My handsome Gilderoy.

O ! sike twa charming een he had,
     A breath as sweet as rose ;
He never ware a Highland plaid,
     But costly silken clothes ;
He gain'd the luve of ladies gay,
     Nane eir tull him was coy ;
Ah ! wae is me ! I mourn the day,
     For my dear Gilderoy.

My Gilderoy and I were born,
     Baith in one toun together,
We scant were seven years beforn
     We 'gan to luve each ither ;
Our daddies and our mammies, they
     Were fill'd wi' mickle joy,
To think upon the bridal day,
     'Twixt me and Gilderoy.

For Gilderoy, that luve of mine,
     Gude faith, I freely bought
A wedding sark of holland fine,
     Wi' silken flowers wrought :
And he gied me a wedding ring,
     Which I receiv'd wi' joy ;
Nae lad nor lassie eir could sing,
     Like me and Gilderoy.

M

Wi' mickle joy we spent our prime,
    Till we were baith sixteen,
And aft we past the langsome time,
    Among the leaves sae green ;
Aft on the banks we 'd sit us thair,
    And sweetly kiss and toy ;
Wi' garlands gay wad deck my hair
    My handsome Gilderoy.

O ! that he still had been content,
    Wi' me to lead his life ;
But, ah ! his manfu' heart was bent
    To stir in feates of strife :
And he in many a venturous deed,
    His courage bauld wad try,
And now this gars mine heart to bleed
    For my dear Gilderoy.

And when of me his leave he tuik,
    The tears they wat mine ee ;
I gave tull him a parting luik,
    ' My benison gang wi' thee !
God speid thee weil, mine ain dear heart,
    For gane is all my joy ;
My heart is rent sith we maun part,
    My handsome Gilderoy.'

My Gilderoy baith far and near,
    Was fear'd in every toun,
And bauldly bare away the gear
    Of many a lawland loun ;
Nane eir durst meet him man to man,
    He was sae brave a boy ;
At length wi' numbers he was tane,
    My winsome Gilderoy.

Wae worth the loon that made the laws,
    To hang a man for gear,
To 'reave of life for ox or ass,
    For sheep, or horse, or mare !

Had not their laws been made sae strick,
  I neir had lost my joy,
Wi' sorrow neir had wat my cheek
  For my dear Gilderoy.

Gif Gilderoy had done amisse,
  He mought hae banisht been;
Ah! what sair cruelty is this,
  To hang sike handsome men!
To hang the flower o' Scottish land,
  Sae sweet and fair a boy!
Nae lady had sae white a hand,
  As thee, my Gilderoy.

Of Gilderoy sae fraid they were,
  They bound him mickle strong;
Tull Edenburrow they led him thair,
  And on a gallows hung:
They hung him high aboon the rest,
  He was sae trim a boy;
Thair dyed the youth whom I lued best,
  My handsome Gilderoy.

Scots Ballad.

The Gypsy Laddie

THE gypsies came to our good lord's gate,
  And wow but they sang sweetly!
They sang sae sweet and sae very compleat
  That down came the fair lady.

And she came tripping down the stair,
  And a' her maids before her;
As soon as they saw her well-far'd face,
  They coost the glamour oer her.

' Gae tak frae me this gay mantile,
  And bring to me a plaidie;
For if kith and kin and a' had sworn,
  I 'll follow the gypsy laddie.

' Yestreen I lay in a well-made bed,
  And my good lord beside me ;
This night I 'll ly in a tenant's barn,
  Whatever shall betide me.'

' Come to your bed,' says Johny Faa,
  ' Oh, come to your bed, my deary ;
For I vow and I swear, by the hilt of my sword,
  That your lord shall nae mair come near ye.'

' I 'll go to bed to my Johny Faa,
  I 'll go to bed to my deary ;
For I vow and I swear, by what past yestreen,
  That my lord shall nae mair come near me

' I 'll mak a hap to my Johny Faa,
  And I 'll mak a hap to my deary ;
And he 's get a' the coat gaes round,
  And my lord shall nae mair come near me.'

And when our lord came home at een,
  And spier'd for his fair lady,
The tane she cry'd, and the other reply'd,
  ' She 's away with the gypsy laddie.'

' Gae saddle to me the black, black steed,
  Gae saddle and make him ready ;
Before that I either eat or sleep,
  I 'll gae seek my fair lady.'

And we were fifteen well-made men,
  Altho' we were nae bonny ;
And we were a' put down for ane,
  A fair young wanton lady.

Scots Ballad.

The Gwyddelod

WE continued our way, and presently saw marks of
a fire in some grass by the side of the road. ' Have
the Gipsiaid been there ? ' said I to my guide.

' Hardly, sir ; I should rather think that the Gwyddeliad
(Irish) have been camping there lately.'

' The Gwyddeliad ? '

' Yes, sir, the vagabond Gwyddeliad, who at present
infeſt these parts much, and do much more harm than the
Gipsiaid ever did.'

' What do you mean by the Gipsiaid ? '

' Dark, handsome people, sir, who occasionally used to
come about in vans and carts, the men buying and selling
horses, and sometimes tinkering, whilſt the women told
fortunes.'

' And they have ceased to come about ? '

' Nearly so, sir ; I believe they have been frightened
away by the Gwyddelod.'

' What kind of people are these Gwyddelod ? '

' Savage, brutish people, sir ; in general without shoes
and ſtockings, with coarse features and heads of hair like
mops.'

' How do they live ? '

' The men tinker a little, sir, but more frequently plunder.
The women tell fortunes, and ſteal whenever they can.'

' They live something like the Gipsiaid.'

' Something, sir ; but the hen Gipsiaid were gentlefolks
in comparison.'

. . . ' Is it a long time since you have seen any of these
Gwyddeliaid ? '

' About two months, sir, and then a terrible fright they
caused me.'

' How was that ? '

' I will tell you, sir ; I had been across the Berwyn to
carry home a piece of weaving work to a person who
employs me. It was night as I returned, and when I was
about halfway down the hill, at a place which is called Allt
Paddy, because the Gwyddelod are in the habit of taking
up their quarters there, I came upon a gang of them, who
had come there and camped and lighted their fire, whilſt
I was on the other side of the hill. There were nearly
twenty of them, men and women, and amongſt the reſt
was a man ſtanding naked in a tub of water with two women
ſtroking him down with clouts. He was a large fierce-
looking fellow, and his body, on which the flame of the fire

glittered, was nearly covered with red hair. I never saw such a sight. As I passed they glared at me and talked violently in their Paddy Gwyddel, but did not offer to molest me. I hastened down the hill, and right glad I was when I found myself safe and sound at my house in Llangollen, with my money in my pocket.'

George Borrow.

Captain Bosvile and the Hindity Family

AFTER walking about half-an-hour I saw a kind of wooden house on wheels drawn by two horses coming down the hill towards me. A short black-looking fellow in brown-top boots, corduroy breeches, jockey coat and jockey cap sat on the box, holding the reins in one hand and a long whip in the other. Beside him was a swarthy woman in a wild flaunting dress. Behind the box out of the fore part of the caravan peered two or three black children's heads. A pretty little foal about four months old came frisking and gambolling, now before now beside the horses, whilst a colt of some sixteen months followed more leisurely behind. When the caravan was about ten yards distant I stopped, and raising my left hand with the little finger pointed aloft, I exclaimed :

' Shoon, Kaulomengro, shoon ! In Dibbel's nav, where may tu be jawing to ? '

Stopping his caravan with considerable difficulty the small black man glared at me for a moment like a wild cat, and then said in a voice partly snappish, partly kind :

' Savo shan tu ? Are you one of the Ingrines ? '

' I am the chap what certain folks calls the Romany Rye.'

' Well, I 'll be jiggered if I wasn't thinking so and if I wasn't penning so to my juwa as we were welling down the chong.'

' It is a long time since we last met, Captain Bosvile, for I suppose I may call you Captain now ? ' . . .

' And now tell me, what brought you into Wales ? '

' What brought me into Wales ? I 'll tell you ; my own fool's head. I was doing nicely in the Kaulo Gav and the neighbourhood, when I must needs pack up and come into these parts with bag and baggage, wife and childer. I

thought that Wales was what it was some thirty years agone
when our foky used to say—for I was never here before—
that there was something to be done in it ; but I was never
more mistaken in my life. The country is overrun with
Hindity mescrey, woild Irish, with whom the Romany foky
stand no chance. The fellows underwork me at tinkering,
and the women outscream my wife at telling fortunes—
moreover they say the country is theirs and not intended
for niggers like we, and as they are generally in vast numbers what can a poor little Roman family do but flee away
before them ? A pretty journey I have made into Wales.
Had I not contrived to pass off a poggado bav engro—a
broken-winded horse—at a fair, I at this moment should be
without a tringoruschee piece in my pocket. I am now
making the best of my way back to Brummagem, and if
ever I come back again to this Hindity country may Cal-
craft nash me.'

'I wonder you didn't try to serve some of the Irish out,'
said I.

'I served one out, brother ; and my wife and childer
helped to wipe off a little of the score. We had stopped
on a nice green, near a village over the hills in Glamorganshire, when up comes a Hindity family, and bids us take
ourselves off. Now it so happened that there was but one
man and a woman and some childer, so I laughed, and told
them to drive us off. Well, brother, without many words,
there was a regular scrimmage. The Hindity mush came
at me, the Hindity mushi at my juwa, and the Hindity
chaves at my chai. It didn't last long, brother. In less
than three minutes I had hit the Hindity mush, who was a
plaguey big fellow, but couldn't fight, just under the point
of the chin, and sent him to the ground with all his senses
gone. My juwa had almost scratched an eye out of the
Hindity mushi, and my chai had sent the Hindity childer
scampering over the green. "Who has got to quit now ?"
said I to the Hindity mush after he had got on his legs,
looking like a man who has been cut down after hanging
just a minute and a half. "Who has got notice to quit,
now, I wonder ?" Well, brother, he didn't say anything,
nor did any of them, but after a little time they all took
themselves off, with a cart they had, to the south. Just

as they got to the edge of the green, however, they turned round and gave a yell which made all our blood cold. I knew what it meant, and said, " This is no place for us." So we got everything together and came away ; and, though the horses were tired, never stopped till we had got ten miles from the place ; and well it was we acted as we did, for, had we stayed, I have no doubt that a whole Hindity clan would have been down upon us before morning and cut our throats.'

George Borrow.

Cashel Byron's Opinion

A FIGHT ? Just so. What is life but a fight ? The curs forfeit or get beaten ; the rogues sell the fight and lose the confidence of their backers ; the game ones, and the clever ones, win the stakes, and have to hand over the lion's share of them to the loafers ; and luck plays the devil with them all in turn. That's not the way they describe life in books ; but that's what it is.

George Bernard Shaw.

Mr. Valiant

THEN said Great-heart to Mr. Valiant-for-Truth, Thou hast worthily behaved thyself ; let me see thy Sword. So he shewed it him.

When he had taken it in his Hand, and looked thereon a while, he said Ha ! It is a right Jerusalem Blade.

VALIANT. It is so. Let a man have one of these Blades, with a Hand to wield it, and skill to use it, and he may venture upon an Angel with it. He need not fear its holding, if he can but tell how to lay on. Its Edges will never blunt. It will cut Flesh, and Bones, and Soul, and Spirit, and all.

GREAT-HEART. But you fought a great while, I wonder you was not weary ?

VALIANT. I fought till my Sword did cleave to my Hand ; and when they were joined together, as if a Sword grew out of my Arm, and when the Blood run thorow my Fingers, then I fought with most Courage.

GREAT-HEART. Thou haſt done well. . . .

Then they took him and washed his Wounds, and gave him of what they had, to refresh him, and so they went on together . . . because Mr. Great-heart was delighted in him, for he loved one greatly that he found to be a man of his Hands.

John Bunyan.

Thurtell and Gypsy Will

WHEN a boy of fourteen, I was present at a prize-fight ; why should I hide the truth ? It took place on a green meadow, beside a running ſtream, close by the old church of E——, and within a league of the ancient town of N——, the capital of one of the eaſtern counties. The terrible Thurtell was present, lord of the concourse ; for wherever he moved he was maſter, and whenever he spoke, even when in chains, every other voice was silent. He ſtood on the mead, grim and pale as usual, with his bruisers around. He it was, indeed, who got up the fight, as he had previously done with respeＣt to twenty others ; it being his frequent boaſt that he had firſt introduced bruising and bloodshed amidſt rural scenes, and trans-formed a quiet slumbering town into a den of Jews and metropolitan thieves. Some time before the commence-ment of the combat, three men, mounted on wild-looking horses, came dashing down the road in the direＣtion of the meadow, in the midſt of which they presently showed themselves, their horses clearing the deep ditches with wonderful alacrity. ' That 's Gypsy Will and his gang,' lisped a Hebrew pickpocket ; ' we shall have another fight.' The word Gypsy was always sufficient to excite my curiosity, and I looked attentively at the newcomers.

I have seen Gypsies of various lands, Russian, Hun-garian and Turkish ; and I have also seen the legitimate children of moſt countries of the world, but I never saw, upon the whole, three more remarkable individuals, as far as personal appearance was concerned, than the three English Gypsies who now presented themselves to my eyes on that spot. Two of them had dismounted, and were holding their horses by the reins. The talleſt, and at the first glance, the most interesting of the two, was almost a giant, for his height could not have been less than six feet three. It is impossible for the imagination to conceive anything more perfectly beautiful than were the features of this man, and the most skilful sculptor of Greece might have taken them as his model for a hero and a god. The forehead was exceedingly lofty, a rare thing in a Gypsy; the nose less Roman than Grecian, fine yet delicate; the eyes large, overhung with long drooping lashes, giving them almost a melancholy expression; it was only when they were highly elevated that the Gypsy glance peered out, if that can be called glance which is a strange stare, like nothing else in this world. His complexion—a beautiful olive; and his teeth of a brilliancy uncommon even amongst these people, who have all fine teeth. He was dressed in a coarse waggoner's slop, which, however, was unable to conceal altogether the proportions of his noble and Herculean figure. He might be about twenty-eight. His companion and his captain, Gypsy Will, was, I think, fifty when he was hanged, ten years subsequently (for I never afterwards lost sight of him), in the front of the jail of Bury St. Edmunds. I have still present before me his bushy black hair, his black face, and his big black eyes, full and thoughtful, but fixed and staring. His dress consisted of a loose blue jockey coat, jockey boots and breeches; in his hand a huge jockey whip, and on his head (it struck me at the time for its singularity) a broad-brimmed, high-peaked Andalusian hat, or at least one very much resembling those worn in that province. In stature he was shorter than his more youthful companion, yet he must have measured six feet at least, and was stronger built, if possible. What brawn!—what bone!—what legs!—what thighs! The third Gypsy, who remained on horseback, looked more like a phantom than anything human. His complexion was the colour of pale dust, and of that same colour was all that pertained to him, hat and clothes. His boots were dusty, of course, for it was midsummer, and his very horse was of a dusty dun. His features were whimsically ugly, most of his teeth were gone, and as to his age, he might be thirty or sixty. He was somewhat lame and halt, but an unequalled rider when once upon his steed, which he was

naturally not very solicitous to quit. I subsequently discovered that he was considered the wizard of the gang.

I have been already prolix with respect to these Gypsies,
but I will not leave them quite yet. The intended combatants at length arrived ; it was necessary to clear the ring,
always a troublesome and difficult task. Thurtell went
up to the two Gypsies, with whom he seemed to be acquainted, and with his surly smile, said two or three words,
which I, who was standing by, did not understand. The
Gypsies smiled in return, and giving the reins of their
animals to their mounted companion, immediately set
about the task which the king of the flash-men had, as I
conjecture, imposed upon them ; this they soon accomplished. Who could stand against such fellows and such
whips ? The fight was soon over—then there was a
pause. Once more Thurtell came up to the Gypsies and
said something—the Gypsies looked at each other and
conversed ; but their words had then no meaning for my
ears. The tall Gypsy shook his head—' Very well,' said
the other in English, ' I will—that 's all.'

Then pushing the people aside, he strode to the ropes,
over which he bounded into the ring, flinging his Spanish
hat high into the air.

GYPSY WILL. ' The best man in England for twenty
pounds ! '

THURTELL. ' I am backer.'

Twenty pounds is a tempting sum, and there were men
that day upon the green meadow who would have shed the
blood of their own fathers for the fifth of the price. But the
Gypsy was not an unknown man, his prowess and strength
were notorious, and no one cared to encounter him. Some
of the Jews looked eager for a moment ; but their sharp
eyes quailed quickly before his savage glances, as he towered
in the ring, his huge form dilating, and his black features
convulsed with excitement. The Westminster bravoes
eyed the Gypsy askance ; but the comparison, if they made
any, seemed by no means favourable to themselves.
' Gypsy ! rum chap—ugly customer—always in train-
ing.' Such were the exclamations which I heard, some of
which at that period of my life I did not understand.

No man would fight the Gypsy.—Yes ! a strong country

fellow wished to win the stakes, and was about to fling up his hat in defiance, but he was prevented by his friends, with ' Fool ! he 'll kill you ! '

As the Gypsies were mounting their horses, I heard the dusty phantom exclaim—

' Brother, you are an arrant ring-maker and a horse-breaker ; you 'll make a hempen ring to break your own neck of a horse one of these days.'

They pressed their horses' flanks, again leaped over the ditches, and speedily vanished, amidst the whirlwinds of dust which they raised upon the road.

George Borrow.

The Bloody Dukkeripen

AND now the second fight commences ; it is between two champions of less renown than the others, but is perhaps not the worse on that account. A tall thin boy is fighting in the ring with a man somewhat under the middle size, with a frame of adamant ; that 's a gallant boy ! he 's a yokel, but he comes from Brummagem, and he does credit to his extraction ; but his adversary has a frame of adamant : in what a strange light they fight, but who can wonder, on looking at that frightful cloud, usurping now one half of heaven, and at the sun struggling with sulphurous vapour ; the face of the boy, which is turned towards me, looks horrible in that light, but he is a brave boy, he strikes his foe on the forehead, and the report of the blow is like the sound of a hammer against a rock ; but there is a rush and a roar overhead, a wild commotion, the tempest is beginning to break loose ; there 's wind and dust, a crash, rain and hail ; is it possible to fight amidst such a commotion ? yes ! the fight goes on ; again the boy strikes the man full on the brow, but it is of no use striking that man, his frame is of adamant. ' Boy, thy strength is beginning to give way, and thou art becoming confused ' ; the man now goes to work, amidst rain and hail. ' Boy, thou wilt not hold out ten minutes longer against rain, hail, and the blows of such an antagonist.'

And now the storm was at its height ; the black thunder-cloud had broken into many, which assumed the wildest

shapes and the strangest colours, some of them unspeakably
glorious ; the rain poured in a deluge, and more than one
waterspout was seen at no great distance : an immense
rabble is hurrying in one direction ; a multitude of men of
all ranks, peers and yokels, prize-fighters and Jews, and the
last came to plunder, and are now plundering amidst that
wild confusion of hail and rain, men and horses, carts and
carriages. But all hurry in one direction, through mud
and mire ; there 's a town only three miles distant, which
is soon reached, and soon filled, it will not contain one-
third of that mighty rabble ; but there 's another town
farther on—the good old city is farther on, only twelve
miles, what 's that ! who will stay here ? onward to the old
town.

Hurry skurry, a mixed multitude of men and horses,
carts and carriages all in the direction of the old town ; and,
in the midst of all that mad throng, at a moment when the
rain gushes were coming down with particular fury, and
the artillery of the sky was pealing as I had never heard it
peal before, I felt someone seize me by the arm—I turned
round and beheld Mr. Petulengro.

' I can't hear you, Mr. Petulengro,' said I ; for the
thunder drowned the words which he appeared to be
uttering.

' Dearginni,' I heard Mr. Petulengro say, ' it thundereth.
I was asking, brother, whether you believe in dukkeripens ? '

' I do not, Mr. Petulengro ; but this is strange weather
to be asking me whether I believe in fortunes.'

' Grondinni,' said Mr. Petulengro, ' it haileth.   I believe
in dukkeripens, brother.'

' And who has more right,' said I, ' seeing that you live
by them ?   But this tempest is truly horrible.'

' Dearginni, grondinni ta villaminni ! It thundereth,
it haileth, and also flameth,' said Mr. Petulengro.   ' Look
up there, brother ! '

I looked up.   Connected with this tempest there was
one feature to which I have already alluded—the wonderful
colours of the clouds.   Some were of vivid green ; others
of the brightest orange ; others as black as pitch.   The
gypsy's finger was pointed to a particular part of the sky.

' What do you see there, brother ? '

' A strange kind of cloud.'

' What does it look like, brother ? '

' Something like a stream of blood.'

' That cloud foreshoweth a bloody dukkeripen.'

' A bloody fortune ! ' said I.   ' And whom may it betide ? '

' Who knows ? ' said the gypsy.

Down the way, dashing and splashing and scattering man, horse and cart to the left and right, came an open barouche, drawn by four smoking steeds, with postillions in scarlet jackets and leather skull-caps.   Two forms were conspicuous in it ; that of the successful bruiser and of his friend and backer, the sporting gentleman of my acquaintance.

' His ! ' said the gypsy, pointing to the latter, whose stern features wore a smile of triumph, as probably recognising me in the crowd, he nodded in the direction of where I stood, as the barouche hurried by.

There went the barouche, dashing through the rain gushes, and in it one whose boast it was that he was equal to ' either fortune.'   Many have heard of that man—many may be desirous of knowing yet more of him.   I have nothing to do with that man's after-life—he fulfilled his dukkeripen.   ' A bad, violent man ! '   Softly, friend ; when thou wouldst speak harshly of the dead, remember that thou hast not yet fulfilled thy own dukkeripen !

George Borrow.

A Lament

STRIKE whom thou wilt, O God.   Alas !
    Enough thy fires have scorchéd me.
Strike down, O God, this hedge—for, ah !
    It cannot else surmounted be.

Transylvanian Gypsy Song.

The Drownded Boy

THERE used to be in the dining-room at Kinmel Park— a very large gentleman's house, where I in generally play at—a very large picture with two three different plates upon

it of our Blessed Saviour, how he was served by the cruel
Jews, just like some poor dear Romano Chal with a lot of
nasty spiteful gorgios round him.   One of the forms was
with his hand on his face, and his fingers extended, and his
hair all over his forehead, looking very pitiful, and as much
as to say, ' Look what I 've come to.'   And my poor
Cousin Billy looked the very same, when sitting down on
the grass, and his wife opposite him, and his poor drownded
boy in some kind of an old building behind him, and did
not know what to do.   It struck me there and then how
very much he looked like that picture.

John Roberts, a Gypsy.

Sorrowful Years

THE wit and the skill
　Of the Father of ill,
Who 's clever indeed,
If they would hope
With their foes to cope
The Romany need.

Our horses they take,
Our waggons they break,
And us they fling
Into horrid cells,
Where hunger dwells
And vermin sting.

When the dead swallow
The fly shall follow
Across the river,
O we 'll forget
The wrongs we 've met,
But till then O never.
　Brother, of that be certain !

George Borrow.

VIII

BLACK ARTS

VIII

Black Arts

My Nurse's Song

OF fairies, witches, Gypsies
    My nourrice sang to me ;
Of Gypsies, witches, fairies
    I 'll sing again to thee.   *Scots Rhyme.*

The Art of the Romany

I 'VE seen you where you never were
    And where you never will be ;
And yet within that very place
    You can be seen by me.
For to tell what they do not know
    Is the art of the Romany.
                            Charles Godfrey Leland.

A Knowledge of Futurity

THERE was another pause, when the young Scot . . .
    asked Hayraddin, ' Whether it was not true that his
people, amid their ignorance, pretended to a knowledge of
futurity, which was not given to the sages, philosophers,
and divines, of more polished society ? '

'We pretend to it,' said Hayraddin, 'and it is with justice.'

' How can it be, that so high a gift is bestowed on so
abject a race ? ' said Quentin.

' Can I tell you ? ' answered Hayraddin—' Yes, I may
indeed ; but it is when you shall explain to me why the
dog can trace the footsteps of a man, while man, the nobler
animal, hath not power to trace those of the dog.   These
powers, which seem to you so wonderful, are instinctive
in our race.   From the lines on the face and on the hand,
we can tell the future fate of those who consult us, even
as surely as you know from the blossom of the tree in
spring, what fruit it will bear in the harvest.'
                            Sir Walter Scott.

Noël

Sur l'Air des Bohemiens

N'AOUTREI sian très Boumian
Qué dounan la bonou fourtunou.
N'aoutrei sian très Boumian
Qu'arrapen pertout vounté sian :
Enfan eimablé et tant doux,
Boutou, boute aqui la croux,
Et chascun té dira
Tout cé qué t'arribara :
Coumençou, Janan, cependan
Dé li veiré la man.

Tu siés, à cé qué vieou,
Egaou à Dieou,
Et siés soun Fis tout adourablé :
Tu siés, à cé qué vieou
Egaou à Dieou,
Nascu per yeou din lou néan :
L'amour t'a fach enfan
Per tout lou genre human :
Unou Viergeou és ta mayré,
Siés na sensou gis dé payré ;
Aco sé vei din ta man.
L'amour t'a fach enfan, etc.

L'ia encare un gran sécret,
Qué Janan n'a pas vougu-diré ;
L'ia encare un gran sécret
Qué fara ben léou soun éfet :
Vèné, vèné, beou Messi,
Mettou, mettou, mette eici,
La pèçou blanquou, ooussi
Per nous fayré réjoui :
Janan, parlara, beou Meina,
Boute aqui per dina.

The Three Magi : A Carol

To a Gypsy Air

WE are three Bohemians
    Who tell good fortune.
We are three Bohemians
Who rob wherever we may be :
Child, lovely and so sweet,
Place, place here, the cross,
And each of us will tell thee
Everything that will happen to thee :
Begin, Janan, however,
Give him the hand to see.

    Thou art, from what I see,
Equal to God.
And thou art his Son all-wonderful :
Thou art, from what I see,
Equal to God.
Born for me in the nothingness :
Love has made you a child
For all the human race :
A virgin is thy mother,
Thou art born without any Father ;
This I see in thy hand.
Love has made you a child, etc.

    There is still a great secret,
Which Janan has not wished to tell ;
There is still a great secret,
Which will soon be brought to pass :
Come, come, beauteous Messiah,
Place, place, place here,
The white piece of money
To make us rejoice :
Janan will tell, beauteous Babe ;
Give something here for dinner.

Soutou tant dé mouyen
L'ia quaouquaren
Per noſté ben dé fort siniſtré ;
Soutou tant dé mouyen
L'ia quaouquaren,
Per noſté ben, dé rigouroux :
Sé l'y vés unou crous
Qu'és lou salut dé tous.
Et si té l'aouzé diré,
Lou sujet dé toun martyré
Es qué siés ben amouroux.
Sé l'y vés unou crous, etc.

L'ia encarou quaouquaren
Oou bout dé ta lignou vitalou :
L'ia encarou quaouquaren
Qué té voou diré Magassen :
Vèné, vèné, beou german,
Dounou, dounou eici ta man,
Et té dévinaran
Quaouquaren dé ben charman :
May vengué d'argen ou tan ben
Sensou, noun sé fay ren.

Tu siés Dieou et mourtaou,
Et coumou taou
Vieouras ben poou dessu la terrou ;
Tu siés Dieou et mourtaou,
Et coumou taou
Saras ben poou din noſte éta ;
May ta divinita
Es su l'éternita :
Siés l'Ooutour dé la vidou,
Toun essence és infinidou,
N'as ren qué sié limita.
May ta Divinita, etc.

Vos-ti pas qué diguen
Quaouquaren à sa santou Mayré ?
Vos-ti pas qué lé fen
Per lou men noſté coumplimen ?

Under these happenings
There is something
For our good, but of ill omen ;
Under these happenings
There is something
For our good, hard to bear :
One sees there a cross
That is the salvation of all.
And if I dare to tell it thee,
The cause of thy martyrdom
Is that thou art right loving.
One sees there a cross, etc.

There is still something
At the end of the line of life :
There is still something
Which Magassen will tell thee :
Come, come, gentle brother,
Give, give here thy hand,
And I will divine for thee
Something very charming :
But let the silver come, for
Without it we do nothing.

Thou art God and mortal,
And as such
Thou wilt live a very short time on earth :
Thou art God and mortal,
And as such
Thou wilt be a very short time in our estate :
But thy Divinity
Is for eternity :
Thou art the Author of life,
Thy essence is infinite,
Thou hast nothing that may be limited.
But thy Divinity, etc.

Wilt thou not that we tell
Something to thy holy mother ?
Wilt thou not that we pay to her
At the least our compliments ?

Bellou Damou, vèné eiça,
N'aoutrei couneissen déjà
Qué din ta bellou man
L'ia un mystéri ben gran.
Tu qué siés pouli, digou li
Quaouquaren de joli.

Tu siés doou sang rouyaou,
Et toun houstaou
Es dei pu haou d'aquesté moundé :
Et toun houstaou
Es dei pu haou, à cé qué vieou ;
Toun Seignour és toun Fieou,
Et soun Payré lou Dieou :
Qué podés-ti may estré ?
Siés la Fiou dé toun Mestré
Et la Mayré dé toun Dieou.
Toun Seignour és toun Fieou, etc.

Et tu, bon Seigné-gran,
Qué siés oou cantoun dé la crupi,
Et tu, bon Seigné-gran,
Vos-ti pas qué véguen ta man ?
Digou, tu crésés bessay
Qué noun rousen alquel ay
Qu'és aqui destaca ?
Roubarian pu-léou lou ga :
Méte aqui dessu, beou Moussa,
N'aven pens-a bégu.

Yéou vèzé din ta man
Qué siés ben gran,
Qué siés ben sant, qué siés ben justè,
Yéou vèzé din ta man
Qué siés ben sant et ben ama :
Ah ! divin marida,
As toujour counserva
Unou sante abstinençou,
Tu gardés la Providençou ;
N'en siés-ti pas ben garda ?
Ah! divin marida, etc.

Fair Lady, come hither,
We others already know
That within thy fair hand
There is a mystery very great.
Thou who art polite, tell her
Something pretty.

Thou art of royal blood,
And thy house
Is of the highest of this world :
And thy house
Is of the highest ; from what I see
The Lord is thy Son,
And his Father is thy God :
What couldest thou be more ?
Thou art the daughter of thy master
And the Mother of thy God.
The Lord is thy Son, etc.

And thou, good old man,
Who art at the corner of the manger,
And thou, good old man,
Wilt thou not that we see thy hand ?
Say, thou fearest perhaps
That we should steal that ass
Which is tied up there ?
We would rather steal the child :
Place something here, fair sir,
We have scarcely drunk to-day.

I see within thy hand
That thou art very great,
That thou art very holy, that thou art very just ;
I see within thy hand
That thou art very holy, and well beloved :
Ah ! divine husband,
Who hast always preserved
A holy abstinence,
Thou guardest Providence ;
Art thou not well guarded ?
Ah! divine husband, etc.

N'aoutrei couneissen ben
Qué siés vengu dédin lou moundé ;
N'aoutrei couneissen ben
Qué tu siés vengu sense argen :
Bel enfan, n'en parlen plus,
Quan tu siés vengu tout nus,
Cregnies, à cé qué vian,
Lou rescontré dei Boumian ;
Qué crégniés, beou Fieou, tu siés Dieou ;
Escoutou, noSté a Dieou.

Si trop dé liberta
Nous a pourta
A dévina toun aventourou :
Si trop dé liberta
Nous a pourta
A té parla trop libramen,
Té prégan humblamen
Dé fayré egalamen
NoStou bonou fourtounou,
Et qué nous en donnés unou
Qué duré eternalamen,
Té prégan humblamen, etc.

XVII Cent. Noël.

A Gypsy Prophetess

NO sooner these remove, but full of Fear,
A Gypsie Jewess whispers in your Ear,
And begs an Alms : An High-PrieSt's Daughter she,
Vers'd in their *Talmud*, and Divinity,
And Prophesies beneath a shady Tree.
Her Goods, a Basket, and old Hay her Bed,
She Strouls, and telling Fortunes gains her Bread :
Farthings, and some small Monies, are her Fees ;
Yet she interprets all your Dreams for these.
Foretels th' EState, when the Rich Uncle dies,
And sees a Sweet-heart in the Sacrifice.

John Dryden.

We others know well
That thou art come into the world ;
We others know well
That thou art come without money :
Fair Child, let us speak no more of it,
Since thou art come quite naked,
Thou fearedst, from what we see,
Meeting with Bohemians ;
Why didst thou fear, fair Son ?—thou art God.
Listen to our farewell.

If too much liberty
Has led us
To divine thy fortune :
If too much liberty
Has led us
To speak to thee too freely,
We pray thee humbly
To give us likewise
A good fortune,
And that thou give us one
Which may last eternally.
We pray thee humbly, etc.

XVII Cent. Carol.

The Death of Richard Hunne

'WEL,' quod the Lordes, 'at the last, yet with muche
worke, we come to somwhat. But wherby thinke
you that he can tell? 'Nay, forsothe, my Lord,' quod he,
'it is a womanne; I woulde she were here with youre
Lordeshyppes nowe.' 'Well,' quod my Lorde, 'woman
or man all is one. She shal be hadde, wheresoever she be.'
'By my fayth, my Lordes,' quod he, 'and she were with
you, she would tell you wonders. For by God, I have
wyst her to tell manye mervaylous thynges ere nowe.'
'Why,' quod the Lordes, 'what have you hearde her
tell?' 'Forsothe, my Lordes,' quod he, 'if a thynge
hadde been stolen, she would have tolde who hadde it.

And therefore I thynke that she could as wel tel who
killed Hunne as who ſtale an horse.'
'Surelye,' sayde the Lordes, 'so thynke all we too, I
trowe. But howe coulde she tel it—by the Devill?'
'Naye, by my trouth I trowe,' quod he, 'for I could
never see her use anye worse waye than lookinge in ones
hand.' Therewith the Lordes laughed and asked 'What
is she?' 'Forsothe, my Lordes,' quod he, 'an Egipcian,
and she was lodged here at Lambeth, but she is gone over
sea now. Howbeit I trowe she be not in her own countrey
yet, for they saye it is a great way hence, and she went over
litle more than a moneth agoe.'   *Sir Thomas More.*

The Gitána of Seville

YES, well may you exclaim 'Ave Maria puriſſima,' ye
dames and maidens of Seville, as she advances towards
you ; she is not of yourselves, she is not of your blood, she
or her fathers have walked to your clime from a diſtance
of three thousand leagues. She has come from the far
Eaſt, like the three enchanted kings to Cologne ; but unlike
them she and her race have come with hate and not with
love. She comes to flatter, and to deceive, and to rob, for
she is a lying prophetess, and a she-Thug ; she will greet
you with blessings which will make your hearts rejoice, but
your hearts' blood would freeze, could you hear the curses
which to herself she murmurs againſt you ; for she says
that in her children's veins flows the dark blood of the
'husbands,' whilſt in those of yours flows the pale tide of
the 'savages,' and therefore she would gladly set her foot
on all your corses firſt poisoned by her hands. For all her
love—and she can love—is for the Romas ; and all her
hate—and who can hate like her ?—is for the Busnees ; for
she says that the world would be a fair world were there
no Busnees, and if the Romaniks could heat their kettles
undiſturbed at the foot of the olive trees ; and therefore
she would kill them all if she could and if she dared. She
never seeks the houses of the Busnees but for the purpose
of prey ; for the wild animals of the sierra do not more
abhor the sight of man than she abhors the countenances
of the Busnees. She now comes to prey upon you and to

scoff at you. Will you believe her words? Fools! do
you think that the being before ye has any sympathy for
the like of you?

She is of the middle stature, neither strongly nor slightly
built, and yet her every movement denotes agility and
vigour. As she stands erect before you, she appears like
a falcon about to soar, and you are almost tempted to believe that the power of volition is hers; and were you to
stretch forth your hand to seize her, she would spring above
the house-tops like a bird. Her face is oval, and her
features are regular but somewhat hard and coarse, for she
was born amongst rocks in a thicket, and she has been
wind-beaten and sun-scorched for many a year, even like
her parents before her; there is many a speck upon her
cheek, and perhaps a scar, but no dimples of love; and her
brow is wrinkled over, though she is yet young. Her
complexion is more than dark, for it is almost that of a
Mulatto; and her hair, which hangs in long locks on
either side of her face, is black as coal, and coarse as the tail
of a horse, from which it seems to have been gathered.

There is no female eye in Seville can support the glance
of hers—so fierce and penetrating, and yet so artful and sly,
is the expression of their dark orbs; her mouth is fine and
almost delicate, and there is not a queen on the proudest
throne between Madrid and Moscow who might not, and
would not, envy the white and even rows of teeth which
adorn it, which seem not of pearl but of the purest elephant's bone of Multan. She comes not alone; a swarthy
two-year-old bantling clasps her neck with one arm, its
naked body half extant from the coarse blanket which,
drawn round her shoulders, is secured at her bosom by a
skewer. Though tender of age it looks wicked and sly,
like a veritable imp of Roma. Huge rings of false gold
dangle from wide slits in the lobes of her ears; her nether
garments are rags, and her feet are cased in hempen sandals.
Such is the wandering Gitána, such is the witch-wife of
Multan, who has come to spae the fortune of the Sevillian
countess and her daughters.

'O may the blessing of Egypt light upon your head,
you high-born lady! (May an evil end overtake your body,
daughter of a Busnee harlot!) and may the same blessing

await the two fair roses of the Nile here flowering by your
side! (May evil Moors seize them and carry them across the
water !)   O listen to the words of the poor woman who is
come from a distant country; she is of a wise people, though
it has pleased the God of the sky to punish them for their
sins by sending them to wander through the world.   They
denied shelter to the Majari, whom you call the queen of
heaven, and to the Son of God, when they flew to the land
of Egypt before the wrath of the wicked king ; it is said
that they even refused them a draught of the sweet waters
of the great river, when the blessed two were athirst.   O
you will say that it was a heavy crime ; and truly so it was,
and heavily has the Lord punished the Egyptians.   He has
sent us a-wandering, poor as you see, with scarcely a
blanket to cover us.   O blessed lady, (Accursed be thy dead
as many as thou mayest have,) we have no money to purchase
us bread ; we have only our wisdom with which to support
ourselves and our poor hungry babes ; when God took
away their silks from the Egyptians, and their gold from
the Egyptians, he left them their wisdom as a resource that
they might not starve.   O who can read the stars like the
Egyptians ? and who can read the lines of the palm like
the Egyptians ?   The poor woman read in the stars that
there was a rich ventura for all of this goodly house, so she
followed the bidding of the stars and came to declare it.
O blessed lady, (I defile thy dead corse,) your husband is at
Granada, fighting with king Ferdinand against the wild
Corohai !   (May an evil ball smite him and split his head !)
Within three months he shall return with twenty captive
Moors, round the neck of each a chain of gold.   (God
grant that when he enter the house a beam may fall upon
him and crush him !)   And within nine months after his
return God shall bless you with a fair chabo, the pledge
for which you have sighed so long !   (Accursed be the
salt placed in its mouth in the church when it is baptized !)
Your palm, blessed lady, your palm, and the palms of all
I see here, that I may tell you all the rich ventura which is
hanging over this good house, (May evil lightning fall
upon it and consume it !) but first let me sing you a song of
Egypt, that the spirit of the Chowahanee may descend more
plenteously upon the poor woman.'

Her demeanour now instantly undergoes a change. Hitherto she has been pouring forth a lying and wild harangue, without much flurry or agitation of manner. Her speech, it is true, has been rapid, but her voice has never been raised to a very high key ; but she now stamps on the ground ; and placing her hands on her hips, she moves quickly to the right and left, advancing and retreating in a sidelong direction. Her glances become more fierce and fiery, and her coarse hair stands erect on her head, stiff as the prickles of the hedgehog ; and now she commences clapping her hands, and uttering words of an unknown tongue, to a strange and uncouth tune. The tawny bantling seems inspired with the same fiend, and, foaming at the mouth, utters wild sounds in imitation of its dam. Still more rapid become the sidelong movements of the Gitána. Movements ! she springs, she bounds, and at every bound she is a yard above the ground. She no longer bears the child in her bosom ; she plucks it from thence, and fiercely brandishes it aloft, till at last, with a yell, she tosses it high into the air like a ball, and then, with neck and head thrown back, receives it, as it falls, on her hands and breast, extracting a cry from the terrified beholders. Is it possible she can be singing ? Yes, in the wildest style of her people ; and here is a snatch of the song in the language of Roma, which she occasionally screams.

> ' On the top of a mountain I stand,
> With a crown of red gold in my hand,—
> Wild Moors come trooping o'er the lea,
> O how from their fury shall I flee, flee, flee ?
> O how from their fury shall I flee ? '

Such was the Gitána in the days of Ferdinand and Isabella, and much the same is she now in the days of Isabel and Christina.   *George Borrow.*

Meg Merrilies

SHE was full six feet high, wore a man's great-coat over the rest of her dress, had in her hand a goodly sloe-thorn cudgel, and in all points of equipment, except her petticoats, seemed rather masculine than feminine. Her dark elf-locks shot out like the snakes of the Gorgon, between

an old-fashioned bonnet called a bongrace, heightening
the singular effect of her strong and weather-beaten features,
which they partly shadowed, while her eye had a wild roll,
that indicated something like real or affected insanity.

'Aweel, Ellangowan,' she said, 'wad it no hae been a
bonnie thing an the leddy had been brought to bed and me
at the fair o' Drumshourloch, no kenning, nor dreaming a
word about it ?   Wha was to hae keepit awa the worrie-
cows, I trow ?—ay, and the elves and gyre-carlings frae
the bonny bairn, grace be wi' it ?   Ay, or said Saint
Colme's charm for its sake, the dear ? '   And without
waiting an answer, she began to sing—

> 'Trefoil, vervain, John's-wort, dill,
> Hinders witches of their will ;
> Weel is them, that weel may
> Fast upon Saint Andrew's day.
>
> Saint Bride and her brat,
> Saint Colme and his cat,
> Saint Michael and his spear,
> Keep the house frae reif and wear.'

This charm she sang to a wild tune, in a high and shrill
voice, and cutting three capers with such strength and
agility as almost to touch the roof of the room, concluded,
'And now, Laird, will ye no order me a tass o' brandy ? '

Sir Walter Scott.

The Gipsy's Camp

HOW oft on Sundays, when I 'd time to tramp,
My rambles led me to a gipsy's camp,
Where the real effigy of midnight hags,
With tawny smoked flesh and tatter'd rags,
Uncouth-brimm'd hat, and weather-beaten cloak,
'Neath the wild shelter of a knotty oak,
Along the greensward uniformly pricks
Her pliant bending hazel's arching sticks ;
While round-topt bush, or briar-entangled hedge,
Where flag-leaves spring beneath, or ramping sedge,
Keep off the bothering bustle of the wind,
And give the best retreat she hopes to find.
How oft I 've bent me o'er her fire and smoke,
To hear her gibberish tale so quaintly spoke,

While the old Sybil forg'd her boding clack
Twin imps the meanwhile bawling at her back ;
Oft on my hand her magic coin 's been ſtruck,
And hoping chink, she talk'd of morts of luck :
And ſtill, as boyish hopes did firſt agree,
Mingled with fears to drop the fortune's fee,
I never fail'd to gain the honours sought,
And Squire and Lord were purchas'd with a groat.
But as man's unbelieving taſte came round,
She furious ſtampt her shoeless foot aground,
Wip'd bye her soot-black hair with clenching fiſt,
While through her yellow teeth the spittle hiſt,
Swearing by all her lucky powers of fate,
Which like as footboys on her actions wait,
That fortune's scale should to my sorrow turn,
And I one day the rash neglect should mourn ;
That good to bad should change, and I should be
Loſt to this world and all eternity ;
That poor as Job I should remain unbleſt ;—
    (Alas, for fourpence how my die is caſt !)
Of not a hoarded farthing be posseſt,
    And when all 's done, be shov'd to hell at laſt !
                                        John Clare.

The Sin of Gypsy Mary

NOW about Gypsy Mary, what I am going to tell you
is the real truth.   One of the Prices she was, kinsfolk
of the Ingrams, and she married my Aunt Silvina's second
son, Black Billy.   And she was a very poor fortune-teller,
and none of our people would show her the genuine way,
because she had such an evil tongue.   So she had to do
the beſt she could to come over the gorgios in her own
way, and 'ticing them to do many a foolish little thing, to
get their money.   And there was one time that she found
out a house to tell fortunes at, and she got a five-pound
note off the woman, and told her to go to the shop and buy
a pound of soap, and to go to some running water and
wash, and was to say, ' I wash myself away from God
Almighty, I wash myself away from God Almighty.'   And
after she did that, the gorgie went mad, and she was taken

O

to the Denbigh Asylum, and died there. But poor Gypsy
Mary had three years' illness for persuading the foolish
woman to do such wickedness, and she was quite unable
to walk during the whole of that time. When they used
to be travelling, she used to be carried upon a donkey;
and her husband used to lift her up and down, and had a
great deal of trouble with her. Still and all she used to
chatter away like a magpie.

John Roberts, a Gypsy.

On Manner

A STROLLING Gipsy will offer to tell your fortune
with a grace and an insinuation of address that would
be admired in a court.   *William Hazlitt.*

Hearing a Fortune

LIKE a queen the Gipsy woman sate,
  With head and face downbent
On the Lady's head and face intent:
For, coiled at her feet like a child at ease,
The Lady sate between her knees
And o'er them the Lady's clasped hands met,
And on those hands her chin was set,
And her upturned face met the face of the crone
Wherein the eyes had grown and grown
As if she could double and quadruple
At pleasure the play of either pupil.

   .   .   .   .   .

—I said, is it a blessing, is it banning,
Do they applaud you or burlesque you—
Those hands and fingers with no flesh on?
When, just as I thought to spring in to the rescue,
At once I was stopped by the Lady's expression:
For it was life her eyes were drinking
From the crone's wide pair above unwinking,

   .   .   .   .   .

As still her cheeks burned and eyes glistened,
As she listened and she listened.

Robert Browning.

Mr. Pepys *believes in* Fortune-telling

Aug. 22*nd*, 1663. . . . After breakfast Mr. Castle and
I walked to Greenwich, and in our way met some Gypsys,
who would needs tell me my fortune, and I suffered one of
them, who told me many things common as others do, but
bade me beware of a John and a Thomas, for they did seek
to do me hurt, and that somebody should be with me this
day se'nnight to borrow money of me, but I should lend
him none. She got ninepence of me. And so I left them.

Sept. 3*rd.* . . . And I to Deptford, and, after a word or
two with Sir J. Minnes, walked to Redriffe and so home.
In my way, it coming into my head, overtaking of a beggar
or two on the way that looked like Gypsys, what the
Gypsys 8 or 9 days ago had foretold, that somebody that
day se'nnight should be with me to borrow money, but
I should lend none ; and looking, when I came to my
office, upon my journall, that my brother John had brought
a letter that day from my brother Tom to borrow £20
more of me, which had vexed me so that I had sent the
letter to my father into the country, to acquaint him of it,
and how little he is beforehand that he is still forced to
borrow. But it pleased me mightily to see how, contrary
to my expectations, having so lately lent him £20, and
belief that he had money by him to spare, and that after
some days not thinking of it, I should look back and find
what the Gypsy had told me to be so true.

Samuel Pepys.

Milton disparages the Art

IN his tenth Section he (Smectymnuus) will needs erect
Figures, and tell Fortunes. . . . But he proceeds, and
the Familiar belike informs him, that *a rich Widow, or a
Lecture, or both, would content me* : whereby I perceive
him to be more ignorant in his art of divining than any
Gipsy. For this I cannot omit without ingratitude to that
Providence above, who hath ever bred me up in plenty,
although my Life hath not bin unexpensive in Learning,
and voyaging about ; so long as it shall please him to lend

me what he hath hitherto thought good, which is enough
to serve me in all honest and liberal occasions, and something over besides, I were unthankful to that highest
Bounty, if I should make my self so poor as to solicit needily
any such kind of *rich hopes* as this Fortune-teller dreams of.
And that he may further learn how his Astrology is wide
all the houses of Heaven in spelling Marriages, I care not
if I tell him thus much profestly, though it be the losing
of my *rich hopes*, as he calls them, that I think with them
who, both in prudence and elegance of Spirit, would chuse
a Virgin of mean fortunes, honestly bred, before the
wealthiest Widow. The Fiend therefore, that told our
Chaldean the contrary was a lying Fiend.

John Milton.

Sir Roger's Line of Life

AS I was Yesterday riding out in the Fields with my
Friend Sir Roger, we saw at a little Distance from us
a Troop of Gypsies. Upon the first Discovery of them,
my Friend was in some Doubt whether he should not
exert the *Justice of the Peace* upon such a Band of lawless
Vagrants ; but not having his Clerk with him, who is a
necessary Counsellour on these Occasions, and fearing that
his Poultry might fare the worse for it, he let the Thought
drop : But at the same Time gave me a particular Account
of the Mischiefs they do in the Country, in stealing People's
Goods and spoiling their Servants. If a stray Piece of
Linen hangs upon an Hedge, says Sir Roger, they are sure
to have it ; if a Hog loses his Way in the Fields, it is ten
to one but he becomes their Prey ; our Geese cannot live
in Peace for them ; if a Man prosecutes them with Severity,
his Hen-roost is sure to pay for it : They generally straggle
into these Parts about this Time of the Year ; and set the
Heads of our Servant-Maids so agog for Husbands, that
we do not expect to have any Business done, as it should be,
whilst they are in the Country. I have an honest Dairy-
Maid who crosses their Hands with a piece of Silver every
Summer ; and never fails being promised the handsomest
young Fellow in the Parish for her Pains. Your Friend
the Butler has been Fool enough to be seduced by them ;

and though he is sure to lose a Knife, a Fork, or a Spoon every Time his Fortune is told him, generally shuts himself up in the Pantry with an old Gypsie for about half an Hour once in a Twelve-month. Sweet-hearts are the things they live upon, which they bestow very plentifully upon all those that apply themselves to them. You see now and then some handsome young Jades among them : The Sluts have often very white Teeth and Black Eyes.

Sir Roger observing that I listened with great Attention to his Account of a People who were so entirely new to me, told me, That if I would they should tell us our Fortunes. As I was very well pleased with the Knight's Proposal, we rid up and communicated our Hands to them. A *Cassandra* of the Crew, after having examined my Lines very diligently, told me, That I loved a pretty Maid in a Corner, that I was a good Woman's Man, with some other Particulars which I do not think proper to relate. My Friend Sir Roger alighted from his Horse, and exposing his Palm to two or three that stood by him, they crumpled it into all Shapes, and diligently scanned every Wrinkle that could be made in it ; when one of them who was older and more Sun-burnt than the rest, told him, That he had a Widow in his Line of Life : Upon which the Knight cryed, Go, go, you are an idle Baggage ; and at the same time smiled upon me. The Gypsie finding he was not displeased in his Heart, told him, after a further Enquiry into his Hand, that his True-love was constant, and that she should dream of him to Night. My old Friend cryed pish, and bid her go on. The Gypsie told him that he was a Batchelour, but would not be so long ; and that he was dearer to some Body than he thought : the Knight still repeated, She was an idle Baggage, and bid her go on. Ah Master, says the Gypsie, that roguish Leer of yours makes a pretty Woman's Heart ake ; you ha'n't that Simper about the Mouth for Nothing—The uncouth Gibberish with which all this was uttered, like the Darkness of an Oracle, made us the more attentive to it. To be short, the Knight left the Money with her that he had crossed her Hand with, and got up again on his Horse.

As we were riding away, Sir Roger told me, that he knew several sensible People who believed these Gypsies now

and then foretold very strange things ; and for Half an
Hour together appeared more jocund than ordinary. In
the Height of his good Humour, meeting a common
Beggar upon the Road who was no Conjuror, as he went
to relieve him he found his Pocket was pickt : That being
a Kind of Palmistry at which this Race of Vermin are very
dexterous.

Joseph Addison.

The Sibyl

DOWN by yon hazel copse, at evening, blaz'd
  The Gipsy's faggot.—There we stood and gaz'd;
Gaz'd on her sun-burnt face with silent awe,
Her tatter'd mantle, and her hood of straw ;
Her moving lips, her caldron brimming o'er ;
The drowsy brood that on her back she bore,
Imps, in the barn with mousing owlet bred,
From rifled roost at nightly revel fed ;
Whose dark eyes flash'd thro' locks of blackest shade,
When in the breeze the distant watch-dog bay'd :
And heroes fled the Sibyl's mutter'd call,
Whose elfin prowess scal'd the orchard wall.
As o'er my palm the silver piece she drew,
And trac'd the line of life with searching view,
How throbb'd my fluttering pulse with hopes and fears,
To learn the colour of my future years !

Samuel Rogers.

A Maid's Lament

LAST *Friday's* eve, when as the sun was set,
  I, near yon stile, three sallow gypsies met,
Upon my hand they cast a poring look,
Bid me beware, and thrice their heads they shook ;
They said that many crosses I must prove,
Some in my worldly gain, but most in love.
Next morn I miss'd three hens and our old cock,
And off the hedge two pinners and a smock.
I bore these losses with a Christian mind,
And no mishaps could feel, while thou wert kind.

But since, alas ! I grew my *Colin's* scorn,
I 've known no pleasure, night or noon, or morn.
Help me, ye gypsies, bring him home again,
And to a conﬅant lass give back her swain.

John Gay.

Upon Cupid

L OVE like a gipsy lately came,
    And did me much importune
To see my hand, that by the same
    He might foretell my fortune.

He saw my palm, and then, said he,
    I tell thee by this score here,
That thou within few months shalt be
    The youthful Prince d'Amour here.

I smil'd, and bade him once more prove,
    And by some cross-line show it,
That I could ne'er be prince of love,
    Though here the princely poet.

Robert Herrick.

The Lady Purbeck's Fortune

H ELP me, wonder here 's a book,
    Where I would for ever look :
Never yet did gipsy trace
Smoother lines in hand or face :
Venus here doth Saturn move
That you should be Queen of Love ;
And the other ﬅars consent ;
Only Cupid 's not content ;
For though you the theft disguise,
You have robb'd him of his eyes.
And to show his envy further,
Here he chargeth you with murther :
Says, although that at your sight
He muﬅ all his torches light ;
Though your either cheek discloses
Mingled baths of milk and roses ;

Though your lips be banks of blisses,
Where he plants, and gathers kisses ;
And yourself the reason why
Wisest men for love may die ;
You will turn all hearts to tinder,
And shall make the world one cinder.

Ben Jonson.

Narcissus

CEPHISUS. Speake then, I pray you, speake, for wee you
    portune
That you would tell our sunnfac't sonne his fortune.
LYRIOPE. Doe not shrink backe, Narcissus, come &
    stand,
Hold vpp & lett the blind man see thy hand.
TYRESIAS. Come, my young sonne, hold vp & catch
    audacitye ;
I see thy hand with the eyes of my capacitye.
Though I speake riddles, thinke not I am typsye,
For what I speake I learnde it of a gipsye,
And though I speake hard woords of curromanstike,
Doe not, I pray, suppose that I am franticke.
The table of thy hand is somewhat ragged,
Thy mensall line is too direct and cragged,
Thy line of life, my sonne, is too, too breife,
And crosseth Venus girdle heere in cheife,
And heere (O dolefull signe) is overthwarte
In Venus mount a little pricke or warte.
Besides heere, in the hillocke of great Jupiter,
Monnsieur la mors lyes lurking like a sheppbiter ;
What can I make out of this hard construction
But dolefull dumpes, decay, death, & destruction ?

Anon.

The Fortune-teller

A GYPSY I wuz born'd
   An' a Gypsy I 'll demain ;
A-tellin' young maids deir forchants,
   Myself I will maintain.

English Gypsy Song.

The Vicar's Daughters

BUT we could have borne all this, had not a fortune-telling gipsy come to raise us into perfect sublimity. The tawny sibyl no sooner appeared, than my girls came running to me for a shilling a-piece to cross her hand with silver. To say the truth, I was tired of being always wise, and could not help gratifying their request, because I loved to see them happy. I gave each of them a shilling ; though for the honour of the family it must be observed, that they never went without money themselves, as my wife always generously let them have a guinea each, to keep in their pockets, but with strict injunctions never to change it. After they had been closeted up with the fortune-teller for some time, I knew by their looks, upon their returning, that they had been promised something great.—' Well, my girls, how have you sped ? Tell me, Livy, has the fortune-teller given thee a pennyworth ? '—' I protest, Papa,' says the girl, ' I believe she deals with somebody that's not right ; for she positively declared, that I am to be married to a 'Squire in less than a twelve-month ! '—' Well, now Sophy, my child,' said I, ' and what sort of a husband are you to have ? '—' Sir, replied she, ' I am to have a Lord soon after my sister has married the 'Squire.'—' How,' cried I, ' is that all you are to have for your two shillings ? Only a Lord and a 'Squire for two shillings ! You fools, I could have promised you a Prince and a Nabob for half the money.' *Oliver Goldsmith.*

The Way of Soothsayers

PRIESTS and soothsayers go the round of rich men's doors and persuade them that they have power from the gods, whereby, if any sin has been committed by a man or his ancestors, they can heal it by charms and sacrifice performed to the accompaniment of feasting and pleasure, and if any man wishes to injure an enemy, at a small cost he may harm just and unjust indifferently ; for with their incantations and magic formulae they say they can persuade the gods to serve their will. *Plato.*

King Bagrat and the Magicians

WHILST the pious king, Bagrat IV. [c. 1048], was in the imperial city of Constantinople, he learnt—a thing marvellous and quite incredible—that there were certain descendants there of the Samaritan race of Simon Magus, called Atsincan, wizards and famous rogues. Now there were wild beasts that used to come and devour the animals kept, for the monarch's chase, in the imperial park. The great emperor Monomachus, learning of this, bade summon the Atsincan, to destroy by their magic art the beasts devouring his game. They, in obedience to the imperial behest, killed a quantity of wild beasts. King Bagrat heard of it, and summoning the Atsincan said : ' How have you killed these beasts ? ' ' Sire,' said they, ' our art teaches us to poison meat, which we put in a place frequented by these beasts ; then climbing a tree, we attract them by imitating the cry of the animals ; they assemble, eat the meat, and drop down dead. Only beasts born on Holy Saturday obey us not. Instead of eating the poisoned meat, they say to us " Eat it yourselves " ; then off they go unharmed.' The monarch, wishing to see it with his own eyes, bade them summon a beast of this sort, but they could find nothing but a dog which they knew had not been born upon that day. The monk, who was present with the King, was moved with the same natural sentiment as we have spoken of above, on the subject of the icons and of the divine representation. He was moved, not with pity only, but with the fear of God, and would have no such doings among Christians, above all before the King, in a place where he was himself. He made the sign of the cross on the poisoned meat, and the animal had no sooner swallowed it than it brought it up, and so did not drop dead. The dog having taken no harm, the baffled wizards begged the King to have the monk, Giorgi, taken into the inner apartments, and to order another dog to be brought. The holy monk gone, they brought another dog, and gave him the poisoned meat : he fell dead instantly. At sight of this King Bagrat and his lords rejoiced exceedingly, and told the marvel to the pious emperor, Constantine Monomachus [1042-54], who shared their satisfaction and thanked God. As to King Bagrat, he said ' With this holy man near me, I fear neither wizards nor their deadly poisons.' *Georgian XII Cent. MS.*

Mrs. Herne and the Grey-haired Brother

IT was about noon on the third day that I sat beneath the shade of the ash tree ; I was not at work, for the weather was particularly hot, and I felt but little inclination to make any exertion. Leaning my back against the tree, I was not long in falling into a slumber. I particularly remember that slumber of mine beneath the ash tree, for it was about the sweetest slumber that I ever enjoyed ; how long I continued in it I do not know ; I could almost have wished that it had lasted to the present time. All of a sudden it appeared to me that a voice cried in my ear, ' Danger ! danger ! danger ! ' Nothing seemingly could be more distinct than the words which I heard ; then an uneasy sensation came over me, which I strove to get rid of, and at last succeeded, for I awoke. The gypsy girl was standing just opposite to me, with her eyes fixed upon my countenance ; a singular kind of little dog stood beside her.

' Ha ! ' said I, ' was it you that cried danger ? What danger is there ? '

' Danger, brother, there is no danger ; what danger should there be ? I called to my little dog, but that was in the wood ; my little dog's name is not danger, but stranger ; what danger should there be, brother ? '

' What, indeed, except in sleeping beneath a tree ; what is that you have got in your hand ? '

' Something for you,' said the girl, sitting down and proceeding to untie a white napkin ; ' a pretty manricli, so sweet, so nice ; when I went home to my people I told my grandbebee how kind you had been to the poor person's child, and when my grandbebee saw the kekaubi, she said : " Hir mi devlis, it won't do for the poor people to be ungrateful ; by my God, I will bake a cake for the young harko mescro." '

' But there are two cakes.'

' Yes, brother, two cakes, both for you ; my grandbebee meant them both for you—but lift, brother, I will have one of them for bringing them. I know you will give me one, pretty brother, grey-haired brother—which shall I have, brother ? '

In the napkin were two round cakes, seemingly made of rich and coftly compounds, and precisely similar in form, each weighing about half a pound.

' Which shall I have, brother ? ' said the gypsy girl.

' Whichever you please.'

' No, brother, no, the cakes are yours, not mine, it is for you to say.'

' Well, then, give me the one neareft you, and take the other.'

' Yes, brother, yes,' said the girl ; and taking the cakes, she flung them into the air two or three times, catching them as they fell, and singing the while. ' Pretty brother, grey-haired brother—here, brother,' said she, ' here is your cake, this other is mine.'

' Are you sure,' said I, taking the cake, ' that this is the one I chose ? '

' Quite sure, brother ; but if you like you can have mine ; there 's no difference however—shall I eat ? '

' Yes, sifter, eat.'

' See, brother, I do ; now, brother, eat, pretty brother, grey-haired brother.'

' I am not hungry.'

' Not hungry ! well, what then—what has being hungry to do with the matter ? It is my grandbebee's cake which was sent because you were kind to the poor person's child ; eat, brother, eat, and we shall be like the children in the wood that the gorgios speak of.'

' The children in the wood had nothing to eat.'

' Yes, they had hips and haws ; we have better. Eat, brother.'

' See, sifter, I do,' and I ate a piece of the cake.

' Well, brother, how do you like it ? ' said the girl, look-ing fixedly at me.

' It is very rich and sweet, and yet there is something ftrange about it ; I don't think I shall eat any more.'

' Fie, brother, fie, to find fault with the poor person's cake ; see, I have nearly eaten mine.'

'That's a pretty little dog.'

'Is it not, brother? that's my juggal, my little sister, as I call her.'

'Come here, Juggal,' said I to the animal.

'What do you want with my juggal?' said the girl.

'Only to give her a piece of cake,' said I, offering the dog a piece which I had just broken off.

'What do you mean?' said the girl, snatching the dog away; 'my grandbebee's cake is not for dogs.'

'Why, I just now saw you give the animal a piece of yours.'

'You lie, brother, you saw no such thing; but I see how it is, you wish to affront the poor person's child. I shall go to my house.'

'Keep still, and don't be angry; see, I have eaten the piece which I offered the dog. I meant no offence. It is a sweet cake after all.'

'Isn't it, brother? I am glad you like it. Offence! brother, no offence at all! I am so glad you like my grandbebee's cake, but she will be wanting me at home. Eat one piece more of grandbebee's cake and I will go.'

'I am not hungry, I will put the rest by.'

'One piece more before I go, handsome brother, grey-haired brother.'

'I will not eat any more, I have already eaten more than I wished, to oblige you; if you must go, good day to you.'

The girl rose upon her feet, looked hard at me, then at the remainder of the cake which I held in my hand, and then at me again, and then stood for a moment or two, as if in deep thought; presently an air of satisfaction came over her countenance, she smiled and said: 'Well, brother, well, do as you please; I merely wished you to eat because you have been so kind to the poor person's child. She loves you so, that she could have wished to have seen you eat it all; good-bye, brother, I dare say when I am gone you will eat some more of it, and if you don't I dare say you have eaten enough to—to—show your love for us. After all, it was a poor person's cake, a Rommany manricli, and all you gorgios are somewhat gorgious. Farewell, brother, pretty brother, grey-haired brother. Come, juggal.'

I remained under the ash tree seated on the grass for a

minute or two, and endeavoured to resume the occupation
in which I had been engaged before I fell asleep, but I felt
no inclination for labour. I then thought I would sleep
again, and once more reclined against the tree, and slum-
bered for some little time, but my sleep was more agitated
than before. Something appeared to bear heavy on my
breast. I struggled in my sleep, fell on the grass, and
awoke ; my temples were throbbing, there was a burning
in my eyes, and my mouth felt parched ; the oppression
about the chest which I had felt in my sleep still continued.
' I must shake off these feelings,' said I, ' and get upon
my legs.' I walked rapidly up and down upon the green
sward ; at length, feeling my thirst increase, I directed my
steps down the narrow path to the spring which ran amidst
the bushes ; arriving there, I knelt down and drank of the
water, but on lifting up my head I felt thirstier than before ;
again I drank, but with the like result ; I was about to drink
for the third time, when I felt a dreadful qualm which
instantly robbed me of nearly all my strength. What can
be the matter with me, thought I ; but I suppose I have
made myself ill by drinking cold water. I got up and made
the best of my way back to my tent ; before I reached it the
qualm had seized me again, and I was deadly sick. I flung
myself on my pallet ; qualm succeeded qualm, but in the
intervals my mouth was dry and burning, and I felt a frantic
desire to drink, but no water was at hand, and to reach the
spring once more was impossible ; the qualms continued,
deadly pains shot through my whole frame ; I could bear
my agonies no longer, and I fell into a trance or swoon.
How long I continued therein I know not ; on recovering,
however, I felt somewhat better, and attempted to lift my
head off my couch ; the next moment, however, the qualms
and pains returned, if possible, with greater violence than
before. I am dying, thought I, like a dog, without any
help ; and then methought I heard a sound at a distance
like people singing, and then once more I relapsed into my
swoon.

I revived just as a heavy blow sounded upon the canvas
of the tent. I started, but my condition did not permit me
to rise ; again the same kind of blow sounded upon the
canvas ; I thought for a moment of crying out and request-

ing assistance, but an inexplicable something chained my tongue, and now I heard a whisper on the outside of the tent. 'He does not move, bebee,' said a voice which I knew. 'I should not wonder if it has done for him already ; however, strike again with your ran ' ; and then there was another blow, after which another voice cried aloud in a strange tone : 'Is the gentleman of the house asleep, or is he taking his dinner?' I remained quite silent and motionless, and in another moment the voice continued : 'What, no answer? what can the gentleman of the house be about that he makes no answer? Perhaps the gentleman of the house may be darning his stockings?' Thereupon a face peered into the door of the tent, at the farther extremity of which I was stretched. It was that of a woman, but owing to the posture in which she stood, with her back to the light, and partly owing to a large straw bonnet, I could distinguish but very little of the features of her countenance. I had, however, recognised her voice ; it was that of my old acquaintance, Mrs. Herne. 'Ho, ho, sir !' said she, 'here you are. Come here, Leonora,' said she to the gypsy girl, who pressed in at the other side of the door ; 'here is the gentleman, not asleep, but only stretched out after dinner. Sit down on your ham, child, at the door ; I shall do the same. There—you have seen me before, sir, have you not ?'

'The gentleman makes no answer, bebee ; perhaps he does not know you.'

'I have known him of old, Leonora,' said Mrs. Herne ; 'and, to tell you the truth, though I spoke to him just now, I expected no answer.'

'It 's a way he has, bebee, I suppose ?'

'Yes, child, it 's a way he has.'

'Take off your bonnet, bebee ; perhaps he cannot see your face.'

'I do not think that will be of much use, child ; however, I will take off my bonnet—there—and shake out my hair—there—you have seen this hair before, sir, and this face——'

'No answer, bebee.'

'Though the one was not quite so grey, nor the other so wrinkled.'

' How came they so, bebee ? '

' All along of this gorgio, child.'

' The gentleman in the house, you mean, bebee.'

' Yes, child, the gentleman in the house. God grant that I may preserve my temper. Do you know, sir, my name ? My name is Herne, which signifies a hairy individual, though neither grey-haired nor wrinkled. It is not the nature of the Hernes to be grey or wrinkled, even when they are old, and I am not old.' . . .

' Time flows on, I engage in many matters, in moſt miscarry. Am sent to prison ; says I to myself, I am become foolish. Am turned out of prison, and go back to the hairy ones, who receive me not over courteously ; says I, for their unkindness, and my own foolishness, all the thanks to that gorgio. Answers to me the child, " I wish I could set eyes upon him, bebee." '

' I did so, bebee ; go on.'

' " How shall I know him, bebee ? " says the child. " Young and grey, tall, and speaks Romanly." Runs to me the child, and says, " I 've found him, bebee." " Where, child ? " says I. " Come with me, bebee," says the child. " That 's he," says I, as I looked at my gentleman through the hedge.'

' Ha, ha ! bebee, and here he lies, poisoned like a hog.'

' You have taken drows, sir,' said Mrs. Herne ; ' do you hear, sir ? drows ; tip him a ſtave, child, of the song of poison.'

And thereupon the girl clapped her hands, and sang—

> ' The Rommany churl
> And the Rommany girl,
> To-morrow shall hie
> To poison the ſty,
> And bewitch on the mead
> The farmer's ſteed.'

' Do you hear that, sir ? ' said Mrs. Herne ; ' the child has tipped you a ſtave of the song of poison : that is, she has sung it Chriſtianly, though perhaps you would like to hear it Romanly ; you were always fond of what was Roman. Tip it him Romanly, child.'

' He has heard it Romanly already, bebee ; 'twas by that I found him out, as I told you.'

' Halloo, sir, are you sleeping ? you have taken drows ;
the gentleman makes no answer. God give me patience ! '
' And what if he doesn't, bebee ; isn't he poisoned like
a hog ? Gentleman ! indeed, why call him gentleman ?
If he ever was one he 's broke, and is now a tinker, a
worker of blue metal.'
' That 's his way, child, to-day a tinker, to-morrow
something else ; and as for being drabbed, I don't know
what to say about it.' . . .
' He is sick, child, sure enough. Ho, ho ! sir, you have
taken drows ; what, another throe ! writhe, sir, writhe, the
hog died by the drow of gypsies ; I saw him stretched
at evening. That 's yourself, sir. There is no hope, sir,
no help, you have taken drow ; shall I tell you your fortune, sir, your dukkerin ? God bless you, pretty gentleman, much trouble will you have to suffer, and much water
to cross ; but never mind, pretty gentleman, you shall be
fortunate at the end, and those who hate shall take off their
hats to you.'
' Hey, bebee ! ' cried the girl ; ' what is this ? what do
you mean ? you have blessed the gorgio ! '
' Blessed him ! no, sure ; what did I say ? Oh, I
remember, I 'm mad ; well, I can't help it, I said what the
dukkerin dook told me ; woe 's me ; he 'll get up yet.'
' Nonsense, bebee ! . . . He 's drabbed, spite of dukkerin.'
' Don't say so, child ; he 's sick, 'tis true, but don't laugh
at dukkerin, only folks do that that know no better. I,
for one, will never laugh at the dukkerin dook. Sick
again ; I wish he was gone.'
' He 'll soon be gone, bebee ; let 's leave him. He 's
as good as gone ; look there, he 's dead.'
' No, he 's not, he 'll get up—I feel it ; can't we hasten
him ? '
' Hasten him ! yes, to be sure ; set the dog upon him.
Here, juggal, look in there, my dog.'
The dog made its appearance at the door of the tent,
and began to bark and tear up the ground.
' At him, juggal, at him ; he wished to poison, to drab
you. Halloo ! '
The dog barked violently, and seemed about to spring
at my face, but retreated.

P

' The dog won't fly at him, child ; he flashed at the dog with his eye, and scared him. He 'll get up.'

' Nonsense, bebee ! you make me angry ; how should he get up ? '

' The dook tells me so, and, what 's more, I had a dream. I thought I was at York, standing amidst a crowd to see a man hung, and the crowd shouted, " There he comes ! " and I looked, and lo ! it was the tinker ; before I could cry with joy I was whisked away, and I found myself in Ely's big church, which was chock full of people to hear the dean preach, and all eyes were turned to the big pulpit ; and presently I heard them say, " There he mounts ! " and I looked up to the big pulpit, and lo ! the tinker was in the pulpit, and he raised his arm and began to preach. Anon, I found myself at York again, just as the drop fell, and I looked up, and I saw, not the tinker, but my own self hanging in the air.'

' You are going mad, bebee ; if you want to hasten him, take your stick and poke him in the eye.'

' That will be of no use, child, the dukkerin tells me so ; but I will try what I can do. Halloo, tinker ! you must introduce yourself into a quiet family, and raise confusion —must you ? You must steal its language, and, what was never done before, write it down Christianly—must you ? Take that—and that ' ; and she stabbed violently with her stick towards the end of the tent.

' That 's right, bebee, you struck his face ; now, once more, and let it be in the eye. Stay, what 's that ? get up, bebee.'

' What 's the matter, child ? '

' Some one is coming, come away.'

' Let me make sure of him, child ; he 'll be up yet.' And thereupon, Mrs. Herne, rising, leaned forward into the tent, and supporting herself against the pole, took aim in the direction of the farther end. ' I will thrust out his eye,' said she ; and, lunging with her stick, she would probably have accomplished her purpose had not at that moment the pole of the tent given way, whereupon she fell to the ground, the canvas falling upon her and her intended victim.

' Here 's a pretty affair, bebee,' screamed the girl.

' He 'll get up yet,' said Mrs. Herne, from beneath the canvas.

' Get up !—get up yourself ; where are you ? where is your—— Here, there, bebee, here 's the door; there, make haste, they are coming.'

' He 'll get up yet,' said Mrs. Herne, recovering her breath ; ' the dook tells me so.'

' Never mind him or the dook ; he is drabbed ; come away, or we shall be grabbed—both of us.'

' One more blow, I know where his head lies.'

' You are mad, bebee ; leave the fellow—gorgio avella.'

And thereupon the females hurried away.

George Borrow.

Poisoning the Porker

LISTEN to me ye Roman lads, who are seated in the straw about the fire, and I will tell how we poison the porker, I will tell how we poison the porker.

We go to the house of the poison-monger, where we buy three pennies' worth of bane, and when we return to our people, we say we will poison the porker ; we will try and poison the porker.

We then make up the poison, and then we take our way to the house of the farmer, as if to beg a bit of victuals, a little broken victuals.

We see a jolly porker, and then we say in Roman language, ' Fling the bane yonder amongst the dirt, and the porker soon will find it, the porker soon will find it.'

Early on the morrow, we will return to the farm-house, and beg the dead porker, the body of the dead porker.

And so we do, even so we do ; the porker dieth during the night; on the morrow we beg the porker, and carry to the tent the porker.

And then we wash the inside well, till all the inside is perfectly clean, till there 's no bane within it, not a poison grain within it.

And then we roast the body well, send for ale to the ale-house, and have a merry banquet, a merry Roman banquet.

The fellow with the fiddle plays, he plays ; the little lassie
sings, she sings an ancient Roman ditty ; now hear the
Roman ditty.

George Borrow.

Warlocks and Gypsies

WITCHES, warlocks and gypsies soon ken ae the
ither.

Scots Proverb.

How to tell a Witch

A WITCH may be known by her hair, which is straight
for three or four inches and then begins to curl—like
a waterfall which comes down smoothly and then rebounds
roundly on the neck.

Charles Godfrey Leland.

Othello and the Egyptian Spell

OTHELLO.   I have a salt and sorry rheum offends me.
  Lend me thy handkerchief.
DESDEMONA.   Here, my lord.
OTHELLO.   That which I gave you.
DESDEMONA.   I have it not about me.
OTHELLO.   Not ?
DESDEMONA.   No, indeed, my lord.
OTHELLO.   That 's a fault.   That handkerchief
  Did an Egyptian to my mother give ;
  She was a charmer, and could almost read
  The thoughts of people ; she told her, while she kept it,
  'Twould make her amiable, and subdue my father
  Entirely to her love, but if she lost it
  Or made a gift of it, my father's eye
  Should hold her loathed, and his spirits should hunt
  After new fancies.   She dying gave it me ;
  And bid me, when my fate would have me wive,
  To give it her.   I did so : and take heed on 't ;
  Make it a darling like your precious eye ;
  To lose 't or give 't away, were such perdition
  As nothing else could match.

DESDEMONA.   Is 't possible ?
OTHELLO.   'Tis true ; there 's magic in the web of it :
A sibyl, that had number'd in the world
The sun to course two hundred compasses,
In her prophetic fury sew'd the work :
The worms were hallow'd that did breed the silk ;
And it was dyed in mummy which the skilful
Conserved of maidens' hearts.

Shakespeare.

Magic

MAGIC did not jump at once into being, as to the thing
itself ; it was not a revelation from hell, made at
once to mankind, to tell them what they might do : the
Devil did not come and offer his service gratis to us, and
representing how useful a slave he would be, solicit us to
take him into pay, and this at once, without ceremony
or introduction. . . .

Not but that the Devil was very ready, when he found
himself made necessary ; I say, he was very ready to
come into the schemes when proposed, and to serve us
in our occasion, and that with a willingness which was
extremely obliging ; which showed him to be a person
of abundance of complaisance, and mighty willing to
engage us, whatever it cost him ; as much as to say, he was
glad he could serve us, was ready to do his utmost for us,
and the like.

Now to go back briefly to the occasion which brought
the magicians to the necessity of seeking to him for assistance, and to take him into the management of their affairs ;
the case was, in short, this : the world, as I have said
already, began to be wiser than the ages before them : the
ordinary magic of the former ages would not pass any
longer for wisdom ; and if the wise men, as they were
called, did not daily produce some new discoveries, it was
evident the price and rate of soothsaying would come
down to nothing. . . .

At first the magicians satisfied the curiosity of the people
by juggle and trick, by framing artificial voices and noises ;
foretelling strange events, by mechanical appearances, and

all the cheats which we find put upon the ignorant people to this day ; and it would be tedious to enumerate the particulars by which they imposed upon one another. You may guess at them by such as are mentioned before ; but principally those who studied the heavenly motions, had great opportunities of recommending themselves for men of craft, pretending to tell fortunes, calculate nativities, resolve doubts, read the lines of nature drawn in the face, palms of the hand, symmetry of the body, moles and marks on the flesh, and the like.

These things they carried to a due length, and we find the success was so much to their advantage, that the whole world, or great part of it, has been gipsey-ridden by them, even to this day.

Daniel Defoe.

The Cousening Art of Sortilege practised especiallie by Aegyptian vagabonds

THE counterfeit *Aegyptians*, which were indeed cousening vagabonds, practising the art called *Sortilegium*, had no small credit among the multitude : howbeit, their divinations were as was their fast and loose, and as the witches cures and hurtes, & as the soothsaiers answers, and as the conjurors raisings up of spirits, and as *Apollos* or the Rood of graces oracles, and as the jugglers knacks of legierdemaine, and as the papists exorcismes, and as the witches charmes, and as the counterfeit visions, and as the couseners knaveries. Hereupon it was said ; *Non inveniatur inter vos menahas,* that is *Sortilegus,* which were like to these Aegyptian couseners.

Reginald Scot, 1584.

The People of Dar-Bushi-Fal

'NOT far from this place is a Char Seharra, or witch-hamlet, where dwell those of the Dar-bushi-fal. These are very evil people, and powerful enchanters ; for it is well known that if any traveller stop to sleep in their Char, they will with their sorceries, if he be a white man, turn him as black as a coal, and will afterwards sell him as a negro. Horses and mules they serve in the same manner, for if they are black, they will turn them red, or any other colour which beſt may please them ; and although the owners demand juſtice of the authorities, the sorcerers always come off beſt. They have a language which they use among themselves, very different from all other languages, so much so that it is impossible to underſtand them. They are very swarthy, quite as much so as mulattos, and their faces are exceedingly lean. As for their legs, they are like reeds ; and when they run, the devil himself cannot overtake them. They tell Dar-bushi-fal with flour ; they fill a plate, and then they are able to tell you anything you ask them. They likewise tell it with a shoe ; they put it in their mouth, and then they will recall to your memory every aĉtion of your life. They likewise tell Dar-bushi-fal with oil ; and indeed are, in every respeĉt, moſt powerful sorcerers.

' Two women, once on a time, came to Fez, bringing with them an exceedingly white donkey, which they placed in the middle of the square called Faz el Bali ; they then killed it, and cut it into upwards of thirty pieces. Upon the ground there was much of the donkey's filth and dung ; some of this they took in their hands, when it ſtraight assumed the appearance of fresh dates. . . . After they had colleĉted much money from the speĉtators, one of them took a needle, and ran it into the tail of the donkey, crying " Arrhe li dar " (Get home), whereupon the donkey inſtantly rose up, and set off running, kicking every now and then moſt furiously ; and it was remarked, that not one single trace of blood remained upon the ground, juſt as if they had done nothing to it. Both these women were of the very same Char Seharra which I have already mentioned. They likewise took paper, and cut it into the shape of a peseta, and a dollar, and a half dollar, until they had made many pesetas and dollars, and then they put them into an earthen pan over a fire, and when they took them out, they appeared juſt fresh from the ſtamp, and with such money these people buy all they want.

' There was a friend of my grandfather, who came frequently to our house, who was in the habit of making this money. One day he took me with him to buy white silk ;

and when they had shown him some, he took the silk in his hand, and pressed it to his mouth, and then I saw that the silk, which was before white, had become green, even as grass. The master of the shop said, " Pay me for my silk." " Of what colour was your silk ? " he demanded. " White," said the man ; whereupon, turning round, he cried, " Good people, behold, the white silk is green " ; and so he got a pound of silk for nothing ; and he also was of the Char Seharra.

'They are very evil people indeed, and the Emperor himself is afraid of them. The poor wretch who falls into their hands has cause to rue ; they always go badly dressed, and exhibit every appearance of misery, though they are far from being miserable. Such is the life they lead.'

George Borrow.

<i>The Gypsy Glamour</i>

I REMEMBER to have heard (certainly very long ago, for at that time I believed the legend) that a gypsy exercised his glamour over a number of people at Hadding-ton, to whom he exhibited a common dung-hill cock, trailing, what appeared to the spectators, a massy oaken trunk. An old man passed with a cart of clover ; he stopped and picked out a four-leaved blade ; the eyes of the spectators were opened, and the oaken trunk appeared to be a bulrush.

Sir Walter Scott.

<i>Taw and the Wizard</i>

' AND ever after that,' said Siani, ' the place was haunted.'

' Who haunted it ? '

' No one rightly knew that. It might have been the serving-man or it might have been the old lady herself, but any way it was a bad spirit, and the family had to leave the house, which fell all into ruins. But the old gate-keeper and his wife lived on at the little lodge, and often in the night they would be awakened by a bellowing like ten thousand bulls. Then they would see a light come through the gate ; it would stop there and laugh. After that the ruined house would be all lit up, and as the light died away the great laughter would come again.

'The people who lived about there were afraid to go near the house, and the fields where we Gypsies used to play, where we found hedgehogs and killed rabbits, were all deserted. At last they sent for a Wise Man to lay the ghost. He, and the minister, and the people all prayed together for four nights in succession, from midnight to one o'clock in the morning, but it was not until the fourth night, after the minister and the people had gone home, that the ghost was laid.' . . .

'What I tell you is true, every word. No one was there, only Taw and the Wise Man, and I to carry the things, for Taw liked me better nor any of her own daughters.' . . .

'The Wise Man took a bottle with water in it ; he lit a candle and put it in the bottle ; he read something from a book. Then he and the old Gypsy woman (I don't like to say her name, God rest her soul ! she was always good to me) knelt down hand in hand by the book and spoke the words together ; I could not hear what they said.' . . .

'The Wise Man blindfolded the old woman and led her across the field ; she carried the bottle and the bad devil that was in it. They went down the steps into the boat-house, and there the two knelt again. Then the old Gypsy gave the bottle to the Wise Man and spoke the words, while he dropped it into the lake. Now the ghost was laid, he was under the water, and troubled the place no more.' . . .

'They came back to the field where they had left me and the book. The Wise Man took a box from his pocket. " There, old woman, take this, open it ! " A toad jumped from the box ; there was a name written on its back. " Breathe into its mouth," he said, " and I will do so after thee." This was to bind her to him, so that he could call on her again. He paid her well for her help ; she bought many things with the money he gave her, new horses, new harps and fiddles for her sons, and new dresses for her daughters.'

M. Eileen Lyster.

A Blood Bond

A ND then one day the Thing happened. Archelaus,
his wife, and sister-in-law had gone to attend a distant
fair—the man to buy and sell horses, the women to tell
fortunes. The girl and her grandmother were the only
Romané left on the field. Piggott was sitting in the girl's
tent pointing pinthorns with his knife, while he entertained her with a lively account of the gypsies of the
Alhambra. Eldorai, a charming barbaric figure, with coral
necklet and half-guinea pieces braided in her hair, crouched
by the fire, her slim bare legs tucked under her. Lazily
and happily he watched her kneading a little flour into
dough, the simple constituent of the *Romani marikli* or
gypsy cake. Suddenly the young girl said in a voice that
thrilled him : ' Stephen '—it was the first time she had
called him by his name—' I want some of your blood.'
' Splendidly dramatic,' thought Piggott, ' this is, no doubt,
the prelude to a new version of the Robber Bridegroom,
or, better still, perhaps to a vampire myth picked up five
centuries ago, when her ancestors sojourned in the Balkans.
However, a young and pretty vampire must be treated with
the respect due to a lady.' Laughingly, he extended his
arm, saying, ' Take it, little witch.' And then Eldorai,
with her eyes fixed upon his, had rolled up his sleeve.
And before he had time to realise what was happening, he
felt himself stabbed in the fore-arm by some pointed
instrument, doubtless one of the pinthorns of his own
fashioning. The blood flowed. In a moment she had
stanched it with the dough. He saw that it made a small
scarlet blot on the paste. Then, though more deliberately,
she had bared her shapely brown arm, and repeated this
strange rite on her own person. Absorbed as an anthro-
pologist observing for the first time some savage ceremony,
Piggott watched her re-knead the dough in which their
blood was now mingled, fashion it into a thin flat cake,
and place it on the red ashes.

His collector's instincts aroused, he waited breathlessly
for the next act in this mystery. In a few minutes the
marikli was baked. Breaking it into two pieces, Eldorai

took one herself and handed the other to Piggott, gazing
intently into his eyes.

And Piggott, following her example, had eaten it.   That
was the incredible part of it.   How he, delicate-minded
and fastidious as he was, could ever have done so he was
afterwards at a loss to comprehend.   He could only come
to the conclusion that he had been hypnotised by the girl,
just as spectators are by the Indian juggler in his famous
rope trick.   But at the time he had felt neither discomfort
nor disgust ; instead, a strange happiness had pervaded his
whole being.   It was not until the next morning, when he
recalled the occurrence with a shudder, that he felt as
though he had taken part in the celebration of some sacri-
legious Black Mass.

Piggott remembered the words that Eldorai had spoken
to him with such extraordinary gravity :   ' And now,
Stephen, you belongs to me and I belongs to you : and I
will come for you, my rom, to the day, no matter wheresoever I be, even if I has to wait until the seven years is
out.'   *Cornhill Magazine*, 1922.

The Sapengro

ONE day it happened that, being on my rambles, I
entered a green lane which I had never seen before ;
at first it was rather narrow, but as I advanced it became
considerably wider ; in the middle was a drift-way with
deep ruts, but right and left was a space carpeted with a
sward of trefoil and clover ; there was no lack of trees,
chiefly ancient oaks, which, flinging out their arms from
either side, nearly formed a canopy, and afforded a pleasing
shelter from the rays of the sun, which was burning fiercely
above.   Suddenly a group of objects attracted my attention.   Beneath one of the largest of the trees, upon the
grass, was a kind of low tent or booth, from the top of
which a thin smoke was curling ; beside it stood a couple
of light carts, whilst two or three lean horses or ponies
were cropping the herbage which was growing nigh.
Wondering to whom this odd tent could belong, I advanced
till I was close before it, when I found that it consisted of
two tilts, like those of waggons, placed upon the ground

and fronting each other, connected behind by a sail or large piece of canvas, which was but partially drawn across the top ; upon the ground in the intervening space was a fire, over which, supported by a kind of iron crow-bar, hung a cauldron. My advance had been so noiseless as not to alarm the inmates, who consisted of a man and woman, who sat apart, one on each side of the fire ; they were both busily employed—the man was carding plaited straw, whilst the woman seemed to be rubbing something with a white powder, some of which lay on a plate beside her. Suddenly the man looked up, and, perceiving me, uttered a strange kind of cry, and the next moment both the woman and himself were on their feet and rushing out upon me.

I retreated a few steps, yet without turning to flee. I was not, however, without apprehension, which, indeed, the appearance of these two people was well calculated to inspire. The woman was a stout figure, seemingly between thirty and forty ; she wore no cap, and her long hair fell on either side of her head, like horse-tails, half way down to her waist ; her skin was dark and swarthy, like that of a toad, and the expression of her countenance was particularly evil ; her arms were bare, and her bosom was but half-concealed by a slight bodice, below which she wore a coarse petticoat, her only other article of dress. The man was somewhat younger, but of a figure equally wild ; his frame was long and lathy, but his arms were remarkably short, his neck was rather bent, he squinted slightly, and his mouth was much awry ; his complexion was dark, but, unlike that of the woman, was more ruddy than livid ; there was a deep scar on his cheek, something like the impression of a halfpenny. The dress was quite in keeping with the figure : in his hat, which was slightly peaked, was stuck a peacock's feather ; over a waistcoat of hide, untanned and with the hair upon it, he wore a rough jerkin of russet hue ; smallclothes of leather, which had probably once belonged to a soldier, but with which pipeclay did not seem to have come in contact for many a year, protected his lower man as far as the knee ; his legs were cased in long stockings of blue worsted, and on his shoes he wore immense old-fashioned buckles.

Such were the two beings who now came rushing upon me ; the man was rather in advance, brandishing a ladle in his hand.

'So I have caught you at laſt,' said he ; 'I 'll teach ye, you young highwayman, to come skulking about my properties ! '

Young as I was, I remarked that his manner of speaking was different from that of any people with whom I had been in the habit of associating. It was quite as ſtrange as his appearance, and yet it nothing resembled the foreign English which I had been in the habit of hearing through the palisades of the prison ; he could scarcely be a foreigner.

'Your properties ! ' said I ; 'I am in the King's Lane. Why did you put them there, if you did not wish them to be seen ? '

'On the spy,' said the woman, 'hey ? I 'll drown him in the sludge in the toad-pond over the hedge.'

'So we will,' said the man, 'drown him anon in the mud.'

'Drown me, will you ? ' said I ; 'I should like to see you ! What 's all this about ? Was it because I saw you with your hands full of ſtraw-plait, and my mother there——'

'Yes,' said the woman ; 'what was I about ? '

MYSELF. 'How should I know ? Making bad money perhaps ! '

And it will be well here to observe that at this time there was much bad money in circulation in the neighbourhood, generally supposed to be fabricated by the prisoners. . . .

'I 'll ſtrangle thee,' said the beldame dashing at me. 'Bad money, is it ? '

'Leave him to me, wifelkin,' said the man interposing ; 'you shall now see how I 'll baſte him down the lane.'

MYSELF. 'I tell you what, my chap, you had better put down that thing of yours ; my father lies concealed within my tepid breaſt, and if to me you offer any harm or wrong, I 'll call him forth to help me with his forked tongue.'

MAN. 'What do you mean, ye Bengui's bantling ? I never heard such discourse in all my life ; playman's speech or Frenchman's talk—which, I wonder ? Your father !

tell the mumping villain that if he comes near my fire, I 'll serve him out as I will you. Take that—— Tiny Jesus ! what have we got here ? Oh, delicate Jesus ! what is the matter with the child ? '

I had made a motion which the viper underſtood ; and now, partly disengaging itself from my bosom, where it had lain perdu, it raised its head to a level with my face, and ſtared upon my enemy with its glittering eyes.

The man ſtood like one transfixed, and the ladle with which he had aimed a blow at me now hung in the air like the hand which held it ; his mouth was extended, and his cheeks became of a pale yellow, save alone that place which bore the mark which I have already described, and this shone now portentously, like fire. He ſtood in this manner for some time ; at laſt the ladle fell from his hand, and its falling appeared to rouse him from his ſtupor.

' I say, wifelkin,' said he in a faltering tone, ' did you ever see the like of this here ? '

But the woman had retreated to the tent, from the entrance of which her loathly face was now thruſt, with an expression partly of terror and partly of curiosity. After gazing some time longer at the viper and myself, the man ſtooped down and took up the ladle ; then, as if somewhat more assured, he moved to the tent, where he entered into conversation with the beldame in a low voice. Of their discourse, though I could hear the greater part of it, I underſtood not a single word ; and I wondered what it could be, for I knew by the sound that it was not French. At laſt, the man, in a somewhat louder tone, appeared to put a queſtion to the woman, who nodded her head affirmatively, and in a moment or two produced a small ſtool, which she delivered to him. He placed it on the ground, close by the door of the tent, firſt rubbing it with his sleeve, as if for the purpose of polishing its surface.

MAN. ' Now, my precious little gentleman, do sit down here by the poor people's tent ; we wish to be civil in our slight way. Don't be angry and say no ; but look kindly upon us and satisfied, my precious little God Almighty.'

WOMAN. ' Yes, my gorgious angel, sit down by the poor bodies' fire, and eat a sweetmeat. We want to ask you a queſtion or two ; only firſt put that serpent away.'

Myself. 'I can sit down and bid the serpent go to sleep, that's easy enough; but as for eating a sweetmeat, how can I do that? I have not got one, and where am I to get it?'

Woman. 'Never fear, my tiny tawny, we can give you one, such as you never ate, I dare say, however far you may have come from.'

The serpent sunk into its usual resting-place, and I sat down on the stool. The woman opened a box, and took out a strange little basket or hamper, not much larger than a man's fist, and formed of a delicate kind of matting. It was sewed at the top; but ripping it open with a knife she held it to me, and I saw, to my surprise, that it contained candied fruits of a dark green hue, tempting enough to one of my age. 'There, my tiny,' said she; 'taste and tell me how you like them.'

'Very much,' said I; 'where did you get them?'

The beldame leered upon me for a moment, then, nodding her head thrice with a knowing look, said: 'Who knows better than yourself, my tawny?'

Now, I knew nothing about the matter; but I saw that these strange people had conceived a very high opinion of the abilities of their visitor, which I was nothing loath to encourage. I therefore answered boldly: 'Ah, who indeed?'

'Certainly,' said the man; 'who should know better than yourself, or so well? And now, my tiny one, let me ask you one thing—you didn't come to do us any harm?'

'No,' said I, 'I had no dislike to you; though if you were to meddle with me——'

Man. 'Of course, my gorgious, of course you would; and quite right too. Meddle with you!—what right have we? I should say it would not be quite safe. I see how it is; you are one of them there'; and he bent his head towards his left shoulder.

Myself. 'Yes, I am one of them—for I thought he was alluding to the soldiers,—you had best mind what you are about, I can tell you.'

Man. 'Don't doubt we will for our own sake; Lord bless you, wifelkin, only think that we should see one of them there when we least thought about it. Well, I have heard of such things, though I never thought to see one ; however, seeing is believing. Well ! now you are come, and are not going to do us any mischief, I hope you will stay ; you can do us plenty of good if you will.'

MYSELF. 'What good can I do you ? '

MAN. 'What good ? plenty ! Would you not bring us luck ? I have heard say that one of them there always does, if it will but settle down. Stay with us, you shall have a tilted cart all to yourself if you like. We 'll make you our little God Almighty, and say our prayers to you every morning.'

MYSELF. 'That would be nice ; and if you were to give me plenty of these things, I should have no objection. But what would my father say ? I think he would hardly let me.'

MAN. 'Why not ? he would be with you, and kindly would we treat him. Indeed, without your father, you would be nothing at all.'

George Borrow.

Saul and the Witch of Endor

NOW Samuel was dead, and all Israel had lamented him, and buried him in Ramah, even in his own city. And Saul had put away those that had familiar spirits, and the wizards, out of the land. And the Philistines gathered themselves together, and came and pitched in Shunem : and Saul gathered all Israel together, and they pitched in Gilboa. And when Saul saw the host of the Philistines, he was afraid, and his heart greatly trembled. And when Saul inquired of the Lord, the Lord answered him not, neither by dreams, nor by Urim, nor by prophets. Then said Saul unto his servants, Seek me a woman that hath a familiar spirit, that I may go to her, and inquire of her. And his servants said to him, Behold, there is a woman that hath a familiar spirit at Endor. And Saul disguised himself, and put on other raiment, and he went, and two men with him, and they came to the woman by night : and he said, I pray thee, divine unto me by the familiar spirit, and bring me him up, whom I shall name unto thee. And the woman said unto him, Behold, thou knowest what

Saul hath done, how he hath cut off those that have familiar
spirits, and the wizards, out of the land : wherefore then
layeſt thou a snare for my life, to cause me to die ?   And
Saul sware to her by the Lord, saying, As the Lord liveth,
there shall no punishment happen to thee for this thing.
Then said the woman, Whom shall I bring up unto thee ?
And he said, Bring me up Samuel.   And when the woman
saw Samuel, she cried with a loud voice : and the woman
spake to Saul, saying, Why haſt thou deceived me ? for
thou art Saul.   And the king said unto her, Be not afraid :
for what saweſt thou ?   And the woman said unto Saul,
I saw gods ascending out of the earth.   And he said unto
her, What form is he of ?   And she said, An old man
cometh up ; and he is covered with a mantle.   And Saul
perceived that it was Samuel, and he ſtooped with his face
to the ground, and bowed himself.

And Samuel said to Saul, Why haſt thou disquieted me,
to bring me up ?   And Saul answered, I am sore diſtressed ;
for the Philiſtines make war againſt me, and God is departed from me, and answereth me no more, neither by
prophets, nor by dreams : therefore I have called thee,
that thou mayeſt make known unto me what I shall do.
Then said Samuel, Wherefore then doſt thou ask of me,
seeing the Lord is departed from thee, and is become thine
enemy ?   And the Lord hath done to him, as he spake by
me : for the Lord hath rent the kingdom out of thine
hand, and given it to thy neighbour, even to David :
because thou obeyedſt not the voice of the Lord, nor
executedſt his fierce wrath upon Amalek, therefore hath
the Lord done this thing unto thee this day.   Moreover
the Lord will also deliver Israel with thee into the hand
of the Philiſtines : and to morrow shalt thou and thy sons
be with me : the Lord also shall deliver the hoſt of Israel
into the hand of the Philiſtines.

Then Saul fell ſtraightway all along on the earth, and was
sore afraid, because of the words of Samuel : and there
was no ſtrength in him ; for he had eaten no bread all the
day, nor all the night.   And the woman came unto Saul,
and saw that he was sore troubled, and said unto him,
Behold, thine handmaid hath obeyed thy voice, and I have
put my life in my hand, and have hearkened unto thy words

which thou spakeſt unto me. Now therefore, I pray thee, hearken thou also unto the voice of thine handmaid, and let me set a morsel of bread before thee ; and eat, that thou mayeſt have ſtrength, when thou goeſt on thy way.   But he refused, and said, I will not eat.   1 *Samuel.*

The Tale of Ariſtomenus

IN speaking these words, and devising with my selfe of our departing the next morrow, leſt Meroe the Witch should play by us as she had done by divers other persons, it fortuned that Socrates did fall asleepe, and slept very soundly, by reason of his travell, and plenty of meat and wine wherewithall hee had filled himselfe.   Wherefore I closed and barred faſt the doores of the chamber, and put my bed behinde the doore, and so layed mee downe to reſt. But I could in no wise sleepe, for the great feare which was in my heart, untill it was about midnight, and then I began to slumber.   But alas, behold suddenly the chamber doores brake open, and lockes, bolts, and poſts fell downe, that you would verily have thought that some Theeves had beene presently come to have spoyled and robbed us.   And my bed whereon I lay being a truckle bed, fashioned in forme of a Cradle, and one of the feet broken and rotten, by violence was turned upside downe, and I likewise was overwhelmed and covered lying in the same.   Then per- ceived I in my selfe, that certaine affeſts of the minde by nature doth chance contrary.   For as tears oftentimes trickle down the cheekes of him that seeth or heareth some joyfull newes, so I being in this fearefull perplexity, could not forbeare laughing, to see how of Ariſtomenus I was made like unto a snaile in his shell.   And while I lay on the ground covered in this sort, I peeped under the bed to see what would happen.   And behold there entred in two old women, the one bearing a burning torch, and the other a sponge and a naked sword : and so in this habit they ſtood about Socrates being faſt asleep.   Then shee which bare the sword sayd unto the other, Behold siſter Panthia, this is my deare and sweet heart, which both day and night hath abused my wanton youthfulnesse.   This is he, who little regarding my love, doth not onely defame me with reproachfull words, but also intendeth to run away. And I shall be forsaken by like craft as Vlysses did use, and shall continually bewaile my solitarinesse as Calipso. Which said, shee pointed towards mee that lay under the bed, and shewed me to Panthia. This is hee, quoth she, which is his Counsellor, and perswadeth him to forsake me, and now being at the point of death he lieth prostrate on the ground covered with his bed, and hath seene all our doings, and hopeth to escape scot-free from my hands, but I will cause that hee shall repent himselfe too late, nay rather forthwith, of his former untemperate language, and his present curiosity. Which words when I heard I fell into a cold sweat, and my heart trembled with feare, insomuch that the bed over me did likewise rattle and shake. Then spake Panthia unto Meroe and said, Sister let us by and by teare him in pieces, or tye him by the members, and so cut them off. Then Meroe (being so named because she was a Taverner, and loved wel good wines) answered, Nay rather let him live, and bury the corps of this poore wretch in some hole of the earth ; and therewithall shee turned the head of Socrates on the other side, and thrust her sword up to the hilts into the left part of his necke, and received the bloud that gushed out, into a pot, that no drop thereof fell beside : which things I saw with myne owne eyes, and as I thinke to the intent she might alter nothing that pertained to sacrifice, which she accustomed to make, she thrust her hand downe into the intrals of his body, and searching about, at length brought forth the heart of my miserable companion Socrates, who having his throat cut in such sort, yeelded out a dolefull cry and gave up the ghost. Then Panthia stopped the wide wound of his throat with the Sponge, and said, O Sponge sprung and made of the sea, beware that thou passe not by running River. This being sayd, the one of them moved and turned up my bed, and then they strid over mee and went their wayes, and the doores closed fast, the posts stood in their old places, and the lockes and bolts were shut againe. But I that lay upon the ground like one without soule, naked and cold, like to one that were more than halfe dead, yet reviving my selfe, and appointed as I thought for the Gallowes, began to say, Alasse what shall become of me to morrow, when my companion shall be found murthered here in the chamber? To whom shall I seeme to tell any similitude of truth, when as I shall tell the trueth in deed? They will say, If thou wert unable to resist the violence of the women, yet shouldest thou have cried for helpe; Wouldst thou suffer the man to be slaine before thy face and say nothing? Or why did they not slay thee likewise? Why did they spare thee that stood by and saw them commit that horrible fact? Wherefore although thou hast escaped their hands, yet thou shalt not escape ours. While I pondered these things with my selfe the night passed on, and so I resolved to take my horse before day, and goe forward on my journy.

Howbeit the wayes were unknowne unto me, and thereupon I tooke up my packet, unlocked and unberred the doors, but those good and faithfull doores which in the night did open of their owne accord, could then scantly be opened with their keyes. And when I was out I cried, O sirrah Hostler where art thou? open the stable doore, for I will ride away by and by. The Hostler lying behinde the stable doore upon a pallet, and halfe asleepe, What (quoth hee) doe you not know that the wayes be very dangerous? What meane you to rise at this time of night? If you perhaps guilty of some heynous crime, be weary of your life, yet thinke you not that wee are such Sots that we will die for you. Then said I, It is well nigh day, and moreover, what can Theeves take from him that hath nothing? Doest thou not know (Foole as thou art) if thou be naked, if ten Gyants should assaile thee, they could not spoyle or rob thee? Whereunto the drowsie Hostler halfe asleepe, and turning on the other side, answered, What know I whether you have murthered your Companion whom you brought in yesternight, or no, and now seeke the meanes to escape away? O Lord, at that time I remember the earth seemed to open, and me thought I saw at hell gate the Dog Cerberus ready to devour mee; and then I verily beleeved, that Meroe did not spare my throat, mooved with pitty, but rather cruelly pardoned mee to bring mee to the Gallowes. Wherefore I returned to my chamber, and there devised with my selfe in what sort I should finish my life. But when I saw that fortune would minister unto mee no other instrument, than that which my bed profered mee, I sayd, O bed, O bed, most dear unto me at this present, which hast abode and suffered with me so many miseries, judge and arbiter of such things as were done here this night, whome onely I may call to witnesse for my innocency, render (I say) unto me some wholsome weapon to end my life, that am most willing to dye. And therewithal I pulled out a piece of the rope wherewith the bed was corded, and tyed one end thereof about a rafter by the window, and with the other end I made a sliding knot, and stood upon my bed, and so put my neck into it, and when I leaped from the bed, thinking verily to strangle my selfe and so dye, behold the rope beeing old and rotten burst in the middle, and I fell downe tumbling upon Socrates that lay under : And even at that same very time the Hostler came in crying with a loud voyce, and sayd, Where are you that made such hast at midnight, and now lies wallowing abed ? Whereupon (I know not whether it was by my fall, or by the great cry of the Hostler) Socrates as waking out of a sleepe, did rise up first and sayd, It is not without cause that strangers do speake evill of all such Hostlers, for this Caitife in his comming in, and with his crying out, I thinke under a colour to steale away somthing, hath waked me out of a sound sleepe. Then I rose up joyfull with a merry countenance, saying, Behold good Hostler, my friend, my companion and my brother, whom thou didst falsly affirme to be slaine by mee this night. And therewithall I embraced my friend Socrates and kissed him, and tooke him by the hand and sayd, Why tarry we ? Why lose wee the pleasure of this faire morning ? Let us goe, and so I tooke up my packet, and payed the charges of the house and departed : and we had not gone a mile out of the Towne but it was broad day, and then I diligently looked upon Socrates throat, to see if I could espy the place where Meroe thrust in her sword : but when I could not perceive any such thing, I thought with my selfe, What a mad man am I, that being overcome with wine yester night, have dreamed such terrible things ? Behold, I see Socrates is sound, safe, and in health. Where is his wound ? where is the Sponge ? Where is his great and new cut ? And then I spake to him

and sayd, Verily it is not without occasion, that Physitians
of experience do affirme, That such as fill their gorges
abundantly with meat and drinke, shall dreame of dire and
horrible sights: for I my selfe, not tempering my appetite
yeſter night from the pots of wine, did seeme to see this
night ſtrange and cruel visions, that even yet I think my
self sprinkled and wet with human blood : whereunto
Socrates made answer and said, Verily I my self dreamed
this night that my throat was cut, and that I felt the paine
of the wound, and that my heart was pulled out of my
belly, and the remembrance thereof makes me now to
feare, for my knees do so tremble that I can scarse goe any
further, and therefore I would faine eat somewhat to
strengthen and revive my spirits. Then said I, Behold
here thy breakefaſt, and therwithall I opened my scrip that
hanged upon my shoulder, and gave him bread and cheese,
and we sate downe under a great Plane tree, and I eat part
with him ; and while I beheld him eating greedily, I perceived that he waxed meigre and pale, and that his lively
colour faded away, insomuch that beeing in great fear,
and remembring those terrible furies of whom I lately
dreamed, the firſt morsell of bread that I put in my mouth
(which was but very small) did so ſticke in my jawes, that
I could neither swallow it downe, nor yet yeeld it up, and
moreover the small time of our being together increased
my feare, and what is hee that seeing his companion die
in the highway before his face, would not greatly lament
and bee sorry ? But when that Socrates had eaten sufficiently hee waxed very thirſty, for indeed he had well nigh
devoured all a whole Cheese : and behold evill fortune !
there was behinde the Plane tree a pleasant running water
as cleere as Cryſtal, and I sayd unto him, Come hither
Socrates to this water and drinke thy fill. And then he
rose and came to the River, and kneeled downe upon the
side of the banke to drinke, but he had scarce touched the
water with his lips, when as behold the wound of his throat
opened wide, and the Sponge suddenly fell into the water,
and after issued out a little remnant of bloud, and his body
being then without life, had fallen into the river, had not
I caught him by the leg and so pulled him up. And after
that I had lamented a good space the death of my wretched

companion, I buried him in the Sands there by the river.

Which done, in great feare I rode through many Out-wayes and desart places, and as culpable of the death of Socrates, I forsooke my countrey, my wife, and my children, and came to Etolia where I married another Wife.

Apuleius.

The Red King and the Witch

IT was the Red King, and he bought ten ducats' worth of victuals. He cooked them, and put them in a press. And he locked the press, and from night to night posted people to guard the victuals.

In the morning, when he looked, he found the platters bare. He did not find anything in them. Then the king said : ' I will give the half of my kingdom to whoever shall be found to guard the press, that the victuals may not go amissing from it.'

The king had three sons. Then the eldest thought with-in himself. ' God ! what, give half the kingdom to a stranger ! It were better for me to watch. Be it unto me according to God's will.'

He went to his father : ' Father, all hail. What, give the kingdom to a stranger ! It were better for me to watch.'

And his father said to him : ' As God will, only don't be frightened by what you may see.'

Then he said : ' Be it unto me according to God's will.' And he went and lay down in the palace. And he put his head on the pillow, and remained with his head on the pillow till towards dawn. And a warm sleepy breeze came and lulled him to slumber. And his little sister arose. And she turned a somersault, and her nails became like an axe, and her teeth like a shovel. And she opened the cup-board, and ate up everything. Then she became a child again, and returned to her place in the cradle, for she was a child at the breast. The lad arose, and told his father that he had seen nothing. His father looked in the press, found the platters bare—no victuals, no anything. His

father said to him : ' It would take a better man than you,
and even he might do nothing.'

His middle son also said : ' Father, all hail ! I am going
to watch to-night.'

' Go, dear ; only play the man.'

' Be it unto me according to God's will.'

And he went into the palace, and put his head on a pillow.
And at ten o'clock came a warm breeze, and sleep seized
him. Up rose his sister, and unwound herself from her
swaddling-bands, and turned a somersault, and her teeth
became like a shovel, and her nails like an axe. And she
went to the press, and opened it, and ate off the platters
what she found. She ate it all, and turned a somersault
again, and went back to her place in the cradle. Day
broke, and the lad arose, and his father asked him and
said : ' It would take a better man than you, and yet he
might not do anything for me, if he were as poor a creature
as you.'

The youngest son arose. ' Father, all hail ! Give me
also leave to watch the cupboard by night.'

' Go, dear ; only don't be frightened with what you see.'

' Be it unto me according to God's will,' said the lad.

And he went and took four needles, and lay down with
his head on the pillow ; and he stuck the four needles in
four places. When sleep seized him, he knocked his head
against a needle, so he stayed awake till dawn. And his
sister arose from her cradle, and he saw. And she turned
a somersault, and he was watching her. And her teeth
became like a shovel, and her nails like an axe. And she
went to the press, and ate up everything. She left the
platters bare. And she turned a somersault, and became
tiny again as she was ; she went to her cradle. The lad,
when he saw that, trembled with fear ; it seemed to him
ten years till daybreak.

And he arose, and went to his father. ' Father, all hail ! '

Then his father asked him : ' Didst see anything,
Peterkin ? '

' What did I see ? What did I not see ? Give me
money and a horse, a horse fit to carry the money, for I
am away to marry me.'

His father gave him ducats in abundance, and he put

them on his horse. The lad went, and made a hole on the border of the city. He made a chest of stone, and placed all the money there, and buried it. He placed a stone cross above, and departed. And he journeyed eight years, and came to the queen of all the birds that fly.

And the queen of the birds asked him : ' Whither away, Peterkin ? '

' Thither where there is neither death nor old age, to marry me.'

The queen said to him : ' Here is neither death nor old age.'

Then Peterkin said to her : ' How comes it that here is neither death nor old age ? '

Then she said to him : ' When I whittle away the wood of all this forest, then death will come and take me, and old age.'

Then Peterkin said : ' One day and one morning death will come and old age, and take me.'

And he departed farther, and journeyed on eight years, and arrived at a palace of copper. And a maiden came forth from that palace, and took him and kissed him. She said : ' I have waited long for thee.'   ·

She took the horse and put him in the stable, and he spent the night there. He arose in the morning, and placed his saddle on the horse.

Then the maiden began to weep, and asked him. ' Whither away, Peterkin ? '

' Thither, where there is neither death nor old age.'

Then the maiden said to him : ' Here is neither death nor old age.'

Then he asked her : ' How comes it that here is neither death nor old age ? '

' Why, when these mountains are levelled and these forests, then death will come.'

' This is no place for me,' said the lad to her. And he departed farther.

Then what said the horse to him ? ' Master, whip me four times, and twice yourself, for you are come to the Plain of Regret. And Regret will seize you, and cast you down, horse and all. So spur your horse, and escape and tarry not.'

He came to a hut. In the hut he beholds a lad, as it were ten years old, who asked him : ' What seekest thou, Peterkin, here ? '

' I seek the place where there is neither death nor old age.' The lad said : ' Here is neither death nor old age. I am the Wind.'

Then Peterkin said : ' Never, never will I go from here.' And he dwelt there a hundred years, and grew no older.

There the lad dwelt, and went out to hunt in the Mountains of Gold and Silver, and he could hardly carry home the game.

Then what said the Wind to him ? ' Peterkin, go unto all the Mountains of Gold and the Mountains of Silver ; but go not to the Mountain of Regret or to the Valley of Grief.'

He heeded not, but went to the Mountain of Regret and the Valley of Grief. And Grief cast him down ; he wept till his eyes were full.

And he went to the Wind : ' I am going home to my father, I will not stay longer.'

' Go not, for your father is dead, and brothers you have no more left at home. A million years have come and gone since then. The spot is not known where your father's palace stood. They have planted melons on it ; it is but an hour since I passed that way.'

But the lad departed thence, and arrived at the maiden's, whose was the palace of copper. Only one stick remained, and she cut it and grew old. As he knocked at the door, the stick fell, and she died. He buried her, and departed thence. And he came to the queen of the birds in the great forest. Only one branch remained, and that was all but through. When she saw him, she said, ' Peterkin, thou art quite young.'

Then he said to her, ' Dost thou remember telling me to stay here ? ' As she pressed and broke through the branch, she too fell and died.

He came where his father's palace stood and looked about him. There was no palace, no anything. And he fell to marvelling : ' God, Thou art mighty.' He only recognised his father's well, and went to the well. His

sister, the witch, when she saw him, said to him : ' I
have waited long for you, dog.' She rushed at him to
devour him, but he made the sign of the cross, and she
perished.

And he departed thence and came on an old man with
his beard down to his belt. ' Father, where is the palace
of the Red King ? I am his son.'

' What is this,' said the old man, ' thou tellest me, that
thou art his son ? My father's father has told me of the
Red King. His very city is no more. Dost thou not see
it is vanished ? And dost thou tell me that thou art the
Red King's son ? '

' It is not twenty years, old man, since I departed from
my father, and dost thou tell me that thou knowest not my
father ? ' (It was a million years since he had left his
home.) ' Follow me, if thou dost not believe me.'

And he went to the cross of stone ; only a palm's breadth
was out of the ground. And it took him two days to get
at the chest of money. When he had lifted out the chest,
and opened it, Death sat in one corner groaning, and Old
Age groaning in another corner.

Then what said Old Age ? ' Lay hold of him, Death.'
' Lay hold of him, yourself.'

Old Age laid hold of him in front, and Death laid hold
of him behind.

The old man took and buried him decently, and planted
the cross near him. And the old man took the money and
also the horse.

Rumanian Gypsy Folk-Tale.

Benison

FEAR no more the heat o' the sun,
    Nor the furious winter's rages ;
Thou thy worldly task hast done,
    Home art gone and ta'en thy wages :
Golden lads and girls all must,
As chimney-sweepers, come to dust.

Fear no more the frown o' the great ;
   Thou art paſt the tyrant's ſtroke ;
Care no more to clothe and eat ;
   To thee the reed is as the oak :
The sceptre, learning, physic, muſt
All follow this and come to duſt.

Fear no more the lightning-flash,
   Nor the all-dreaded thunder-ſtone ;
Fear not slander, censure rash ;
   Thou haſt finish'd joy and moan :
All lovers young, all lovers muſt
Consign to thee and come to duſt.

     No exorciser harm thee !
     Nor no witchcraft charm thee !
     Ghoſt unlaid forbear thee !
     Nothing ill come near thee !
     Quiet consummation have ;
     And renowned be thy grave !

                               Shakeſpeare.

IX

A GYPSY BESTIARY

IX

A Gypsy Bestiary

An Affair of Egypt

IT is an affair of Egypt, brother, and I shall not acquaint
you with it ; peradventure it relates to a horse or an ass,
or peradventure it relates to a mule or a macho.

George Borrow.

Some Auguries of Innocence

A ROBIN REDBREAST in a Cage
Puts all Heaven in a rage. . . .
The wild Deer, wand'ring here & there,
Keeps the Human Soul from Care.

William Blake.

The Horse and the Bear

AMONG animals the Gypsy has two favourites, and
his choice is characteristic. His predilection for the
horse (or in its default the mule) shows his sympathy with
what might be called the heroic instinct of the steed, the
only one of our four-footed companions that rises to a
comprehension of our spiritual desires. . . . The horse
alone appears to understand and sympathize with the
agonising impatience of our heart, the anxieties of love,
our fiery hatreds, our ambitious illusions, when, speedy
even as our thoughts, he rushes through space to bring us
to the desired goal. . . .

Is it not a paradox that Gypsies are perfect horse-dealers
but indifferent riders ? It is immaterial. Their way of
life allows them no luxury, and makes the actual possession
of a horse unnecessary ; but they feel its superiority over

other domestic animals, and know that it alone can afford them any real help, in that it aids their flight. Moreover Gypsies are peculiarly alive to that feeling which seems to double the strength of a man and impart new force to his limbs when, a flying centaur, he uses its strength as his own, and forms one being with his steed. Without practising riding as an art, the Gypsy knows full well how to hold sway over his horse : he wanders here and there with him, he comes to a perfect understanding with him, and learns to enjoy his companionship. He is convinced that the horse has higher impulses than those of mere eating or drinking, and can be a hero and poet in his fashion just as the Gypsy in his ; so the Tsigan, who feels himself wholly misunderstood by those who appear to be his fellow-creatures, is glad to make a brother and comrade of this dumb friend.

.   .   .   .   .   .

For an entirely different reason the Gypsy also loves his bear, catches and tames him, until at last he can make a casual income by the exhibition of the creature's grotesque dances. So he seeks and hunts bears, especially in the Carpathians, where they are not so fierce by nature. Sport with this animal when once he is tamed is an outlet for the Gypsy's love of drollery and burlesque, and of all that is ludicrous—moods of which he would be considered incapable by anyone who saw him solemnly strutting about in a new braided coat, or stricken by some raging fever, or brooding dumbly over his misery. But when he takes his bear out on parade, he is just as amused as the spectator at the clumsy gambollings and droll antics of this uncouth creature, which is fool enough to allow itself to be muzzled, and to dance to another man's piping. The Gypsy despises the bear in the same degree as he respects the horse. The applause of the crowd yields him a certain measure of content, when he reflects that they cannot compel *him* to wear a muzzle or dance to another man's tune. And if this gratification brings him a few coppers into the bargain, then he welcomes these as one of the agreeable windfalls in his happy-go-lucky life.

Franz Liszt.

The Irish Cob

AND it came to pass that, as I was standing by the door of the barrack stable, one of the grooms came out to me, saying, ' I say, young gentleman, I wish you would give the cob a breathing this fine morning.'

' Why do you wish me to mount him ? ' said I ; ' you know he is dangerous. I saw him fling you off his back only a few days ago.'

' Why, that's the very thing, master. I'd rather see anybody on his back than myself ; he does not like me ; but, to them he does, he can be as gentle as a lamb.'

' But suppose,' said I, ' that he should not like me ? '

' We shall soon see that, master,' said the groom ; ' and, if so be he shows temper, I will be the first to tell you to get down. But there's no fear of that ; you have never angered or insulted him, and to such as you, I say again, he'll be as gentle as a lamb.'

' And how came you to insult him,' said I, ' knowing his temper as you do ? '

' Merely through forgetfulness, master. I was riding him about a month ago, and having a stick in my hand, I struck him, thinking I was on another horse, or rather thinking of nothing at all. He has never forgiven me, though before that time he was the only friend I had in the world ; I should like to see you on him, master.'

' I should soon be off him ; I can't ride.'

' Then you are all right, master ; there's no fear. Trust him for not hurting a young gentleman, an officer's son who can't ride. If you were a blackguard dragoon, indeed, with long spurs, 'twere another thing ; as it is, he'll treat you as if he were the elder brother that loves you. Ride ! he'll soon teach you to ride, if you leave the matter with him. He's the best riding master in all Ireland, and the gentlest.'

The cob was led forth ; what a tremendous creature ! I had frequently seen him before, and wondered at him ; he was barely fifteen hands, but he had the girth of a metropolitan dray-horse ; his head was small in comparison with his immense neck, which curved down nobly to his wide

R

back; his chest was broad and fine, and his shoulders models of symmetry and strength; he stood well and powerfully upon his legs, which were somewhat short. In a word, he was a gallant specimen of the genuine Irish cob, a species at one time not uncommon, but at the present day nearly extinct.

'There!' said the groom, as he looked at him, half admiringly, half sorrowfully, 'with sixteen stone on his back, he'll trot fourteen miles in one hour; with your nine stone, some two and a half more, ay, and clear a six-foot wall at the end of it.'

'I'm half afraid,' said I; 'I had rather you would ride him.'

'I'd rather so, too, if he would let me; but he remembers the blow. Now, don't be afraid, young master, he's longing to go out himself. He's been trampling with his feet these three days, and I know what that means; he'll let anybody ride him but myself, and thank them; but to me he says, "No! you struck me."'

'But,' said I, 'where's the saddle?'

'Never mind the saddle; if you are ever to be a frank rider, you must begin without a saddle; besides, if he felt a saddle, he would think you don't trust him, and leave you to yourself. Now, before you mount, make his acquaintance—see there, how he kisses you and licks your face, and see how he lifts his foot, that's to shake hands. You may trust him—now you are on his back at last; mind how you hold the bridle—gently, gently! It's not four pair of hands like yours can hold him if he wishes to be off. Mind what I tell you—leave it all to him.'

Off went the cob at a slow and gentle trot, too fast and rough, however, for so inexperienced a rider. I soon felt myself sliding off, the animal perceived it too, and instantly stood stone still till I had righted myself; and now the groom came up: 'When you feel yourself going,' said he, 'don't lay hold of the mane, that's no use; mane never yet saved man from falling, no more than straw from drowning; it's his sides you must cling to with your calves and feet, till you learn to balance yourself. That's it, now abroad with you; I'll bet my comrade a pot of beer that you'll be a regular rough rider by the time you come back.'

And so it proved; I followed the directions of the groom, and the cob gave me every assistance. How easy is riding, after the first timidity is got over, to supple and youthful limbs; and there is no second fear. The creature soon found that the nerves of his rider were in proper tone. Turning his head half round, he made a kind of whining noise, flung out a little foam, and set off.

In less than two hours I had made the circuit of the Devil's Mountain, and was returning along the road, bathed with perspiration, but screaming with delight; the cob laughing in his equine way, scattering foam and pebbles to the left and right, and trotting at the rate of sixteen miles an hour.

Oh, that ride! that first ride! most truly it was an epoch in my existence; and I still look back to it with feelings of longing and regret. People may talk of first love—it is a very agreeable event, I dare say—but give me the flush, and triumph, and glorious sweat of a first ride, like mine on the mighty cob! My whole frame was shaken, it is true; and during one long week I could hardly move foot or hand; but what of that? By that one trial I had become free, as I may say, of the whole equine species. No more fatigue, no more stiffness of joints, after that first ride round the Devil's Hill on the cob.

Oh, that cob! that Irish cob! —may the sod lie lightly over the bones of the strongest, speediest, and most gallant of its kind! Oh! the days when, issuing from the barrack-gate of Templemore, we commenced our hurry skurry just as inclination led—now across the fields—direct over stone walls and running brooks—mere pastime for the cob! —sometimes along the road to Thurles and Holy Cross, even to distant Cahir!—what was distance to the cob?

George Borrow.

The Tsigan to his Steed

HURRY on, my little horse!
There is far to go, far to go, but hurry on!
When once we get home, then will I give you dear little oats.
I will give you dear little hay and a drop of water.

I have business to do—we must gallop.

You shall not be bartered or sold—I will shut you up within gates, I will bind up your legs, I will remember of you that you were a good little horse.

I never had such a horse.

Such a horse you were that you made me lose my head.

And after that I fed you a dear little bran-mash, when you made me lose my head!

Now on!

May the wolves devour you!

Russian Gypsy Song.

Marshland Shales

I WAS standing on the castle hill in the midst of a fair of horses. . . .

The reader is already aware that I had long since conceived a passion for the equine race, a passion in which circumstances had of late not permitted me to indulge. I had no horses to ride, but I took pleasure in looking at them; and I had already attended more than one of these fairs : the present was lively enough, indeed horse fairs are seldom dull. There was shouting and whooping, neighing and braying ; there was galloping and trotting ; fellows with highlows and white stockings, and with many a string dangling from the knees of their tight breeches, were running desperately, holding horses by the halter, and in some cases dragging them along ; there were long-tailed steeds, and dock-tailed steeds of every degree and breed ; there were droves of wild ponies, and long rows of sober cart horses ; there were donkeys, and even mules : the last rare things to be seen in damp, misty England, for the mule pines in mud and rain, and thrives best with a hot sun above and a burning sand below. There were— oh, the gallant creatures! I hear their neigh upon the wind ; there were—goodliest sight of all—certain enormous quadrupeds only seen to perfection in our native isle, led about by dapper grooms, their manes ribanded and their tails curiously clubbed and balled. Ha! ha!—how distinctly do they say, ha! ha!

An old man draws nigh, he is mounted on a lean pony,

and he leads by the bridle one of these animals ; nothing
very remarkable about that creature, unless in being smaller
than the reſt and gentle, which they are not ; he is not of
the sightlieſt look ; he is almoſt dun, and over one eye a
thick film has gathered. But ſtay ! there *is* something
remarkable about that horse, there is something in his
aćtion in which he differs from all the reſt. As he advances,
the clamour is hushed ! all eyes are turned upon him—
what looks of intereſt—of respećt—and, what is this ?
people are taking off their hats—surely not to that ſteed !
Yes, verily ! men, especially old men, are taking off their
hats to that one-eyed ſteed, and I hear more than one deep-
drawn ah !

‘ What horse is that ? ’ said I to a very old fellow, the
counterpart of the old man on the pony, save that the laſt
wore a faded suit of velveteen, and this one was dressed in
a white frock.

‘ The beſt in mother England,’ said the very old man,
taking a knobbed ſtick from his mouth, and looking me
in the face, at firſt carelessly, but presently with something
like intereſt ; ‘ he is old like myself, but can ſtill trot his
twenty miles an hour. You won’t live long, my swain ;
tall and overgrown ones like thee never does ; yet, if you
should chance to reach my years, you may boaſt to thy
great-grand-boys, thou haſt seen Marshland Shales.’

Amain I did for the horse what I would neither do for
earl or baron, doffed my hat ; yes ! I doffed my hat to the
wondrous horse, the faſt trotter, the beſt in mother England ;
and I too drew a deep ah ! and repeated the words of the
old fellows around. ‘ Such a horse as this we shall never
see again ; a pity that he is so old.’

George Borrow.

Tam Marshall’s Sousie Beaſt

TO this speech, in which, perhaps, the jealousy of
rivalry embittered the cup of offence that had been
proffered to the lips of his kindred, the man of Drysdale
replied with a loud and discordant laugh, something like
the shrieking scream of the owl when, with expanded
wings, it comes pounce on its prey. His face grew black

as death, and even dilated with the infernal smile which curled his lips, and his whole frame quivered with rage—it was only for a moment. He seized the mortal weapon, which lay at his feet, by the point, and launched it with amazing force at the head of the cousin of Kate Marshall. But he had to combat with a man far more cool, and equally desperate as himself. He ducked his head as a water-hen does when the fowler's gun flashes; the dangerous missile grazed his hair as he sunk, and flying far beyond, sunk deep into the pannier of an old ass, the property of the Patriarch himself, which, covered with a worn mantle, and caparisons of untanned leather, stood ruminating over a sheaf of fresh grain in the corner. The ass, at this aggression, addressed to the hand from which the harm proceeded a deep and dolorous bray—a moving cry of the most pathetic expostulation; and, snapping its halter in two, came rushing between the gypsey combatants, effectually shielding them from the mortal thrusts which, with bared swords, they were aiming at each other.

During this period of controversy and aggression, the chieftain sat on the old pannier with most perfect composure and unconcern; he heard all, but heeded none; and seemed by his silence to decide that the death of one or two of the most ferocious and turbulent of his gang would be an acceptable event. He even applied himself with more than common diligence to the construction of a silver mouthpiece for the living cow's horn, and I cannot say that his skill in this elegant craft was abated by the mortal conclusion to which his dependants seemed hastening; nay, he even gave one 'tout' on the instrument, for the apparent purpose of proving the merit of his labour; but as it was uttered at the moment the dirks were drawn, I suspect he internally considered it as a bugle note to battle. But this composure was soon to be shaken. The moment he perceived what had befallen his ancient and favourite ass, he started from his seat with unexpected agility, and pulling a silver-mounted pistol from his girdle, cocked it, and unbuckled the panniers of the animal. The ashen hue of his cheek waxed of a kindlier colour when, on removing the caparisons, he discovered that the missile had drawn blood, but only penetrated skin deep. It had

been thrown from a hand so desperate and so powerful,
that it forced its way through, among two bunches of horn
spoons and the lid of a brass sauce-pan. The old man
uncocked his pistol, replaced it in his belt, and, stroking
the neck of the old and conscious animal, said, with a
visible and tender kindness, 'Thou auld sonsie beast—
thou best piece of ass's flesh that ever cropped corn—thou
that hast balanced spoons on thy back to Mall Marshall
and her seventeen lad weans, and seen them all laid under
the green turf, waes me ! The living hand that harms thy
life shall soon belong to a dead man, else let never man
trust a spark wi' powder mair.' So saying, he led the aged
animal back to its stance, adding a piece of wheat bread to
its pittance of corn, and then slowly returned and resumed
his seat.

Allan Cunningham.

Metempsychosis

WHEN I was a child I was beating a burra, but my
father stopped my hand and chided me. ' Hurt not
the animal,' said he, ' for within it is the soul of your own
sister.'

George Borrow.

Clara's Old Gentleman

THE man said his name was James Vanis. His sister's
Clara Vanis. She was a slight, well-formed girl, with
a decidedly, but not strongly marked Gypsy countenance.
Not handsome but strikingly intelligent. She spent the
eight days with us, and obtained much of the admiration,
and almost affection, of every inmate of the family. Without anything approaching to forwardness or boldness, she
was free from any embarrassing timidity. . . . She soon
learned to milk, with which she was much pleased. Her
brother being a tinker, brazier, tinner, umbrella-mender,
&c., &c., she had acquired a knowledge and an expert-
ness which few servants possess. On their asking her if
she would be glad to see her brother when he came for her,
she almost screamed out, ' Oh ! no—I hope he won't
come ! If he does I shall be ready to creep into a bottle ! '

On seeing a mouse, she said that they used often to have
dormice which they called the *seven sleepers*. We kept two
young hedgehogs in a box in the kitchen to clear us of
blackclocks. They only came out in the evening. On
firſt seeing one of them she appeared quite delighted, as
if she had met with an old acquaintance ; she snatched it up
in her hand, exclaiming, ' Oh ! you old gentleman ; but
I 'll make you both whiſtle and sing ! ' On being asked
how she would do that, she said by squeezing his toes.

Samuel Roberts.

The Seven Sleepers

DOST thou know which are the Seven Sleepers ? The
hedgehog, the snake, the dormouse, the squirrel, the
snail, the bee and the frog.

Ithal Lee, a Gypsy.

Recipe for Keeping One's Youth

A GOOD recipe for keeping one's youth is surely to go
a gypsying and eat a roaſted hedgehog.

William Hazlitt.

Father Hedgehog and the Gypsies

' WHAT in the hedge do you think has happened to
the six ? ' said Father Hedgehog.
' Oh, don't tell me ! ' cried my mother ; ' I am so
nervous.' (Which she was, and rather foolish as well,
which used to irritate my father, who was haſty tempered,
as I am myself.)
' They 've been taken by gipsies and flitted,' said he.
' What do you mean by *flitted* ? ' inquired my mother.
' A ſtring is tied round the hind-leg of each, and they are
tethered in the grass behind the tent, juſt as the donkey
is tethered. So will they remain till they grow fat, and
then they will be cooked.'
' And will the donkey be cooked when he is fat ? ' asked
my mother.

' Upon my whine,' said he, ' they live on the fat of the
land. Scraps of all kinds, apples, and a dish of bread and
milk under their very noses. I sat inside a gorse bush on
the bank, and watched them till my mouth watered.'

The next day he reported—

' They 've cooked one—in clay. There are only five
now.'

And the next day—

' They 've cooked another. Now there are only four.'

' There won't be a cousin left if I wait much longer,'
thought I.

On the morrow there were only three.

My mother began to cry. ' My poor dear nephews and
nieces ! ' said she (though she had never seen them).
' What a world this is ! '

' We must take it as we eat eggs,' said my father, with
that air of wisdom which naturally belongs to the sayings
of the head of the family, ' the shell with the yolk. And
they have certainly had excellent victuals.'

. . . . . .

' But they [the Gypsies] are a set of people,' continued
Father Hedgehog, in a voice as sour as a green crab, ' who
if they hear us talking, or catch us walking abroad, will
kill your mother and me, and temper up two bits of clay
and roll us up in them. Then they will put us into a fire
to bake, and when the clay turns red they will take us out.
The clay will fall off and our coats with it. What remains
they will eat—as we eat snails.'

Juliana Horatia Ewing.

The Gipsy Naturalist

NOW here 's what a friend of mine once saw. . . . He
was going home one moonlight night by a footpath
through the woods when he heard a very strange noise
a little distance ahead, a low whistling sound, very sharp,
like the continuous twittering of a little bird with a voice
like a bat, or a shrew, only softer, more musical. He
went on very cautiously until he spied two hedgehogs
standing in the path facing each other, with their noses
almost or quite touching. He remained watching and

liſtening to them for some moments, then tried to go a little nearer and they ran away. . . .

'But no doubt,' I said, 'you 've seen other queer things in hedgehogs and in other little animals which I should like to hear.'

Yes, he had, firſt and laſt, seen a good many queer things both by day and night, in woods and other places, he replied, and then continued : ' But you see it 's like this. We see something and say, " Now that 's a very curious thing ! " and then we forget all about it. You see, we don't lay no ſtore by such things ; we ain't scolards and don't know nothing about what 's said in books. We see something and say, *That 's* something we never saw before and never heard tell of, but maybe others have seen it, and you can find it in the books. So that 's how 'tis, but if I hadn't forgotten them I could have told you a lot of queer things.'

W. H. Hudson.

Hedgehogs in Heaven

THE only indication of a belief in a future ſtate which I ever deteƈted in an old Gypsy woman, was that she once dreamed she was in heaven. It appeared to her as a large garden, full of fine fat hedgehogs.

Richard Liebich.

The Baker's Daughter

' Well, God 'ield you ! They say the owl was a baker's daughter.
Lord ! we know what we are, but know not what we may be.'
Hamlet, iv. 5.

ONCE when our blessed Lord was on earth, a-going about trying people's consciences, he ſtopped at a baker's shop and asked de young ooman to give him a drink of water. ' Could you give me a drink of water, miss ? ' he says werry polite, ' and I 'd be *so* much obliged to you.' ' Oh, no ! ' she says, ' we haven't none too much water for ourselves, and it 's a werry long ſtep to go and fetch it.' ' O-o-o-o-o-h, no-o-o-o-oh ! ' says he, a-copying her, ' oo-oo-oh, noo-ooh ! you goes just like a howlet, miss, and a howlet you shall be all the days of your life, and live in a hole in a rotten tree, and only come out of nights, and if you comes out in de day, all de birds in de sky shall have a peck at you.'

Gypsy Legend.

The Owl

DOWNHILL I came, hungry, and yet not starved ;
Cold, yet had heat within me that was proof
Against the North wind ; tired, yet so that rest
Had seemed the sweetest thing under a roof.

Then at the inn I had food, fire and rest,
Knowing how hungry, cold and tired was I.
All of the night was quite barred out except
An owl's cry, a most melancholy cry

Shaken out long and clear upon the hill,
No merry note, nor cause of merriment,
But one telling me plain what I escaped
And others could not, that night, as in I went.

And salted was my food, and my repose,
Salted and sobered, too, by the bird's voice
Speaking for all who lay under the stars,
Soldiers and poor, unable to rejoice.

Edward Thomas.

Fishing in the Alwen

THERE are three colours in this river, cream colour, mud colour, and beer colour. . . .

Thou wilt never find a salmon in the river Alwen until the foxglove is in full bloom. . . .

And it would be the same with my dear God in heaven ! If he were to cast his line in this river, and had not the right fly, he would catch nothing.

Harry Wood, a Gypsy.

The Salmon and the Trout

FOR by cause that the Samon is the mooſt ſtately fyssh that ony man maye angle to in fresshe water. Therfore I purpose to begynn at hym. The samon is a gentyll fysshe : but he is comborous for to take. For comynly he is but in depe places of grete ryuers. And for the more parte he holdyth the myddys of it : that a man maye not come at hym. And he is in season from Marche unto Myghelmas. In whyche season ye shall angle to hym wyth thyse baytes whan ye maye gete theym. Fyrſte wyth a redde worme in the begynnynge & endynge of the season. And also wyth a bobbe that bredyth in a dunghyll. And specyally wyth a souerayn bayte that bredyth on a water docke. And he bytith not at the grounde : but at yᵉ flote. Also ye may take hym : but it is seldom seen with a dubbe at suche tyme as whan he lepith in lyke fourme & manere as ye doo take a troughte or a gryaylynge. And thyse baytes ben well prouyd baytes for the samon.

The Troughte for by cause he is a right deyntous fyssh and also a ryght feruente byter we shall speke nexte of hym. He is in season fro Marche unto Myghelmas. He is on clene grauely grounde & in a ſtreme. Ye may angle to hym all tymes wyth a grounde lyne lyenge or rennynge : sauyng in leppynge tyme, and thenne wyth a dubbe. And erly wyth a rennynge grounde lyne, and forth in the daye wyth a flote lyne. Ye shall angle to hym in Marche wyth a menew hangyd on your hoke by the nether nesse wythout flote or plumbe : drawynge up & downe in the ſtreme tyll ye fele hym taſte. In the same tyme angle to hym wyth a grounde lyne with a redde worme for the mooſt sure. In Aprill take the same baytes ; & also Inneba other wyse namyd vii eyes. Also the canker that bredyth in a grete tree and the redde snayll. In May take yᵉ ſtone flye and the bobbe under the cowe torde and the sylke worme : and the bayte that bredyth on a fernn leyf. In Juyn take a redde worme & nyppe of the heed : and put on thyn hoke a codworme byforn. In Juyll take the grete redde worme and the codworme togyder. In Auguſt take a flesshe flye & the grete redde worme and the fatte of the bakon : and

bynde abowte thy hoke. In Septembre take the redde
worme and the menew. In Octobre take the same : for
they ben specyall for the trought all tymes of the yere.
From Aprill tyll Septembre ye trought leppyth : thenne
angle to hym wyth a dubbyd hoke acordynge to the
moneth. *Dame Juliana Berners, c. 1450.*

The Angler's Tackle

1

A WAY to the brook,
  All your tackle outlook,
    Here 's a day that is worth a year's wishing ;
See that all things be right,
For 'tis a very spite
  To want tools when a man goes a fishing.

2

Your rod with tops two,
For the same will not do
  If your manner of angling you vary :
And full well you may think,
If you troll with a pink,
  One too weak will be apt to miscarry.

3

Then basket, neat made
By a Master in 's trade,
  In a belt at your shoulders must dangle ;
For none e'er was so vain
To wear this to disdain,
  Who a true brother was of the angle.

4

Next, pouch must not fail,
Stuff'd as full as a mail,
  With wax, cruels, silks, hair, furs and feathers,
To make several flies,
For the several skies,
  That shall kill in despite of all weathers.

5

The boxes and books
For your lines and your hooks,
   And, though not for strict need notwithstanding,
Your scissors, and your hone
To adjust your points on,
   With a net to be sure for your landing.

6

All these being on,
'Tis high time we were gone,
   Down, and upward, that all may have pleasure ;
Till, here meeting at night,
We shall have the delight
   To discourse of our fortunes at leisure.

7

The day 's not too bright,
And the wind hits us right,
   And all Nature does seem to invite us ;
We have all things at will
For to second our skill,
   As they all did conspire to delight us.

8

Or stream now, or still,
A large panier will fill,
   Trout and grayling to rise are so willing ;
I dare venture to say
'Twill be a bloody day,
   And we shall be weary of killing.

9

Away then, away,
We lose sport by delay,
   But first leave all our sorrows behind us ;
If misfortune do come,
We are all gone from home,
   And a fishing she never can find us.

                                        Charles Cotton.

The Poacher

WHEN I was bound apprentice in famous Lincoln-
shire,
I sarved my master truly for nearly seven long year,
Till I took up with poaching as you shall quickly hear—
For it 's my delight of a shiny night in the season of the
year.

As me and my companions were setting of a snare,
The game-keeper was watching us, for him we did not
care ;
For we can wrestle and fight, my boys, and jump out anywhere ;
For it 's my delight of a shiny night in the season of the
year.

As me and my companions were setting four or five,
And taking of them up again, we took the hare alive ;
We popped her into a bag, my boys, and through the wood
did steer ;
For it 's my delight of a shiny night in the season of the
year.

I threw her o'er my shoulder, and wandered through the
town ;
We called inside a neighbour's house, and sold her for a
crown ;
We sold her for a crown, my boys, but I did not tell you
where ;
For it 's my delight of a shiny night in the season of the
year.

Well, here 's success to poaching, for I do think it fair ;
Bad luck to ev'ry game-keeper that would not sell his deer ;
Good luck to ev'ry housekeeper that wants to buy a hare ;
For it 's my delight on a shiny night in the season of the
year.

English Folk-Song.

The Romani Magpie

NOW, as we walked there lighted on the road before us a ' Romani magpie ' or water-wagtail, and Christopher son of Pyramus, chanted the Gipsy formula :

' Is it any kin to me, it will fly, it will fly ;
Is it any kin to me, it will fly, it will fly.'

No, it scarce hopped aside to let us pass, so Christopher proclaimed that we should see strange Gipsies ; and lo ! a turn in the lane brought us in sight of what seemed to verify his words—two tattered, low, smoked tents, pitched in a hollow by the wayside.

Francis Hindes Groome.

The Water-Wagtail

DURING the flight into Egypt, while the Virgin Mary and St. Joseph were crossing the desert with the child Jesus, a quail saw them, and immediately cried out—' Aqui vai, aqui vai ! ' (Here they go, here they go !) Mary heard the sinful quail, and pressing her blessed charge closer to her bosom, she turned and said—' Oh quail, be cursed ! For this evil deed henceforth and for ever thou shalt be unable to rise high into the air, but be doomed to skim near the surface of the earth, so that thy enemies can slay thee.' It happened that a little wagtail heard the wicked quail and, silently following the fugitives, it pitifully swept the desert sand over their footprints with its long tail, so that their enemies might not be able to track them. Mary saw the pretty bird at its self-appointed task, and she blessed the wagtail, and promised that it should for evermore be held sacred by man. And so to this day a wagtail is never wantonly killed, and fortunate indeed is that man who chances to see a wagtail in his path in the early morning.

Gypsy Legend.

A Good Omen

A K'O *romano cheriklo : dikása i kalén.*
Lo! here is the Romany bird! we shall meet
Gypsies.

Gypsy Proverb.

Snake-Lore

'NOW, our old people had a curious way with snakes,'
said Nathan's Welsh Gypsy wife. 'When one of us
children killed an adder, my daddy would cut it in half
with a whip or a stick, and the head he would put on the
right side of the road, and the tail on the left. Then my
mother would walk between them first, my daddy next
to her, and all we children after them in a row, from the
eldest down to the littlest. And my poor mother used to
say some funny words to herself, what none of us never
knew or ever did ; but for certain when we used to go
through that performance, my mother would not be long
before she had a pocketful of gold.'

A pitying smile played on Silvanus' face, as he gravely
observed, 'That was a superstition, Alabina, and superstitions are things I never vindicates.'

Francis Hindes Groome.

Happy Boz'll

ONEST upon a time there was a Romano, and his name
was Happy Boz'll, and he had a German-silver grinding-barrow, and he used to put his wife and child on the
top, and he used to go that quick along the road he 'd beat
all the coaches. Then he thought this grinding-barrow
was too heavy and clumsy to take about, and he cut it up
and made tent-rods of it. And then his dickey got away,
and he didn't know where it was gone to ; and one day
he was going by the tent, and he said to himself ' Bless my
soul, wherever 's that dickey got to ? ' And there was a
tree close by, and the dickey shouted out and said, ' I 'm

here, my Happy, getting you a bit of stick to make a fire.'
Well, the donkey come down with a lot of sticks, and he
had been up the tree a week getting fire-wood. Well
then Happy had a dog, and he went out one day, the dog
one side the hedge and him the other. And then he saw
two hares. The dog ran after the two ; and as he was
going across the field, he cut himself right through with
a scythe ; and then one half ran after one hare, and the
other after the other. Then the two halves of the dog
catched the two hares ; and then the dog smacked together
again ; and he said, ' Well, I 've got 'em, my Happy ' ;
and then the dog died. And Happy had a hole in the knee
of his breeches, and he cut a piece of the dog's skin after
it was dead, and sewed it in the knee of his breeches. And
that day twelve months his breeches-knee burst open and
barked at him. And so that 's the end of Happy Boz'll.

Francis Hindes Groome.

X
EGIPTE SPECHE

X

Egipte Speche

A Test

' CAN you rokra Romany ?
        Can you play the bosh ?
        Can you jal adrey the staripen ?
    Can you chin the cost ? '

' Can you speak the Roman tongue ?
    Can you play the fiddle ?
        Can you eat the prison-loaf ?
    Can you cut and whittle ? '

George Borrow.

One Use of Gypsy

THE young people often ask : What good is there in
    the Romany tongue ?   I answers : Ye are all fools !
There is plenty, plenty of good in it, and plenty, plenty of
our people would have been transported or hung, but for
the old, poor Roman language.   A word in Romany said
in time to a little girl, and carried to the camp, has caused
a great purse of money and other things which had been
stolen, to be stowed underground ; so that when the constables came they could find nothing, and had not only
to let the Gypsy they had taken up go his way, but also to
beg his pardon.

George Borrow.

Languages the Pedigree of Nations

I AM not very willing that any language should be totally
    extinguished.   The similitude and derivation of lan-
guages afford the most indubitable proof of the traduction
of nations, and the genealogy of mankind.   They add

277

often physical certainty to historical evidence ; and often supply the only evidence of ancient migrations, and of the revolutions of ages which left no written monuments behind them.

'Every man's opinions, at least his desires, are a little influenced by his favourite studies. My zeal for languages may seem, perhaps, rather over-heated, even to those by whom I desire to be well-esteemed. To those who have nothing in their thoughts but trade or policy, present power, or present money, I should not think it necessary to defend my opinions ; but with men of letters I would not unwillingly compound, by wishing the continuance of every language, however narrow in its extent, or however incommodious for common purposes, till it is reposited in some version of a known book, that it may be always hereafter examined and compared with other languages, and then permitting its disuse.'

Samuel Johnson.

The Tongue

L A véritable histoire de la race Tchinghianée est dans l'étude de leur idiome.

Alexandros Paspates.

A Talk in Egipcion

E GIPT is a countrey ioyned to Iury ; The countrey is plentyfull of wine, corne, and Hony.

Ther be many great wyldernes, in the which be many great wylde beastes. In the which wildernes liuid many holy fathers, as it apperyth in *vitas patrum*. The people of the country be swarte, and doth go disgisyd in theyr apparel, contrary to other nacyons : they be lyght fyngerd, and vse pyking ; they haue litle maner, and euyl loggyng, & yet they be pleas[a]unt daunsers. Ther be few or none of the Egipcions that doth dwel in Egipt, for Egipt is repleted now with infydele alyons. There mony is brasse and golde. Yf there be any man that wyl learne parte of theyr speche, Englyshe and Egipt speche foloweth.

Good morow ! *Lach ittur ydyues !*
How farre is it to the next towne ?   *Cater myla barforas ?*
You be welcome to the towne.   *Maysta ves barforas.*
Wyl you drynke some wine ?   *Mole pis lauena ?*
I wyl go wyth you.   *A vauatosa.*
Sit you downe, and dryncke.   *Hyste len pee.*
Drynke, drynke ! for God sake !   *Pe, pe, deue lasse !*
Mayde, geue me bread and wyne !
Achae, da mai manor la veue !
Geue me fleshe !   *Da mai masse !*
Mayde, come hyther, harke a worde !
Achae, a wordey tusse !
Geue me aples and peeres !   *Da mai paba la ambrell !*
Much good do it you !   *Iche misto !*
Good nyght !   *Lachira tut !*

Andrew Borde.

The Third Volume of Reports

JACKMAN. If we here be a little obscure, 'tis our pleasure ;
for rather than we will offer to be our own interpreters,
we are resolved not to be understood ; yet if any man
doubt of the significancy of the language, we refer him to
the Third Volume of Reports, set forth by the learned in
the laws of canting, and published in the gipsy tongue.

Ben Jonson.

Tinker's Talk

PRINCE HENRY. . . . Sirrah, I am sworn brother to a
leash of drawers ; and can call them all by their christian
names, as—Tom, Dick, and Francis.   They take it already
upon their salvation, that, though I be but Prince of Wales,
yet I am the king of courtesy ; and tell me flatly I am no
proud Jack, like Falstaff ; but a Corinthian, a lad of mettle,
a good boy, and when I am King of England, I shall command all the good lads in Eastcheap. . . . To conclude, I
am so good a proficient in one quarter of an hour, that I
can drink with any tinker in his own language during my
life.

Shakespeare.

Pedlars' French

MOREOVER in counterfeiting the Egyptian rogues, they have devised a language among themselves which they name Canting, but others Pedlers French, a speach compacte thirtie yeares since of English and a great number of od words of their owne devising, without all order or reason; and yet such is it, as none but themselves are able to understand. The first deviser thereof was hanged by the necke, a just reward no doubt for his deserts, and a common end to all of that profession.

William Harrison, 1577.

An Obscure and Mystical Language

MR. ONGLEY said he thought it his duty to rise on this occasion to inform the House, that in a certain part of Kent there was an established body of Egyptians, who were frequently accused of committing great enormities, but could not be brought to condign punishment, because the obscure and mystical language, which prevailed among them, made it frequently impossible to procure evidence or arraign them more than if they were dumb; and that lately an offender of this body had escaped, because he could neither understand nor be understood.

Hansard, 1772.

A Forbidden Language

ABOUT noon we arrived at a small village in the neighbourhood of a high lumpy hill. ' There is no Calo house in this place,' said Antonio, ' we will therefore go to the posada of the Busné, and refresh ourselves, man and beast.' We entered the kitchen, and sat down at the board, calling for wine and bread. There were two ill-looking fellows in the kitchen, smoking cigars. I said something to Antonio in the Calo language.

' What is that I hear ? ' said one of the fellows, who was distinguished by an immense pair of mustaches. ' What is that I hear ? Is it in Calo that you are speaking before me,

and I a Chalan and national? Accursed gypsy, how dare
you enter this posada and speak before me in that speech?
Is it not forbidden by the law of the land in which we are,
even as it is forbidden for a gypsy to enter the mercado?
I tell you what, friend, if I hear another word of Calo come
from your mouth, I will cudgel your bones and send you
flying over the house-tops with a kick of my foot.'
'You would do right,' said his companion; 'the inso-
lence of these gypsies is no longer to be borne. When
I am at Merida or Badajoz I go to the mercado, and there
in a corner stand the accursed gypsies, jabbering to each
other in a speech which I understand not. "Gypsy gentleman," say I to one of them, "what will you have for that
donkey?" "I will have ten dollars for it, Caballero
nacional," says the gypsy; "it is the best donkey in all
Spain." "I should like to see its paces," say I. "That you
shall, most valorous!" says the gypsy, and jumping upon
its back, he puts it to its paces, first of all whispering something into its ear in Calo, and truly the paces of the donkey
are most wonderful, such as I have never seen before. "I
think it will just suit me"; and, after looking at it awhile,
I take out the money and pay for it. "I shall go to my
house," says the gypsy; and off he runs. "I shall go to
my village," say I, and I mount the donkey. "Vamonos,"
say I, but the donkey won't move. I give him a switch,
but I don't get on the better for that. "How is this?"
say I, and I fall to spurring him. What happens then,
brother? The wizard no sooner feels the prick than he
bucks down, and flings me over his head into the mire.
I get up and look about me; there stands the donkey
staring at me, and there stand the whole gypsy canaille
squinting at me with their filmy eyes. "Where is the
scamp who has sold me this piece of furniture?" I shout.
"He is gone to Granada, valorous," says one. "He is gone
to see his kindred among the Moors," says another. "I
just saw him running over the field, in the direction of ——,
with the devil close behind him," says a third. In a word
I am tricked. I wish to dispose of the donkey; no one,
however, will buy him; he is a Calo donkey, and every
person avoids him. At last the gypsies offer thirty rials for
him; and after much chaffering I am glad to get rid of him

at two dollars. It is all a trick, however ; he returns to his master, and the brotherhood share the spoil amongst them. All which villainy would be prevented, in my opinion, were the Calo language not spoken ; for what but the word of Calo could have induced the donkey to behave in such an unaccountable manner ? '

Both seemed perfectly satisfied with the justness of this conclusion, and continued smoking till their cigars were burnt to stumps, when they arose, twitched their whiskers, looked at us with fierce disdain, and dashing the tobacco-ends to the ground, strode out of the apartment.

' These people seem no friends to the gypsies,' said I to Antonio, when the two bullies had departed, ' nor to the Calo language either.'

' May evil glanders seize their nostrils,' said Antonio ; ' they have been jonjabadoed by our people. However, brother, you did wrong to speak to me in Calo, in a posada like this ; it is a forbidden language ; for, as I have often told you, the king has destroyed the law of the Calés. Let us away, brother, or these juntunes (*sneaking scoundrels*) may set the justicia upon us.'

George Borrow.

cA Licence for Gentiles

WHEN the gentiles enquire of me what is so and so in Romani, I say: 'Show me your licence.' And when they ask : ' What licence ? ' I reply : ' Your licence to ask questions.' Then their mouths are closed.

Harry Wood, a Gypsy.

The Tongue of Mr. Petulengro

' DON'T speak contemptuously of Mr. Petulengro,' said I, ' nor of anything belonging to him. He is a dark mysterious personage ; all connected with him is a mystery, especially his language ; but I believe that his language is doomed to solve a great philological problem.'

George Borrow.

A Primaeval Speech

I MAY be doomed perhaps to encounter the smile or the frown of fastidious levity, when in the course of these discussions I shall gravely appeal to the authority of the *Gipsey Language*, which we have ever been accustomed to regard as the idle jargon of a forlorn and abandoned crew,

> ' So wither'd and so wild in their attire,
> That look not like the inhabitants o' the Earth
> And yet are on 't.'

The Gipsey Language, as it is now spoken, may probably be considered as the most ancient form of Speech which is at present extant in the world. The causes, by which the mutation of other languages has been affected, have not extended their influence to the fate and fortunes of the wandering Gipsies ; and with them only is preserved a faithful record of Primaeval Speech. . . . Thus it is that the great revolutions of mankind may have been originally effected by this despised and rejected race. . . . In our own age a language has been lost : it shall be my province to record and preserve another.

Walter Whiter.

Mutilated Remains

SELBORNE, *Oct.* 2, 1775.

DEAR SIR,—We have two gangs, or hordes of gypsies, which infest the south and west of *England*, and come round in their circuit two or three times in the year. One of these tribes calls itself by the name of *Stanley*, of which I have nothing particular to say ; but the other is distinguished by an appellative somewhat remarkable. As far as their harsh gibberish can be understood they seem to say that the name of their clan is *Curleople* : now the termination of this word is apparently *Grecian* : and, as *Mezeray* and the gravest historians all agree that these vagrants did certainly migrate from *Egypt* and the East, two or three centuries ago, and so spread by degrees over *Europe*, may not this name, a little corrupted, be

the very name they brought with them from the *Levant* ?
It would be matter of some curiosity, could one meet with
an intelligent person among them, to inquire whether,
in their jargon, they still retain any *Greek* words : the
Greek radicals will appear in hand, foot, head, water,
earth, &c. It is possible, that, amidst their cant and corrupted dialect, many mutilated remains of their native
language might still be discovered.

Gilbert White of Selborne.

A Distinct and Proper Language

THAT the language exists I have no doubt, though I
should rather think the number to which it is known
is somewhat exaggerated. I need not point out to you
the difference between the *cant* language or *slang* used by
thieves or flash men in general, and the peculiar dialect said
to be spoken by the Gipsies. . . . My own opinion leads
me to think that the Gipsies have a distinct and proper
language, but I do not consider it is extensive enough to
form any settled conclusion. . . . There is little doubt
however that it is a dialect of the Hindostanee, from the
specimens produced by Grellmann, Hoyland and others
who have written on the subject. But the author has,
besides their authority, personal occasion to know that an
individual out of mere curiosity and availing himself with
patience and assiduity of such opportunities as offered, has
made himself capable of conversing with any Gipsy whom
he meets, or can, like the royal Hal, drink with any tinker
in his own language.

Sir Walter Scott.

Sonnet à Sarasvati

EPOUSE de Brahma, clémente majesté,
Déesse du langage, auguste Souveraine,
Toi, qui du sacrifice es l'arbitre et la reine,
Sarasvati, pardonne à ma témérité !

J'ose t'offrir un livre humblement enfanté
Sous le soleil lointain où, pieuse et sereine,
Travaille en ton honneur la modeſte Lorraine,
Afin que le Sanscrit soit par tous adopté.

Dans la Littérature, aujourd'hui languissante,
C'eſt du Gange héroïque amener l'eau puissante,
Et de l'Enseignement rajeunir les hivers !

Je voue à cette étude une ardeur sans génie :
Et pourtant, s'il te plaît, Mère de l'harmonie,
Mes rimes apprendront à lire de beaux vers.

Leupol.

The Seven Languages

FRAMPTON BOSWELL (desirous, apparently, of parading our joint erudition). ' Now, what might you call that, Mr. Groome ? ' (pointing to the kettle-prop).

MYSELF. ' That ? Oh ! a *saſter*, I suppose.'

FRAMPTON. ' H'm ! well, yes ! that 's not so bad, but *kekavisko saſter* would be properer.'

MRS. CUNNINGHAM (a brush and basket hawker). ' There, now ! Mr. Boswell, and I ain't no Gypsy woman, but I 've know'd *saſter* for a kettleſtick since I weren't no higher than one.'

FRAMPTON. ' There's plenty Gypsies don't know it, Mrs. Cunningham, but, Gypsy or no Gypsy, you 're a very old-fashioned sort of a traveller, I 'm thinking.'

OLD HENRY CUNNINGHAM (philosophically). ' It 's juſt like this, you see. There 's the Romany caint, and there 's the Gaelic caint, and they 're both on 'em no better than a jibberidge.'

MYSELF. ' Well, I 'm not quite so certain of that. Gaelic, of course that 's gibberish ; but wouldn't you say, Frampton, Romani was a kind of language ? '

FRAMPTON (authoritatively). ' No, I shouldn't, Mr. Groome. Leaſtwise, it isn't one of the Seven Languages.'

Francis Hindes Groome.

As the Birds sing

THE speech of the Tchingané is rude, sharp, strongly accentuated, and somewhat difficult to comprehend. Properly spoken it is harmonious enough, though rendered hoarse and almost distasteful by the wild tribes who employ it. 'We speak,' say they themselves, 'as the birds sing, but we sing as the lions roar.'

Chambers's Journal, 1878.

A Rising Rookery

THE women set up a cry, 'Kiomi! Kiomi!' like a rising rookery. Their eyes and teeth made such a flashing as when you dabble a hand in a dark waterpool. The strange tongue they talked, with a kind of peck of the voice at a word, rapid, never high or low, and then a slide of similar tones all round,—not musical, but catching and incessant,—gave me an idea that I had fallen upon a society of birds, exceedingly curious ones. They welcomed me kindly, each of them looking me in the face a bright second or so.

George Meredith.

Anglicized Hindoos

WHILE this conversation passed, I heard them speaking to each other in a language which had the effect of Irish, but with more shrill tones ; and the first man, notwithstanding his English physiognomy, as well as the others, spoke with a foreign accent, not unlike that of half-anglicized Hindoos. I mentioned this peculiarity, but he assured me that neither he nor any of the party had been out of England. I now enquired about their own language, when one of them said it was *Maltese*, but the other said it was their *cant* language. I asked their names for various objects which I pointed out ; but after half a dozen words, the first man enquired, if I had 'ever heard of one Sir Joseph Banks—for,' said he, 'that gentleman once paid me a guinea for telling him twenty words in our lan-

guage.' Perceiving therefore that he rated this species
of information very high, and aware that the subject has
been treated at large by many authors, I forbore to press
him further.

Sir Richard Phillips.

A Gipsy Vocabulary

A GIPSY vocabulary is a list of the Gipsy's ideas and a
clue to the Gipsy's thoughts. I have often learnt
from the words that he has taught me traits of his character which he would have wished to conceal. In this way
I have learnt his petty crimes, and private vices, and by
what means he procures a livelihood. By observing what
words he has not, I can form an opinion as to the extent
of his ignorance. He speaks to me out of the abundance
of his heart the words which reveal his most common
thoughts.

T. W. Norwood.

The Dance of Joy

WHEN Gypsies meet, even if they have come from
widely separated parts of the earth, they greet one
another with the familiar cry : *Han dume Romnitschel ?*
' Are ye Romnichel ? '—and straightway begins the dance
of joy.

Alfred Graffunder.

The Gypsy Meeting

WHO 'S your mother, who 's your father ?
Do thou answer me in Romany,
And I will answer thee.

A Hearne I have for mother !
A Cooper for my father !
Who 's your father, who 's your mother ?
I have answer'd thee in Romany,
Now do thou answer me.

A Smith I have for father !
A Lee I have for mother !
True Romans both are we—
For I 've answer'd thee in Romany,
And thou haſt answer'd me.

George Borrow.

A Lesson in Romany

' PHARAOH lived in Egypt.'
   ' So did we once, brother.'
 ' And you left it ? '
 ' My fathers did, brother.'
 ' And why did they come here ? '
 ' They had their reasons, brother.'
 ' And you are not English ? '
 ' We are not gorgios.'
 ' And you have a language of your own ? '
 ' Avali.'
 ' This is wonderful.'
  ' Ha, ha ! ' cried the woman, who had hitherto sat knit-
ting, at the farther end of the tent, without saying a word,
though not inattentive to our conversation, as I could
perceive, by certain glances, which she occasionally caſt
upon us both. ' Ha, ha ! ' she screamed, fixing upon me
two eyes, which shone like burning coals, and which were
filled with an expression both of scorn and malignity, ' it
is wonderful, is it, that we should have a language of our
own ? What, you grudge the poor people the speech they
talk among themselves ? That 's juſt like you gorgios,
you would have every body ſtupid, single-tongued idiots,
like yourselves. We are taken before the Poknees of the
gav, myself and siſter, to give an account of ourselves. So
I says to my siſter's little boy, speaking Rommany, I says
to the little boy who is with us, run to my son Jasper, and
the reſt, and tell them to be off, there are hawks abroad.
So the Poknees queſtions us, and lets us go, not being able
to make anything of us ; but, as we are going, he calls us
back. " Good woman," says the Poknees, " what was
that I heard you say juſt now to the little boy ? " " I was
telling him, your worship, to go and see the time of day,

and, to save trouble, I said it in our language." "Where
did you get that language?" says the Poknees. "'Tis
our own language, sir," I tells him, "we did not steal it."
"Shall I tell you what it is, my good woman?" says the
Poknees. "I would thank you, sir," says I, "for 'tis
often we are asked about it." "Well, then," says the
Poknees, "it is no language at all, merely a made-up
gibberish." "Oh, bless your wisdom," says I, with a
curtsey, "you can tell us what our language is, without
understanding it!" Another time we meet a parson.
"Good woman," says he, "what's that you are talking?
Is it broken language?" "Of course, your reverence,"
says I, "we are broken people; give a shilling, your
reverence, to the poor broken woman." Oh, these gor-
gios! they grudge us our very language!'
   'She called you her son, Jasper?'
   'I am her son, brother.'
   'I thought you said your parents were . . .'
   'Bitchadey pawdel; you thought right, brother. This
is my wife's mother.'
   'Then you are married, Jasper?'
   'Ay, truly; I am husband and father. You will see
wife and chabo anon.'
   'Where are they now?'
   'In the gav, penning dukkerin.'
   'We were talking of language, Jasper.'
   'True, brother.'
   'Yours must be a rum one?'
   ''Tis called Rommany.'
   'I would gladly know it.'
   'You need it sorely.'
   'Would you teach it me?'
   'None sooner.'
   'Suppose we begin now?'
   'Suppose we do, brother.'
   'Not whilst I am here,' said the woman, flinging her
knitting down, and starting upon her feet; 'not whilst
I am here shall this gorgio learn Rommany. A pretty
manœuvre, truly; and what would be the end of it? I
goes to the farming ker with my sister, to tell a fortune,
and earn a few sixpences for the chabes. I sees a jolly pig

in the yard, and I says to my sister, speaking Rommany, " Do so and so," says I ; which the farming man hearing, asks what we are talking about.   " Nothing at all, master," says I, " something about the weather " ; when who should start up from behind a pale, where he has been listening, but this ugly gorgio, crying out, " They are after poisoning your pigs, neighbour ! " so that we are glad to run, I and my sister, with perhaps the farm-engro shouting after us.   Says my sister to me, when we have got fairly off, " How came that ugly one to know what you said to me ? "   Whereupon I answers, " It all comes of my son Jasper, who brings the gorgio to our fire, and must needs be teaching him."   " Who was fool there ? " says my sister.   " Who, indeed, but my son Jasper," I answers. And here should I be a greater fool to sit still and suffer it ; which I will not do.   I do not like the look of him ; he looks over-gorgeous.   An ill day to the Romans when he masters Rommany ; and, when I says that, I pens a true dukkerin.'
    ' What do you call God, Jasper ? '
    ' You had better be jawing,' said the woman, raising her voice to a terrible scream ; ' you had better be moving off, my gorgio ; hang you for a keen one, sitting there by the fire, and stealing my language before my face.   Do you know whom you have to deal with ?   Do you know that I am dangerous ?   My name is Herne, and I comes of the hairy ones ! '
    And a hairy one she looked !   She wore her hair clubbed upon her head, fastened with many strings and ligatures ; but now, tearing these off, her locks, originally jet black, but now partially grizzled with age, fell down on every side of her, covering her face and back as far down as her knees.   No she-bear of Lapland ever looked more fierce and hairy than did that woman, as standing in the open part of the tent, with her head bent down, and her shoulders drawn up, seemingly about to precipitate herself upon me, she repeated, again and again,—
    ' My name is Herne, and I comes of the hairy ones ! ' . . .
    ' I call God Duvel, brother.'
    ' It sounds very like Devil.'
    ' It doth, brother, it doth.'   *George Borrow.*

The Three Words

'LOOK here, Uncle! If you 'll give me five shillings, I 'll tell you three words you do not know.'

'Not I, my friend; not if I know it. Tell me what are the words in English, and I 'll bet the five shillings I know Gypsy for them.'

'Yes, that 's fair, Ike. Tell the gentleman in English, and see if he does not know the Gypsy.'

'Well, Uncle. Tell me how you would say, "Put the saddle and bridle on the horse, and go to the fair."'

'*Chiv* the *boshto*, and *solivardo 'pré* the *grei*, and *jal* to the *welgaurus*.' (Put the saddle and bridle on the horse, and go to the fair.)

'That 's not quite right, Uncle. I would say, "*Dordi, chawóli, jal* and *lel* the *boshto* and *solivardo. And* the *vardo akei*, and *chiv* the *grei adré lesti*, and *mook's jal* to the *welingaurus*, and have some *peias*." (Hi, mates, go and get the saddle and bridle. Bring the cart here, and put the horse to, and let us go to the fair, and have some fun.) That 's the right way to say what I asked you.'

'All right, Mr. H——; I see: six of one, and half a dozen of the other. And what are the other words?'

'Tell me, Uncle, what the sun is in Gypsy.'

'The sun. Well, I call that *Kam* (Sun).'

'No, friend. It 's *Tam*, not *Kam*. And what is a Signpost?'

'A *Siker-droméngro* (Show-road-thing), or a *Sikerméngro* (Showman).'

'Well, a *Sikerméngro* might do, but that is a Show. We call a Signpost a *Pookering-kosht* (a Telling-post), but I see you know plenty of Gypsy, and I dare say you know more words than any of us, but "the great secret" you will never know. Only real Gypsies know *that*, and they will never tell *you*.'

He went out, but returned not long after, and said,—

'Tell me, what is a *beurus*?'

'A brewery?'

'No, a *beurus*.'

'A *Livena-kel*in'-*Kair* (beer-making house)?'

' No, that 's a brew-house.   I said a *beurus*.'
' Well, I don't know that word at all.'
' It 's a parlour, Uncle.   The beſt room of the house.
I thought I would find something you did not know,
besides the " great secret," and *that* you will never get to
know.'

Bath Smart & H. T. Crofton.

Low Wagram Folks

I PRESENTLY saw her returning with another female,
of slighter build, lower in ſtature, and apparently much
older.   She came towards me with much smiling, smirk-
ing, and nodding, which I returned with as much smiling
and nodding as if I had known her for threescore years.
She motioned me with her hand to enter the house.   I
did so.   The other woman returned down the hill, and
the queen of the Gypsies entering, and shutting the door,
confronted me on the floor, and said in a rather musical,
but slightly faltering voice :
' Now, sir, in what can I oblige you ? '
Thereupon, letting the umbrella fall, which I invariably
carry about with me in my journeyings, I flung my arms
three times up into the air, and in an exceedingly dis-
agreeable voice, owing to a cold which I had had for some
time, and which I had caught amongſt the lakes of Lough-
maben, whilſt hunting after Gypsies whom I could not find,
I exclaimed :
' Sossi your nav ?   Pukker mande tute's nav !   Shan
tu a mumpli-mushi, or a tatchi Romany ? '
Which, being interpreted into Gorgio, runs thus :
' What is your name ?   Tell me your name !   Are you
a mumping woman, or a true Gypsy ? '
The woman appeared frightened, and for some time said
nothing, but only ſtared at me.   At length, recovering
herself, she exclaimed, in an angry tone, ' Why do you talk
to me in that manner, and in that gibberish ?   I don't
underſtand a word of it.'
' Gibberish ! ' said I ; ' it is no gibberish ; it is Zingarrijib, Romany rokrapen, real Gypsy of the old order.'
' Whatever it is,' said the woman, ' it 's of no use speak-

ing it to me.   If you want to speak to me, you must speak
English or Scotch.'

'Why, they told me as how yer were a Gypsy,' said I.

'And they told you the truth,' said the woman ; 'I am
a Gypsy, and a real one ; I am not ashamed of my
blood.'

'If yer were a Gyptian,' said I, 'yer would be able to
speak Gyptian ; but yer can't, not a word.'

'At any rate,' said the woman, 'I can speak English,
which is more than you can.   Why, your way of speaking
is that of the lowest vagrants of the roads.'

'Oh, I have two or three ways of speaking English,'
said I ; 'and when I speaks to low wagram folks, I speaks
in a low wagram manner.'

'Not very civil,' said the woman.

'A pretty Gypsy ! ' said I ; 'why, I'll be bound you
don't know what a *churi* is ! '

The woman gave me a sharp look ; but made no reply.

'A pretty queen of the Gypsies ! ' said I ; 'why, she
doesn't know the meaning of *churi* ! '

'Doesn't she?' said the woman, evidently nettled;
'doesn't she ? '

'Why, do you mean to say that you know the meaning
of *churi* ? '

'Why, of course I do,' said the woman.

'Hardly, my good lady,' said I ; 'hardly ; a *churi* to you
is merely a *churi*.'

'A *churi* is a knife,' said the woman, in a tone of defiance ;
'a *churi* is a knife.'

'Oh, it is,' said I ; 'and yet you tried to persuade me that
you had no peculiar language of your own, and only knew
English and Scotch : *churi* is a word of the language in
which I spoke to you at first, Zingarrijib, or Gypsy language ; and since you know that word, I make no doubt
that you know others, and in fact can speak Gypsy.   Come ;
let us have a little confidential discourse together.'

The woman stood for some time, as if in reflection, and
at length said : 'Sir, before having any particular discourse with you, I wish to put a few questions to you, in
order to gather from your answers whether it is safe to
talk to you on Gypsy matters.   You pretend to under-

Stand the Gypsy language : if I find you do not, I will hold no further discourse with you : and the sooner you take yourself off the better. If I find you do, I will talk with you as long as you like.'

George Borrow.

Comparative Philology

NO ! *rye*, no matter where you goes,
　Sarch high or low where'er you please,
You 'll never find another talk
　So good as our old *Romines.*

What do you call this here in French ?
　Cuttow ! That 's Cant, or mumpish quite.
In Jarman ? *Messer !* Well it hain't
　A messer if you use it right.

Or take a talk one onderstands
　Like Henglish ; still it 's all the same.
Knife ! Well now, *rye*, I axes you,
　What is that only just a name ?

But *Churi !* There you has it straight,
　A *churi* IS a *churi, rye.*
A *churi* is the thing hitself,
　And not a name you calls it by.

Jubilee Book, Phil. Inst., Edin.

The Tongue of 200 Years ago

' DO you know what patteran means ? '
　' Of course, Ursula ; the gypsy trail, the handful of grass which the gypsies strew in the roads as they travel, to give information to any of their companions who may be behind, as to the route they have taken. The gypsy patteran has always had a strange interest for me, Ursula.'
　' Like enough, brother ; but what does patteran mean ? '
　' Why, the gypsy trail, formed as I told you before.'
　' And you know nothing more about patteran, brother ? '
　' Nothing at all, Ursula ; do you ? '

' What 's the name for the leaf of a tree, brother ? '

' I don't know,' said I ; ' it 's odd enough that I have asked that question of a dozen Romany chals and chies, and they always told me that they did not know.'

' No more they did, brother ; there 's only one person in England that knows, and that 's myself—the name for a leaf is patteran. Now there are two that knows it—the other is yourself.'

' Dear me, Ursula ; how very strange ! I am much obliged to you. I think I never saw you look so pretty as you do now.'

.   .   .   .   .

So patteran signified leaf, the leaf of a tree ; and no one at present knew that but myself and Ursula, who had learnt it from Mrs. Herne, the last, it was said, of the old stock ; and then I thought what strange people the gypsies must have been in the old time. They were sufficiently strange at present ; but they must have been far stranger of old ; they must have been a more peculiar people—their language must have been more perfect—and they must have had a greater stock of strange secrets. I almost wished that I had lived some two or three hundred years ago, that I might have observed these people when they were yet stranger than at present. I wondered whether I could have introduced myself to their company at that period, whether I should have been so fortunate as to meet such a strange, half-malicious, half good-humoured being as Jasper, who would have instructed me in the language, then more deserving of note than at present. What might I not have done with that language, had I known it in its purity ? Why, I might have written books in it ; yet those who spoke it would hardly have admitted me to their society at that period, when they kept more to themselves. Yet I thought that I might possibly have gained their confidence, and have wandered about with them, and learnt their language, and all their strange ways, and then—and then—and a sigh rose from the depth of my breast ; for I began to think, ' Supposing I had accomplished all this, what would have been the profit of it ? and in what would all this wild gypsy dream have terminated ? '

George Borrow.

The Rommany Jōter

IF a Gipsy is lost and cannot find his way in the night, he cries out 'Hup—hup—*Rom-ma-ny, Rom-ma-ny jōter!*' When the children cannot find the tent, it is the same cry, '*Rom-ma-ny jōter.*'

And one night my father, sixty years ago, was walking through the woods to his tent, and he heard a little cry like little ladies talking real old Gipsy, and so he went from one great tree to the other, and after a while he saw a little lady, and she was crying out as if for her life '*Rom-ma-ny, Rom-ma-ny jōter!*' So my father cried again '*Rom-ma-ny chal akai!*' But as he hallooed, there came a great blast of wind, and the little ladies and all flew away in the sky like birds in a storm, and all he heard was a laughing, and '*Rom-ma-ny jōter!*' softer and softer, till all was done.

And you can see by that that the goblins, and fairies, and ghosts, and witches, and all talk real old Gipsy, because that is the old Egyptian language that was talked in the Scripture land.

Charles Godfrey Leland.

XI

SCHOLAR GYPSIES

XI

Scholar Gypsies

El Aficionado

THROUGHOUT my life the Gypsy race has always had a peculiar interest for me. Indeed I can remember no period when the mere mention of the name of Gypsy did not awaken within me feelings hard to be described. I cannot account for this—I merely state a fact.

George Borrow.

The Call

. . . THE same whom in my Schoolboy days
  I listened to ; that Cry
Which made me look a thousand ways
  In bush, and tree, and sky. . . .

And I can listen to thee yet ;
  Can lie upon the plain
And listen, till I do beget
  That golden time again.

William Wordsworth.

The Glamour of the 'G'

JUST as Gautier was troubled whenever he saw the middle 'g' of Hugo trampling across the page of a book, so for me there is the same magic in the first 'g' of Gypsy. *Arthur Symons.*

A Magic Thread

THE word 'Gipsy' seems to have a magic thread running through it, beginning at the tip end of 'G' and ending with the tail end of 'y.' Geese have tried to gobble it, ducks swallow it, hens scratched after it, peacocks pecked it, dandy cocks crowed over it, foxes have hid it, dogs have fought for it, cats have sworn and spit over it, pigs have tried to gulp it as the daintiest morsel, parrots have chatted about it, hawks, eagles, jackdaws, magpies, ravens and crows have tried to carry it away as a precious jewel, and in the end all have put it down as a thing they could neither carry nor swallow. *George Smith, of Coalville.*

The Romany Rye

AND as I wandered along the green, I drew near to a place where several men, with a cask beside them, sat carousing in the neighbourhood of a small tent. ' Here he comes,' said one of them, as I advanced, and standing up he raised his voice and sang :—

> ' Here the Gypsy gemman see,
> With his Roman jib and his rome and dree—
> Rome and dree, rum and dry
> Rally round the Rommany Rye.'

It was Mr. Petulengro, who was here diverting himself with several of his comrades ; they all received me with considerable frankness. ' Sit down, brother,' said Mr. Petulengro, ' and take a cup of good ale.'

I sat down. ' Your health, gentlemen,' said I, as I took the cup which Mr. Petulengro handed to me.

' Aukko tu pios adrey Rommanis. Here is your health in Romany, brother,' said Mr. Petulengro ; who, having refilled the cup, now emptied it at a draught.

' Your health in Romany, brother,' said Tawno Chikno, to whom the cup came next.

' The Rommany Rye,' said a third.

' The Gypsy gentleman,' exclaimed a fourth, drinking.

And then they all sang in chorus :—

> ' Here the Gypsy gemman see,
> With his Roman jib and his rome and dree—
> Rome and dree, rum and dry
> Rally round the Rommany Rye.'

' And now, brother,' said Mr. Petulengro, ' seeing that you have drunk and been drunken, you will perhaps tell us where you have been, and what about ? '

George Borrow.

The Oxford Scholar

THAT one man shold be able to bind the thoughts of another, and determine them to their particular objeḍs; will be reckon'd in the firſt rank of *Impossibles* : Yet by the power of advanc'd *Imagination* it may very probably be effeḍed ; and *ſtory* abounds with Inſtances. I 'le trouble the Reader but with one ; and the hands from which I had it, make me secure of the truth on 't. There was very lately a Lad in the *University* of *Oxford*, who being of very pregnant and ready parts, and yet wanting the encouragement of preferment ; was by his poverty forc'd to leave his ſtudies there, and to caſt himself upon the wide world for a livelyhood. Now, his necessities growing dayly on him, and wanting the help of friends to relieve him ; he was at laſt forced to joyn himself to a company of *Vagabond Gypsies*, whom occasionly he met with, and to follow their Trade for a maintenance. Among these extravagant people, by the insinuating subtilty of his carriage, he quickly got so much of their love, and eſteem ; as that they discover'd to him their *Myſtery* : in the praḍice of which, by the pregnancy of his wit and parts he soon grew so good a proficient, as to be able to out-do his Inſtruḍours. After he had been a pretty while well exercis'd in the Trade ; there chanc'd to ride by a couple of *Scholars* who had formerly bin of his acquaintance. The *Scholars* had quickly spyed out their old friend, among the *Gypsies* ; and their amazement to see him among such society, had wellnigh discover'd him : but by a sign he prevented their owning him before that Crew : and taking one of them aside privately, desired him with his friend to go to an *Inn*, not far diſtant thence, promising there to come to them. They accordingly went thither, and he follows : after their firſt salutations, his friends enquire how he came to lead so odd a life as that was, and to joyn himself with such a *cheating beggerly* company. The *Scholar-Gypsy* having given them an account of the necessity, which drove him to that kind of life ; told them, that the people he went with were not such *Impoſtours* as they were taken for, but that they had a *traditional* kind of *learning* among them, and could do wonders by the power of *Imagination*, and that himself had learnt much of their Art, and improved it further then themselves could. And to evince the truth of what he told them, he said, he 'd remove into another room, leaving them to discourse together ; and upon his return tell them the sum of what they had talked of : which accordingly he perform'd, giving them a full account of what had pass'd between them in his absence. The *Scholars* being amaz'd at so unexpected a discovery, earnestly desir'd him to unriddle the *mystery*. In which he gave them satisfaction, by telling them, that what he did was by the power of *Imagination*, his Phancy *binding* theirs ; and that himself had dictated to them the discourse, they held together, while he was from them : That there were warrantable wayes of heightening the *Imagination* to that pitch, as to bind anothers ; and that when he had compass'd the whole *secret*, some parts of which he said he was yet ignorant of, he intended to leave their company, and give the world an account of what he had learned.

Joseph Glanvill.

The Scholar Gipsy

. . . AND near me on the grass lies Glanvil's book—
    Come, let me read the oft-read tale again,
        The Story of that Oxford scholar poor,
    Of pregnant parts and quick inventive brain,
        Who, tir'd of knocking at Preferment's door,
            One summer morn forsook
    His friends, and went to learn the Gipsy lore,
        And roam'd the world with that wild brotherhood,
        And came, as most men deem'd, to little good,
    But came to Oxford and his friends no more.

    But once, years after, in the country lanes,
        Two scholars, whom at college erst he knew,
        Met him, and of his way of life inquir'd.
    Whereat he answer'd that the Gipsy crew,
        His mates, had arts to rule as they desir'd
            The workings of men's brains ;

And they can bind them to what thoughts they will :
' And I,' he said, ' the secret of their art,
When fully learn'd, will to the world impart :
But it needs heaven-sent moments for this skill ! '

This said, he left them, and return'd no more,
But rumours hung about the country side,
That the lost Scholar long was seen to stray,
Seen by rare glimpses, pensive and tongue-tied,
In hat of antique shape, and cloak of grey,
The same the Gipsies wore.
Shepherds had met him on the Hurst in spring ;
At some lone alehouse in the Berkshire moors,
On the warm ingle bench, the smock-frock'd
boors
Had found him seated at their entering.

But, 'mid their drink and clatter, he would fly :
And I myself seem half to know thy looks,
And put the Shepherds, Wanderer, on thy trace ;
And boys who in lone wheatfields scare the rooks
I ask if thou hast pass'd their quiet place ;
Or in my boat I lie
Moor'd to the cool bank in the summer heats,
Mid wide grass meadows which the sunshine
fills,
And watch the warm green-muffled Cumner hills,
And wonder if thou haunt'st their shy retreats.

For most, I know, thou lov'st retiréd ground.
Thee, at the ferry, Oxford riders blithe,
Returning home on summer nights, have met
Crossing the stripling Thames at Bablock-hithe,
Trailing in the cool stream thy fingers wet,
As the slow punt swings round :
And leaning backwards in a pensive dream,
And fostering in thy lap a heap of flowers
Pluck'd in shy fields and distant Wychwood bowers,
And thine eyes resting on the moonlit stream :

And then they land, and thou art seen no more.
Maidens who from the distant hamlets come
To dance around the Fyfield elm in May,
Oft through the darkening fields have seen thee roam,
Or cross a stile into the public way.
Oft thou hast given them store
Of flowers—the frail-leaf'd, white anemone—
Dark bluebells drench'd with dews of summer eves,
And purple orchises with spotted leaves—
But none has words she can report of thee.

And, above Godstow Bridge, when haytime 's here
In June, and many a scythe in sunshine flames,
Men who through those wide fields of breezy grass
Where black-wing'd swallows haunt the glittering
            Thames,
To bathe in the abandon'd lasher pass,
        Have often pass'd thee near
Sitting upon the river bank o'ergrown :
        Mark'd thy outlandish garb, thy figure spare,
        Thy dark vague eyes, and soft abstracted air ;
But, when they came from bathing, thou wert gone.

At some lone homestead in the Cumner hills,
        Where at her open door the housewife darns,
        Thou hast been seen, or hanging on a gate
To watch the threshers in the mossy barns.
        Children, who early range these slopes and late
        For cresses from the rills,
Have known thee watching, all an April day,
        The springing pastures and the feeding kine ;
        And mark'd thee, when the stars come out and shine,
Through the long dewy grass move slow away.

In Autumn, on the skirts of Bagley Wood,
        Where most the Gipsies by the turf-edg'd way
        Pitch their smok'd tents, and every bush you see
With scarlet patches tagg'd and shreds of grey,
        Above the forest ground call'd Thessaly—
        The blackbird picking food

Sees thee, nor stops his meal, nor fears at all ;
So often has he known thee past him stray
Rapt, twirling in thy hand a wither'd spray,
And waiting for the spark from Heaven to fall.

And once, in winter, on the causeway chill
Where home through flooded fields foot-travellers go,
Have I not pass'd thee on the wooden bridge
Wrapt in thy cloak and battling with the snow,
Thy face towards Hinksey and its wintry ridge ?
And thou hast climb'd the hill
And gain'd the white brow of the Cumner range ;
Turn'd once to watch, while thick the snowflakes
fall,
The line of festal light in Christ-Church hall—
Then sought thy straw in some sequester'd grange.

But what—I dream ! Two hundred years are flown
Since first thy story ran through Oxford halls,
And the grave Glanvil did the tale inscribe
That thou wert wander'd from the studious walls
To learn strange arts, and join a Gipsy tribe :
And thou from earth art gone
Long since, and in some quiet churchyard laid ;
Some country nook, where o'er thy unknown
grave
Tall grasses and white flowering nettles wave—
Under a dark red-fruited yew-tree's shade.

Matthew Arnold.

Thyrsis speaks

. . . WHY faintest thou ?   I wandered till I died.
Roam on ! the light we sought is shining still.
Dost thou ask proof ?   Our Tree yet crowns the
hill,
Our Scholar travels yet the loved hillside.

Matthew Arnold.

U

Doctor Boorde : Ipse dixit

OF noble England, of Ireland and of Wales,
    And also of Scotland, I haue tolde som tales ;
And of other Londes I haue shewed my mynd ;
He that wyl trauell, the truthe he shall fynd.
After my conscyence I do wryte truly,
Although that many men wyl say that I do lye ;
But for that matter, I do greatly pas,
But I am as I am, but not as I was.
And where[as] my metre is ryme dogrell,
The effect of the whych no wyse man wyll depell,
For he wyll take the effect of my mynde,
Although to make meter I am full blynde. . . .

. . . For I doo speke of many countryes & regions, and
of the natural dysposicyon of the inhabitours of the same,
with other necessary thynges to be knowen, specially for
them the whiche doth pretende to trauayle the countrees,
regions, and prouinces, that they may be in a redines to
knowe what they should do whan they come there ; And
also to know the money of the countre, & to speke parte
of the language or speache that there is vsed, by the whiche
a man may com to a forder knowledge.

Andrew Borde.

Here 's to Whiter's Health

'HERE 'S Parr's health, and Whiter's.'
    ' Who is Whiter ? '
' Don't you know Whiter ?   I thought everybody knew
Reverend Whiter the philologist, though I suppose you
scarcely know what that means.   A man fond of tongues
and languages, quite out of your way—he understands
some twenty ; what do you say to that ? '
    ' Is he a sound man ? '
    ' Why, as to that, I scarcely know what to say : he has got
queer notions in his head—wrote a book to prove that
all words came originally from the earth—who knows ?
Words have roots, and roots live in the earth ; but, upon

the whole I should not call him altogether a sound man, though he can talk Greek nearly as fast as Parr.'

' Is he a round man ? '

' Ay, boy, rounder than Parr ; I 'll sing you a song, if you like, which will let you into his character :—

" Give me the haunch of a buck to eat, and to drink Madeira old,
And a gentle wife to rest with, and in my arms to fold,
An Arabic book to study, a Norfolk cob to ride,
And a house to live in shaded with trees, and near to a river side ;
With such good things around me, and blessed with good health
     withal,
Though I should live for a hundred years, for death I would not
     call."

' Here 's to Whiter's health ! '

George Borrow.

Mr. Bryant

TUESDAY, JANUARY 8TH (1788).—This evening, according to my present plan of freedom, as Mrs. Delany came not to the lodge, I went myself to Mrs. Delany, and left the tea-table to its original state. I had the courage to make my visit from seven to ten o'clock.

I met Mr. Bryant, who came by appointment to give me that pleasure. He was in very high spirits, full of anecdote and amusement. He has as much good-humoured chit-chat and entertaining gossiping as if he had given no time to the classics and his studies, instead of having nearly devoted his life to them. One or two of his little anecdotes I will try to recollect.

. . . He spoke upon the Mysteries, or origin of our theatrical entertainments, and repeated the plan and conduct of several of these strange compositions, in particular one he remembered which was called ' Noah's Ark,' and in which that patriarch and his sons, just previous to the Deluge, made it all their delight to speed themselves into the ark without Mrs. Noah, whom they wished to escape ; but she surprised them just as they had embarked, and made so prodigious a racket against the door that, after a long and violent contention, she forced them to open it, and gained admission, having first contented them by being kept out till she was thoroughly wet to the skin.

These moſt eccentric and unaccountable dramas filled
up the chief of our conversation : and whether to consider them moſt with laughter, as ludicrous, or with horror,
as blasphemous, remains a doubt I cannot well solve.

Frances Burney.

Hoyland the Quaker

' I HAVE avoided much intercourse with this class,
fearing the fate of Mr. Hoyland, who being a Quaker,
was shot by one of Cupid's darts from a black-eyed Gipsy
girl ; *and J. S. may do well to be cautious.*'

George Offor.

G. B.

A LAD who twenty tongues can talk,
And sixty miles a day can walk ;
Drink at a draught a pint of rum,
And then be neither sick nor dumb ;
Can tune a song and make a verse,
And deeds of Northern kings rehearse ;
Who never will forsake his friend
While he his bony fiſt can bend ;
And though averse to brawl and ſtrife,
Will fight a Dutchman with a knife ;
O that is juſt the lad for me,
And such is honeſt six-foot-three.

George Borrow.

A Gypsy's Impression of Borrow

' A LMOST a giant—a very noble-looking gentleman,
as it might be the Mayor of England.'

Isaac Heron.

George Borrow

T HREE hundred years since Borrow would have been
a gentleman adventurer : he would have dropped
quietly down the river, and ſteered for the Spanish Main,
bent upon making carbonadoes of your Don.   But he

came too late for that, and falling upon no sword and
buckler age but one that was interested in Randal and
Spring, he accepted that he found, and did his best to turn
its conditions into literature. As he had that admirable
instinct of making the best of things which marks the true
adventurer, he was on the whole exceeding happy. There
was no more use in sailing for Javan and Gadire ; but at
home there were highways in abundance, and what is
your genuine tramp but a dry-land sailor ? The Red Man
is exhausted of everything but sordidness ; but under that
round-shouldered little tent at the bend of the road, beside
that fire artistically built beneath that kettle of the comfortable odours, among those horses and colts at graze
hard by, are men and women more mysterious and more
alluring to the romantic mind than any Mingo or Comanch
that ever traded a scalp. While as for your tricks of fence
—your immortal *passado*, your *punto reverso*—if that be no
longer the right use for a gentleman, have not Spring and
Langan fought their great battle on Worcester racecourse ?
and has not Cribb of Gloucestershire—that renowned,
heroic, irresistible Thomas—beaten Molyneux the negro
artist in the presence of twenty thousand roaring Britons ?
and shall the practice of an art which has rejoiced in such a
master as the illustrious Game Chicken, Hannibal of the
Ring, be held degrading by an Englishman of sufficient
inches who, albeit a Tory and a High Churchman, is at
bottom as thoroughgoing a Republican as ever took the
word of command from Colonel Cromwell ? And if all
this fail, if he get nobody to put on the gloves with him,
if the tents of the Romany prove barren of interest, if the
king's highway be vacant of adventure as Mayfair, he has
still philology to fall back upon, he can still console himself
with the study of strange tongues, he can still exult in a
peculiar superiority by quoting the great Ab Gwylim
where the baser sort of persons is content with Shakespeare. So that what with these and some kindred diver-
sions—a little horse-whispering and ale-drinking, the
damnation of Popery, the study of the Bible—he can
manage not merely to live but to live so fully and richly as
to be the envy of some and the amazement of all. That,
as life goes and as the world wags, is given to few. Add

to it the credit of having written as good a book about
Spain as ever was written in any language, the happiness
of having dreamed and partly lived that book ere it was
written, the perfect joy of being roundly abused by everybody, and the consciousness of being different from everybody and of giving at least as good as ever you got at
several things the world is silly enough to hold in worship
—as the Toryism of Sir Walter, or the niceness of Popery,
or the pleasures of Society : and is it not plain that Borrow
was a man uncommon fortunate, and that he enjoyed life
as greatly as most men not savages who have possessed
the fruition of this terrestrial sphere ?

William Ernest Henley.

The Carter's Opinion of Lavengro

' A RE you a carter ? ' said I. No answer. ' One of
Twm o'r Nant's people ? ' No answer. ' Famous
fellow that Twm o'r Nant, wasn't he ? Did you ever hear
how he got the great tree in at Carmarthen Gate ? What is
wood per foot at present ? Whom do you cart for ? Or
are you your own master ? If so, how many horses do
you keep ? '
    To not one of these questions, nor to a dozen others
which I put, both in English and Welsh, did my friend
with the brush return any verbal answer, though I could
occasionally hear a kind of stifled giggle proceeding from
him. Having at length thoroughly brushed not only my
clothes, but my boots and my hat, which last article he
took from my head, and placed on again very dexterously,
after brushing it, he put the brush down on the dresser,
and then advancing to me made me a bow, and waving his
forefinger backwards and forwards before my face, he said,
with a broad grin : ' Nice gentleman—will do anything
for him but answer questions, and let him hear my discourse.
Love to listen to his pleasant stories of foreign lands, ghosts
and tylwith teg ; but before him, deem it wise to be mum,
quite mum. Know what he comes about. Wants to
hear discourse of poor man, that he may learn from it
poor man's little ways and invirmities, and mark them down

in one small, little book to serve for fun to Lord Palmer-
ston and the other great gentlefolks in London. Nice
man, civil man, I don't deny ; and clebber man too, for
he knows Welsh, and has been everywhere—but fox—old
fox—lives at Plas y Cadno.'

George Borrow.

Romany Ryes

IF the ' Romany Rye ' is, as Groome defined him, one,
not a Gypsy, who loves the race and has mastered the
tongue, Borrow did not invent him. Already students
had busied themselves with the language ; already Gypsy
scholars like Glanvill's,—or Matthew Arnold's ?—' had
roam'd the world with that wild brotherhood.' But they
had been scattered through the many centuries since the
first Gypsy had appeared in Europe. It was Borrow, who
hearing the music of the wind on the heath, and feeling the
charm of the Gypsy's life, made others hear and feel with
him, till, where there had been but one Romany Rye, there
were now a score, learning more of Romany in a few years
than earlier scholars had in hundreds, and, less fearful
than Glanvill's youth, giving the world their knowledge
of the language and the people who spoke it. A very
craze for the Gypsy spread throughout the land. I know
of nothing like it save the ardour with which the Félibrige
took root in Provence. Language in both cases—with
the Félibres their own, with the Romany Ryes that of the
stranger—led to sympathy and fellowship. There were
the same meetings, the same rivalries and friendships, the
same collaboration, the same exaltation even.

Elizabeth Robins Pennell.

On the First Members of the Gypsy Lore Society

SO that now there are five of us—and a rum lot they are,
as the Devil said when he looked over the ten Com-
mandments.

Charles Godfrey Leland.

The Archduke Josef as Myth

THERE was once a tribe of poor Gypsies, and their chief said to his people : ' Up ! let us go to the land of the Gypsies, let us go to Josef our King.'

The grandam said : ' O children, do not go to King Josef, for in the city of Kutchela ye will have to work all day, and be for ever hoeing the ground ; I tell you that is not for us.'

The men did not hearken to her, and travelled far, very far, until they came to the city of Kutchela. There at one time was the land of the Gypsies.

King Josef spoke to them : ' Sweet Gypsies, in my land there dwells a big ogress, a great big ogress, as tall as a tree of the forest. This big ogress has six tusks, and with her six tusks she devours a man every day. Men, my sweet men, she will devour you all. And I shall weep bitterly, O my sweet Gypsies, when I have no men left.'

And valiant Tchurko answered : ' O great black King ! I am not afraid. I will hie me straightway to this big woman, and it is I who will devour her. I have huge teeth.'

The lad reached the great silver city, where dwelt poor Josef, King of the Gypsies, and the ogress with the six tusks. As soon as he got there, she said to the lad : ' Stay here with me ; I will not eat thee up, if thou canst tell me how many hairs there are on the head of Josef the King.'

Tchurko answered : ' Do thou tell me how many stars there are in the sky, for so many hairs are there on the head of King Josef.'

' Good ! ' said the ogress, ' but tell me how many mountains there are in the world.'

The poor lad looked out upon the silver city, and answered : ' There are as many mountains in the world, thou black monster, as there are houses in the silver city.'

' Good ! ' said the ogress, ' and now tell me how many tusks I have.'

The lad had heard that she had six tusks, so he answered : ' Thou hast six tusks.'

The ogress said : ' See !   I have only five tusks.   I will eat thee up.'   And she ate up the poor lad.

And the Devil came out of Egypt, and devoured poor King Josef.

In those days we had a land of our own, now we have none : we toil and moil, we are condemned to wander, and we have no sweet land of our own.

Peter Karčić, a Bosnian Gypsy.

A Great Collector

I OFTEN found myself in the midst of the tents, alone among a horde of Zaparis (the Gypsies of my predilection), who would press around me, hurling words at me from every side, each correcting the other, and calling his fellows stupid and ignorant.   Some of them in their zeal would snatch my hand, so that I might only record the word they themselves proffered me, all others being spurious and not Romani.   I must confess that I never had occasion to complain of their conduct towards me.   A little medical attention to their sick enabled me to make some valuable acquaintances.

The most fruitful of my expeditions were those made to some tents which were pitched every spring on the heights above Constantinople.   These fierce and sinister-looking copper-smiths and sieve-makers proved most helpful to me.   I visited their tents, supplied their needs and attended them and their numerous brood in all the ailments they suffered from.   As soon as I appeared, they would abandon work and damp down their fires ; the wife would quit the huge bellows, and the women and children would pour out of the tents and gather round me.   Seated on a three-legged stool, surrounded by more than thirty of them, I used to write down not only what they were actually telling me, but also all the phrases of the children who were squabbling in our midst, and of the parents who were trying to silence them.   And all the while the youngsters would be rummaging in my pockets, and the elders smoking my tobacco.   By the time I left, my instructors had succeeded in rifling me of all my small change, and I turned homewards, followed by a crowd of imps from the other tents, wholly exhausted, and covered with vermin. These visits were repeated time after time, and, in spite of all such discomforts, brought me a handsome reward.

Alexandros Paspates.

The Romany Soul

ONE twilight we found [in Aberystwyth] a couple whom I can never forget. It was an elderly Gypsy and his wife. The husband was himself characteristic; the wife was more than merely picturesque. I have never met such a superb old Romany as she was ; indeed, I doubt if I ever saw any woman of her age, in any land or any range of life, with a more magnificently proud expression or such unaffected dignity. It was the whole poem of ' Crescentius ' living in modern time in other form.

When a scholar associates much with Gypsies there is developed in him in due time a perception or intuition of certain kinds of men or minds, which it is as difficult to describe as it is wonderful. He who has read Matthew Arnold's ' Gypsy Scholar ' may, however, find therein many apt words for it. I mean very seriously what I say ; I mean that through the Romany the demon of Socrates acquires distinctness ; I mean that a faculty is developed which is as strange as divination, and which is greatly akin to it. . . .

And by this *duk* I read in a few words in the Romany woman an eagle soul, caged between the bars of poverty, ignorance, and custom ; but a great soul for all that. Both she and her husband were of the old type of their race, now so rare in England, though commoner in America. They spoke Romany with inflection and conjugation ; they remembered the old rhymes and old words. Little by little, the old man seemed to be deeply impressed, indeed awed, by our utterly inexplicable knowledge. I wore a velveteen coat, and had on a broad, soft, felt hat.

' You talk as the old Romanys did,' said the old man. ' I hear you use words which I once heard from old men who died when I was a boy. I thought those words were lying in graves which have long been green. I hear songs and sayings which I never expected to hear again. You talk like Gypsies, and such Gypsies as I never meet now ; and you look like Gorgios. But when I was still young, a few of the oldest Romany chals still wore hats such as you have ; and when I first looked at you, I thought of them. I don't understand you. It is strange, very strange.'

' It is the Romany soul,' said his wife. ' People take to what is in them ; if a bird were born a fox, it would love to fly.'

Charles Godfrey Leland.

Hardy on Leland

CHARLES LELAND—a man of higher literary rank than ever was accorded him—told some of his gipsy tales at the Savile Club, including one of how he visited at a country mansion, and while there went to see a gipsy family living in a tent on the squire's land. He talked to them in Romany, and was received by the whole family as a bosom friend. He was told by the head gipsy that his, the gipsy's, brother would be happy to know him when he came out of gaol, but that at present he was doing six months for a horse. While Leland was sitting by the fire drinking brandy-and-water with this friend, the arrival of some gentlemen and ladies, fellow-guests at the house he was staying at, was announced. They had come to see the gipsies out of curiosity. Leland threw his brandy from his glass into the fire, not to be seen tippling there, but as they entered it blazed up in a blue flare much to their amazement, as if they thought it some unholy libation, which added to their surprise at discovering him. How he explained himself I cannot remember.

Thomas Hardy.

The Palmer

NOW when I heard that thou wert gone
Afar across the sea,
I little thought how very far
That journey was to be.

And when I heard that thou wouldst tread
In half-known lands alone,
I little thought thy footsteps sped
Unto the all unknown.

I knew how soon to every tongue
Thy tongue was quickly turned,
Now if thou speakest, 'tis in that
Which mortal never learned.

There may be happiness in death,
As many sing or say,
But oh! in finding happiness
Thou 'st taken ours away.

Charles Godfrey Leland.

Sir Richard Burton

WHETHER there may not be also a tinge of Arab or perhaps of Gypsy blood in Burton's race is a point which is perhaps open to question. For the latter suspicion an excuse may be found in the incurable restlessness which has beset him since his infancy, a restlessness which has effectually prevented him from ever settling long in any one place, and the singular idiosyncrasy which his friends have often remarked—the peculiarity of his eyes. ' When it [the eye] looks at you,' says one who knows him well, ' it looks through you, and then, glazing over, seems to see something behind you. Richard Burton is the only man (not a Gypsy) with that peculiarity, and he shares with them the same horror of a corpse, deathbed scenes, and graveyards, though caring little for his own life.' When to this remarkable fact be added the scarcely less interesting detail that Burton is one of the half dozen distinctively Romany names, it is evident that the suspicion of Sir Richard Burton having a drop of Gypsy blood in his descent—crossed and commingled though it be with an English, Scottish, French and Irish strain—is not altogether unreasonable.

Francis Hitchman.

A Gypsy Philanthropist

[After reading aloud George Smith's letter on 'the wretched condition of some eight to ten thousand little gipsy children.']

I CEASED, and looked around upon the dirt, squalor, ignorance, and misery before me. Sticks—a small stack of them stood outside the tent ; stones—there were walls, loose boulders, mountains, indeed, of stone ; grass—ay, a meadow-full of grass ; and mud—yon road assuredly was muddy. . . . But how did the hedge-bottom heathens, the plague-spots, look ? Conscience-stricken ? Why, they looked much as you or I might look on reading a libel upon ourselves and families, written by no mere enemy, but by an enemy we deeply scorned. This in itself was proof of heathendom ; yet, after all, it might be conscience that kept them thus silent, fixed and quivering. To break which silence I asked Silvanus what he had to say.

Nothing apparently. He simply stooped and picked up Lementina's teapot, an old-fashioned oddity, which china-maniacs might have fondled, but which here stood poked among the glowing embers. He picked it up and hurled it against the opposite stone wall, remarking quietly, ' There 's your teapot all to atoms, Lementina, and ' (with an outburst) ' I wish to *mi-Duvel* George Smith's head were into it.' Then the old man fell to a passion of sobbing ; Lementina, with a grim consenting smile, said ' *Mishto*, Israel ! ' and the rest broke forth into tumultuous din. One dominant wish seemed to possess them all, ' to see the man as had gone and made that letter.' Their words were earnest, heathenishly forcible, and I think had I preached a crusade to Coalville, the hills would have rung with their Romani *Deus vult*. *Francis Hindes Groome.*

The Compleat Rye

BESIDES acting as private secretary, legal, medical, and spiritual adviser, general arbiter and tobacco-jar to his Romany friends, the complete Rai is supposed to possess a more or less exact knowledge of divination. The

Gypsy assumption that one has successfully made all know-
ledge one's province is often not a little embarrassing, yet
I like to think that something more than this delusion
suggested to old Gray's mind his beautiful comparison of a
Romany Rai, surrounded by a group of eagerly inquiring
Gypsies, to ' Christ sittin' in de midst of his disciples.'

J.G.L.S., 1892.

To Francis Hindes Groome

SCHOLAR Gypsy, Brother, Student,
    Peacefully I kiss thy forehead,
Quietly I depart and leave
    Thee whom I loved—' Good night.'

Sunny, smiling was the morning ;
    A light heart was thine, when, as a youth,
Thou didst strike life's trail
    And take the ancient road.

The birds sang in the woods,
    Man and maid laughed on thee,
The hills, fields, and water thou didst love
    The golden summer illuminated.

Then come the rain, cold, and wind ;
    All the day thou hast tramped bravely.
Now thou growest weary, night comes on.
    It is time to pitch thy tent.

Across death's dark stream
    I give thee my hand ; and what
Thou wouldst have desired for thyself
    I wish thee—Mayst thou sleep well.

Trans. by Theodore Watts-Dunton.

A Romany Rawnee

DURING one of these long walks Rudi said they wanted
    me to come the next evening, when they would play
as they never had before ; I had not heard yet all their violins
could tell.   They were going from Philadelphia in a week

now. Yes, it made them sad. Not for many months could they turn their faces toward the Hungarian plain, and Marie, and the deep, green forests. They must play first in other American towns, and it would be lonely for them when I was not near. Would I come? Would I listen?

There was but one answer to make as we walked together under the stars, with the last passionate cry of the Czardas still ringing in my ears. I was infatuated with the gipsies, my friends told me in reproach. Perhaps I was.

They went back to the Männerchor for their last week. It was near the shell-shaped band-stand in among the plants in tubs, where we had first met, that they were waiting when J. and I passed through the turnstile. The leader with unwonted ceremony stepped forward to greet me and lead the way to the table they called mine. His wife was sitting there.

I knew them so well now that before they spoke I was conscious of their unusual excitement. When they spoke it was with strangely boisterous gaiety; their eyes shone with a new light; there was triumph in their smiles. The little soft-eyed man for the first time wished me ' *Latcho ratti*,' while Rudi speechless danced about my chair. The gipsy with the scar was as gay as were the others.

What did it mean? I cannot explain why I was uneasy. I was not afraid, not distrustful. And yet instinctively I wished I had not come. The evening would not pass as had the many I had spent dreaming my own dreams, my thoughts far away in other gardens, on other hillsides, while I listened to their music : of this I was sure before I had been with them ten minutes. And when they played? Rudi was right. Never before had I heard all that violins and cymbal could tell.

Their music was entirely Hungarian. One Czardas after another quickened into frenzy in the warm still night, while the waiters rushed in and out among the tables, and the Germans drank deep and long from their beer-mugs. But now the wail of sorrow was at once silenced by a pæan of joy. They came to me again during the first interval, and the Czardas had not quieted them. The leader sent for a bottle of Hungarian wine. Was it that, and not the music, which had gone to their heads? I stilled the suspicion as disloyal even before it took definite shape. Indeed had theirs been ordinary intoxication it would have troubled me less. There was something far more alarming in the solemnity with which the leader filled the glasses, and all, clinking mine, drank to me in the wine of their country, and cried aloud their ' Servus ! Viva ! Eljen ! '

I grew more uneasy at these uncanny sounds, which I have since learned are harmless. Even as they drank, I determined to leave the garden as soon as the gipsies returned to the band-stand, and not to wait for the last friendly farewell after the Rakotzy had beaten a dismissal. Again they played a Czardas, all fire and passion.

But I rose to go. Without seeing, I knew that their eyes followed my every movement. ' *Latcho ratti !* ' I said to the leader's wife, who could speak but Hungarian.

Sitting with her were two fellow-countrymen, not gipsies, whom she had met for the first time that night. She was talking with them, and at my ' good night ' turned in surprise. She took both my hands and forced me into my chair.

I told her in English, though I knew she could not understand, that I must catch a train, that I could not wait. And I struggled to get up. She protested almost with tears. She held my hands tight, she looked to Sandor, she half rose, hesitated, and then suddenly spoke to the Hungarians at her side, while, all the time, the gipsies watched and played a remonstrance. One of the Hungarians lifted his hat : ' She begs you not to go,' he said.

' Tell her, please, that I have a train to catch.'

There was despair in her face, and she clung to my hands. Again he translated : ' She says Sandor has something of importance to talk to you about. You cannot go.'

' But I must ! I must ! ' I cried. The more she insisted, the more eager was I to be gone,—not to hear that something Sandor had to say. I could not draw my hands from hers, and again she spoke to her interpreter fast and earnestly, never once looking from me. There was a twinkle in his eye, but he said gravely and respectfully :

' Madam, she implores that you stay. Sandor to-night will ask for your hand in marriage for his brother. He is wealthy. He plays well. He will take you to many lands, to his beautiful Hungary. You will be rich, you will have the gipsy music with you always.'

This then was what it meant. I had been living my own romance in their music ; they had been making one for me.

' It 's impossible,' I said. ' I must catch my train. It 's all a dreadful mistake. I cannot stay another minute. I 'm so sorry ! '

And I wrenched my hands from hers. Without a look at the band-stand, though I felt all their eyes upon me, and trembled at the madness of the Czardas, I fled from the garden and the gipsies to Ninth and Green streets, through the depot, into the cars. The train had not started before I regretted my flight. Was ever yet woman's curiosity put to so cruel a test ? I had a lover among the gipsies ; so much I knew. But which one of these swarthy men was Sandor's brother, and indeed which Sandor was it who had a brother ? Rudi loved the dark-eyed Marie in his Karpathian home, but then one or two more wives to a Hungarian gipsy would be no great matter. Herr Josef with the flashing opals and the velvet coat seemed the Croesus of the band. Was it he whom I had refused with such reckless incoherence ? Or was it the big bass-viol player who wanted a new mother for his boy ? Or the flageolet-player, the full tenderness of whose pantomime I had not grasped ? Or that soft-eyed, shy creature, or the mysterious one with the scarred cheek ? I could not go back and ask. Never now would I know the lover, with whom I might have wandered from land to land, at whose side, under the starlit skies of Hungary, I might forever have listened to the gipsy music.

Elizabeth Robins Pennell.

Victoria R.

SUNDAY, 25TH DECEMBER (XMAS DAY 1836).—At a little before 2, dearest Lehzen, Victoire and I went out and came home at 3. As we were approaching *the camp*, we met Rea coming from it, who had been sent there by Mamma to enquire into the story of these poor wanderers. He told us (what I was quite sure of before) that all was quite true, that the poor young woman and baby were doing very well, though very weak and miserable, and that what they wanted chiefly was fuel and nourishment. Mamma has ordered broth and fuel to be sent tonight, as also 2 blankets ; and several of our people have sent old flannel things for them. Mamma has ordered that the broth and fuel is to be sent each day till the woman is recovered. Lehzen sent them by our footmen a little worsted knit jacket for the poor baby, and when we drove by, Aunt Sarah, the old woman and the Husband all looked out and bowed most gratefully. Rea gave them directly a sovereign. I cannot say how happy I am that these poor creatures are assisted, for they are such a nice set of Gipsies, so quiet, so affectionate to one another, so discreet, not at all forward or importunate, and *so* grateful ; so unlike the gossiping, fortune-telling race-gipsies ; and this is such a peculiar and touching case. Their being assisted makes me quite merry and happy today, for yesterday night when I was safe and happy at home in that cold night and today when it snowed so and everything looked white, I felt quite unhappy and grieved to think that our poor gipsy friends should perish and shiver for want ; and now today I shall go to bed happy, knowing they are better off and more comfortable. . . .

THURSDAY, 29TH DECEMBER. . . . At 12 we went out with dear Lehzen and came home at 2. Everything still looked very white and the ground rather slippery but not so much as yesterday. It snowed part of the time we were walking. I saw Aunt Sarah and the least pretty of the two sisters-in-law, who has returned, in a shop in Esher. How I *do* wish I could do something for their *spiritual* and *mental* benefit and for the education of their children and in particular for the poor little baby who I have known since its birth, in the admirable manner Mr. Crabbe in his *Gipsies' Advocate* so strongly urges ; he beseeches and urges those who have kind hearts and Christian feelings to think of these poor wanderers, who have many good qualities and who have many good people among them. He says, and alas ! I *too well* know its truth, from experience, that whenever any poor Gipsies are encamped anywhere and crimes and robberies &c. occur, it is invariably laid to their account, which is shocking ; and if they are always looked upon as vagabonds, how *can* they become good people ? I trust in Heaven that the day may come when *I* may do something for these poor people, and for this particular family ! I am sure that the little kindness which they have experienced from us will have a good and lasting effect on them ! . . .

SUNDAY, 8TH JANUARY, 1837. . . . It is today a week that we took leave of our poor good friends the Gipsies, and I am quite sorry when I pass the spot so long enlivened by their little camp, and behold it empty and deserted, and with almost no trace to be seen of their ever having been there. They had been there more than a month, for they encamped there about 5 days after we arrived here and have been there ever since until last Wednesday or Thursday. To *my* feeling, the chief ornament of the Portsmouth Road is gone since their departure. But this is their life ; they are happy and grateful and we have done them some good. The place and spot may be forgotten, but the Gipsy family Cooper will *never* be obliterated from my memory ! . . .

Queen Victoria's Diaries, 1836-7.
By permission : from ' The Girlhood of Queen Victoria,'
published by Mr. John Murray.

A Gypsy Poet

AS early in the morning
Before the tents I pass,
'Tis good for me to see you there,
You little Roman lass.

In pity and wide wonder
My face your dark eyes scan :
' Who art thou, and what ailest thee,
Thou big unhappy man ? '

' I am a Gypsy poet, dear,
And Scholar Gypsy true :
If all the strongest names be named
Then mine is namèd too.

' And what ails me, Egyptian child,
Ails many of our crew :
If all the world's worst ills were named
Then mine were namèd too.'

Adapted from Heine.

Count Arnaldos

I

WHO had ever such adventure,
  Holy priest, or virgin nun,
As befel the Count Arnaldos
  At the rising of the sun ?

II

On his wrist the hawk was hooded,
  Forth with horn and hound went he,
When he saw a stately galley
  Sailing on the silent sea.

III

Sails of satin, masts of cedar,
  Burnish'd poop of beaten gold—
Many a morn you 'll hood your falcon
  Ere you such a bark behold.

IV

Sails of satin, masts of cedar,
  Golden poops may come again,
But mortal ear no more shall listen
  To yon grey-hair'd sailor's strain.

V

Heart may beat, and eye may glisten,
  Faith is strong, and Hope is free,
But mortal ear no more shall listen
  To the song that rules the sea.

VI

When the grey-hair'd sailor chaunted,
  Every wind was hush'd to sleep—
Like a virgin's bosom panted
  All the wide reposing deep.

VII

Bright in beauty rose the star-fish
From her green cave down below,
Right above the eagle poised him—
Holy music charm'd them so.

VIII

' Stately galley ! glorious galley !
God hath pour'd his grace on thee !
Thou alone mayst scorn the perils
Of the dread devouring sea !

IX

' False Almeria's reefs and shallows,
Black Gibraltar's giant rocks,
Sound and sand-bank, gulf and whirlpool,
All—my glorious galley mocks ! '—

X

' For the sake of God, our maker ! '—
(Count Arnaldos' cry was strong,)
' Old man, let me be partaker
In the secret of thy song ! '—

XI

' Count Arnaldos ! Count Arnaldos !
Hearts I read, and thoughts I know—
Wouldst thou learn the ocean secret,
In our galley thou must go.'—

Spanish Ballad.

XII
ENVOY

XII

Envoy

Mr. Petulengro's Opinion of Life and Death

'WHAT is your opinion of death, Mr. Petulengro?'
said I, as I sat down beside him.
'My opinion of death, brother, is much the same as that
in the old song of Pharaoh, which I have heard my grandam sing :—

> "Cana marel o manus chivios andé puv,
> Ta rovel pa leste o chavo ta romi."

When a man dies, he is cast into the earth, and his wife and
child sorrow over him. If he has neither wife nor child,
then his father and mother, I suppose ; and if he is quite
alone in the world, why, then, he is cast into the earth, and
there is an end of the matter.'
'And do you think that is the end of a man?'
'There's an end of him, brother, more's the pity.'
'Why do you say so?'
'Life is sweet, brother.'
'Do you think so?'
'Think so ! There's night and day, brother, both
sweet things ; sun, moon, and stars, brother, all sweet
things ; there's likewise a wind on the heath. Life is
very sweet, brother ; who would wish to die?'
'I would wish to die——'
'You talk like a gorgio—which is the same as talking
like a fool—were you a Rommany Chal you would talk
wiser. Wish to die, indeed ! A Rommany Chal would
wish to live for ever !'
'In sickness, Jasper?'
'There's the sun and stars, brother.'
'In blindness, Jasper?'
'There's the wind on the heath, brother ; if I could
only feel that, I would gladly live for ever. Dosta, we'll
now go to the tents and put on the gloves ; and I'll try
to make you feel what a sweet thing it is to be alive,
brother !'

George Borrow.

329

Notes

I. THE DARK RACE

PAGE
3. CERVANTES. 'La Gitanilla de Madrid.' (*Novelas Exemplares*. 1614.)

4. SYMONS. 'In Praise of Gypsies.' (*Journal of the Gypsy Lore Society*, n.s. i. 295-7.)

5. RUSKIN. 'The Madonna and the Gypsy.' (*Roadside Songs of Tuscany*. 1885.)

5. LOWELL. 'The Nomades'; stanzas 5 and 6. (*Under the Willows*. 1869.)

6. BORROW. *The Romany Rye*; vol. i. chap. ix. 1857. *cukkerin* and *dukkerin* means ' cuckooing and telling fortunes.'

8. HOPKINS. 'Inversnaid'; the last stanza. (From *Poems*, ed. Robert Bridges. 1918.)

8. JEFFERIES. 'Just before Winter.' (*Field and Hedgerow*. 1889.)

10. RUSKIN. From ' The Gipsies,' a poem offered by J. R. (*aet.* 17) in 1837 for the Newdigate Prize, which was won, however, by the more academic lines of Dean Stanley (cp. p. 21). A high compassion characterizes these juvenile verses. In the lines quoted Ruskin endeavours to enter into the social feelings of the Gypsy, but without any true knowledge.

11. IRVING. 'Gipsies.' (*Bracebridge Hall*. 1822.)

12. WAUGH. *Jannock*; chap. iii. [1873]. The scene is in North Lancashire by the River Duddon. The Gypsies described are perhaps some of the Grays.

13. BÉRANGER. ' Les Bohémiens.' (*Chansons Inédites*. 1828.)

15. H. SMITH. *Miscellaneous Poems*, 1846. The book referred to in stanza 5 is the popular *History and Curious Adventures of Bampfylde-Moore Carew* (1745). This ' King of the Mendicants ' was, however, not a Gypsy, and his account of Gypsy rites and ceremonials is purely fictitious.

16. C. SMITH. A Gypsy jest, quoted in the original Romani, *J. G. L. S.* iii. 245.

17. BORROW. *The Zincali*, Pt. II. chap. i. (1841), with the title ' The Steeds of the Egyptians drink the Waters of the Guadiana.' According to Borrow ' the Gitanos of Estremadura call themselves in general Chai or Chabos, and say that their original country was Chal or Egypt.' In the compound *Romanichal* (a generic name for the Gypsies), *chal*, however, is merely a variant of *chavo*, ' son ' or ' lad.' This song is written in Firdausi's measure. Cp. ' The Black Zigan,' p. 31.

331

PAGE

17. FIRDAUSI (*ob.* 1024). From the Persian epic the *Shâhnâma*, trans. A. G. and E. Warner; vol. vii. sect. 39. We have here the legendary account of the importation of the Gypsies into Persia by the monarch Bahram Gur—Omar's 'great Hunter'—the same story being related in prose half a century earlier by the Arabian historian Hamza of Ispahan. The prevalence of such a myth shows that the Luri or Gypsies must have been settled in Persia some time before the beginning of the tenth century. The Persian text of this passage, with English prose translation, is given by Col. Harriott in *Trans. of the Royal Asiatic Society* (1830), vol. ii. pp. 527-8.

19. SYMON SIMEONIS. From the *Itineraria* of this Irish Franciscan monk, who made the pilgrimage to the Holy Land in 1322. This early reference to the Gypsies in Europe was first noted by Jacob Bryant in *Archaeologia* (1785).

19. HUGO. *Notre Dame de Paris*, Bk. v. chap. iii.; trans. J. C. Beckwith. The novelist probably took his facts from Estienne Pasquier's *Recherches de la France*. 1596.

20. BROWNE. *Pseudodoxia Epidemica*; Bk. VI. chap. xiii. 1646.

21. STANLEY. From 'The Gipsies' (Oxford Prize Poem). 1837.

22. VON HOFMANNSWALDAU. An Epitaph quoted by Pischel in his *Heimat der Zigeuner*. An English translation of this article, by D. E. Yates, is given in *J. G. L. S.* n.s. ii. 292 *sqq.* :—
'In stern wanderings I spent my life;
Two lines will teach you who I've been.
Egypt, Hungary, Switzerland, Beelzebub, and Swabia,
Have named, reared, fed, slain and buried me.'

22. VOLTAIRE. *Essai sur les mœurs et l'esprit des nations*; chap. civ. 1756.

23. PHILLIPS. 'A Morning's Walk from London to Kew.' (*Monthly Magazine*; Oct. 1816, Jan. 1817.) Cp. Borrow's somewhat uncharitable sketch of Sir Richard as 'the Publisher' in *Lavengro*, chap. xxx. and *passim*.

25. S. ROBERTS. A pleasant outburst in the chapter on English Gypsies in Roberts' work *The Gypsies: their origin, continuance and destination; or the Sealed Book Opened* (1836). Roberts held that the Gypsies were Egyptians dispersed by divine decree.

25. LELAND. *The Gypsies*. 1882.

25. BORROW. *The Zincali*; pref. to 2nd ed. 1843. 'Miss Pinfold' was the daughter of Charlie Pinfold, who was beaten by Jem Mace in a fight for a purse of £10, on Norwich Hill, about 1850.

26. BUNYAN. This passage from *Grace Abounding* (1666), considered in conjunction with Bunyan's swarthy complexion and tinker's trade, to which I may add such typical feats as converting the leg of his prison chair into a flute, supports the

PAGE

view that the author of *The Pilgrim's Progress* was of Gypsy race. See W. Simson *passim*. The theory has been further confirmed by Groome's discovery of an entry in a Cornish Parish Register, recording the baptism in 1586 of a certain ' James, sonne of Nicholas Bownia, an Egiptiä rogue.'

26. JONSON. *A Masque of the Metamorphosed Gypsies.* 1621.

27. DEKKER. *Lanthorne and Candle-light* ; chap. viii. 1608. ' Moonmen,' as in the previous extract, was an Elizabethan name for the Gypsies, which did not live long. Cp. Shakespeare, 1 *Henry IV*. i. ii. 30: ' Let us be Diana's foresters, gentlemen of the shade, minions of the moon.' We find the same fancy in Baudrimont, who says of the Basque Gypsies (1862), ' Leurs exploits ont plus souvent été éclairés par la lune que le soleil.' Dekker's picturesque account shows some personal knowledge of their habits. He is, for instance, the first writer to describe the Gypsy trail or *patrin* (Borrow's *patteran*, see p. 294). His reference to the fine undergarments worn beneath the outward rags is convincing, while his picture of several Gypsies astride of a single horse may be compared with Shakespeare's simile in *As You Like It* (v. 3), ' both in a tune, like two gipsies on a horse.'

28. WYNNE. From Borrow's translation of the *Bardd Cwsc*, 1703 (The Sleeping Bard), a prose allegorical narrative, written by the Rector of Llandanwg somewhat in the manner of Quevedo's *Visions*. The Gypsies described are probably members of the ' Teulu Abram Wd.,' shortly before the permanent settlement of this tribe, who were the first to enter Wales. A later reference to this famous family of Wood is found in the Interlude *Pleser a Gofid (Pleasure and Grief)* of Twm o'r Nant (Thomas [Edwards] of the Dingle), where ' Aunty Sal from the South ' enquires :

' Do you know Abram Wood, my cousin ; he travels Wales and England ? '

to which Rondol replies :

' Oh I have seen some Sypsiwns about the world, stealing very eagerly, and the infernal " gêr " did a dirty trick at Welshpool—frightenin' the Sessions out of the hall by their hellish fierce tricks.'

30. COWPER. ' The Sofa.' (*The Task* ; Bk. i. 1785.) I omit the two lines—

' They swathe the forehead, drag the limping limb, And vex their flesh with artificial sores,'

in which Cowper falsely attributes to the Gypsies the loathly practice of the Palliards, or ' beggars who counterfeit sores '— a variety of English rogue described by Harman in his *Caveat for Commen Cursitors* (1566). Nor, it may be added, does the Gypsy appetite for *mulo mas* or ' carrion ' extend to ragout de chicn. ll. 14-16 may contain an allusion to the *baro χoχiben* or 'grand deception' (Borrow's *hokkano baro*) ; see the reference to the 'great secret' in 'The Three Words,' p. 291. A 'great secret' truly !—but one which I must never disclose.

31. FIRDAUSI. From the *Sháhnáma*, in Borrow's translation (*The Zincali*, Pt. II. chap. i.). Where precisely this passage occurs in Firdausi's vast epic I may be forgiven for not knowing, but that it is really a translation is evidenced by the metre in which Borrow renders it. Borrovians may recall that one of the expedients resorted to by his friends, when desirous of restoring him to good temper, was to invite him to recite Persian poetry, which he did with great fervour and with happy result.

31. HAZLITT. 'On Personal Identity.' (*Monthly Magazine* ; Jan. 1828.)

31. BORROW. 'Book of the Wisdom of the Egyptians.' (*Romano Lavo-Lil.*) 1874.

32. MIDDLETON AND ROWLEY. *The Spanish Gipsie* ; Act IV. sc. i. Acted 1623 ; publ. 1653.

II. THE ROAMING LIFE

35. CATULLUS. Carmen XLVI.

35. CHAUCER. Prologue (*Canterbury Tales*), in the text of Skeat, but with 'April' for 'Aprille,' as with Bridges.

35. BROME. *A Joviall Crew* or *The Merry Beggars*. 1641.

36. SPENSER. From *Muiopotmos* ; stanza 27.

36. CROFTON. From the Introduction to *The Dialect of the English Gypsies*. 1875.

37. SITWELL. *The Visit of the Gypsies* ; pp. 140-1. See note to p. 109.

38. JEFFERIES. 'Just before Winter.' (*Field and Hedgerow*.)

39. GEORGE ELIOT. The opening verse of a song from *The Spanish Gypsy* (1868), a poem which the authoress modestly compares in motive to the great Greek tragedies, and in spirit to the work of the Elizabethan dramatists. See her *Life as related in her Letters and Journals*, vol. iii. chap. xv.

39. YOXALL. *The Rommany Stone*. 1902.

40. VAMBÉRY. From *Arminius Vambéry : his Life and Adventures written by Himself*.

40. SHAKESPEARE. Song of Autolycus in *Winter's Tale* ; Act IV. sc. iii.

40. HAZLITT. 'On Going a Journey.' (*New Monthly Magazine*. 1822.)

41. STEVENSON. 'The Vagabond.' (*Songs of Travel*. 1896.) A happy rendering of this poem into deep Romani will be found in the *Romani Versions* of Sir Donald MacAlister of Tarbert. The first stanza runs thus :—

> 'Ak'o tacho jivibén,
> Sau vavra nakáva,
> Savimásko tem oprál,
> Drom poshál te java.
> Me sová 're piro vesht,
> Pani piá mârésa :
> Ak'o jivibén ki mai,
> Fededér jivésa ? '

42. GALSWORTHY. *In Chancery* ; chap. vii.

42. LEIGH HUNT. From his *Autobiography* ; chap. xxiii.

43. BUNYAN. *Pilgrim's Progress* ; Pt. II.

43. DE QUINCEY. *Confessions of an English Opium-Eater.* 1822.

44. KINGSLEY. Part of a rhyming Invitation to Tom Hughes and Tom Taylor, before these three friends set out on a walking-tour in Wales, in Aug. 1856. Tom Taylor, dramatist and editor of *Punch*, was, and signed himself, a 'Romany Rai' : his 'Gypsey Experiences,' contributed to the *Illustrated London News*, 1851, are reprinted (with running commentary from the Romanichals) in Groome's *In Gipsy Tents*, chap. x.

45. DICKENS. *Martin Chuzzlewit* ; chap. xxxvi.

45. SACKVILLE-WEST. A stanza from 'Fallen Youth' in *Orchard and Vineyard.* 1921.

46. E. THOMAS. *Poems.* 1920. 'Helen of the roads' is Helena, daughter of Eudda or Octavius, wife to the Emperor Maximus, and mother of Constantine, who gave her name to the Sarn Helen (Helen's causeway), the Ffordd Gam Elen (the winding way of Helen), and many another ancient track in Wales.

48. SWINBURNE. From *The Tale of Balen* ; vii.

48. MANGAN. *Poems.* 1859. The last three stanzas of an 'Apocryphal' translation from the Arabic.

49. HODGSON. *Eve and Other Poems.* 1913.

50. BRIDGES. *The Testament of Beauty* ; Bk. I. I quote these lines in the form in which I first met them, when privileged to read this noble poem in proof.

50. BAUDELAIRE. *Les Fleurs du Mal* ; xiii. Thus Englished by Arthur Symons :—

'GYPSIES ON THE ROAD

' The tribe of fortune-tellers with ardent eyes
   Move on along a road, carrying upon
   Their backs their children, or letting one by one
Satiate its fierce thirst on breasts that never rise.

'Men walk on foot, gazing without surprise,
Beside their caravans, toward the sun
To seek chimeras that they have not won,
With gloomy grief beneath the leaden skies.

'In his retreat, the sudden grasshopper,
Seeing them pass, repeats his double whirr ;
Cybele, who loves them, makes the grass more green,

'Makes deserts flower, water from rocks to flow,
Before these wanderers, who in vision know
Dark empires of those futures they have seen.'

51. BROWNING. 'Flight of the Duchess'; sect. xiii. 1845.

51. PUSHKIN. *Tzigane* (1827); translated from the original by my
friend Oliver Elton, and printed *J. G. L. S.* (3rd ser. vii. 3-4).
A French prose translation of the whole poem is found in
Mérimée's *Les Bohémiens*, which gave Tolstoy 'a new con-
ception of Pushkin's genius.' Tolstoy himself was enchanted
by the singing of Gypsy choirs, and, as his son Count Sergius
tells us, once contemplated writing a story about Gypsy life.

53. GLATIGNY. *Les Vignes Folles.* 1860.

54. MATTHEW ARNOLD. From 'Resignation' (*The Strayed Reveller
and Other Poems.* 1849.)

55. MASEFIELD. 'Vagabond.' (*Salt Water Ballads.* 1902.)

56. BUNYAN. *Pilgrim's Progress* ; Pt. II.

III. FIELD AND SKY

59. SHAKESPEARE. *As You Like It*; Act II. sc. 5. Sir Charles
Strachey's happy conjecture (*J. G. L. S.* iii. 96-9) that all the
allusions here are to Gypsy life, and that *ducdame* itself is a
Gypsy word, has been accepted by Shakespeare's latest textual
editor, Mr. John Dover Wilson, in the new Cambridge
edition : ' The word is one of those textual cruxes in
Shakespeare to which great attention has been given, Furness'
Variorum edition devoting three pages to it. The probable if
not certain solution has now however been known for some
years, though it has not as yet, we believe, been set forth
completely in print. The word is in short a corruption or
mishearing of the Romani *dukrá mē*, which became *dukdá mē*
by the not infrequent change of *r* to *d*, these letters being
closely connected in pronunciation in Romani. The expression, which means "I foretell, I tell fortunes or prophesy,"
fits the context perfectly. As the call of the Gipsy fortune-
teller at fairs or public gatherings, it is a " Greek (=sharper's)
invocation to call fools into a circle." The interpretation
also renders the reference to " the first-born of Egypt "
intelligible. . . . The point of Jaques' skit upon Amiens' song

is now obvious : the members of the banished court are so
many amateur Gipsies, forced to lead this uncomfortable life
by the " stubborn will " of the Duke, who as the elder
brother is " the first-born of Egypt." ' Further evidence,
showing that Gypsies were in Shakespeare's mind at the time
he wrote this play, is to be found in the speech of the Second
Page (v. 3) : ' I' faith, i' faith, and both in a tune, like two
gipsies on a horse.' (Cp. note to Dekker, p. 27.)

60. KEATS. With the title ' Meg Merrilies,' in a playful letter to
his sister Fanny Keats, July 2, 1818.

61. DICKENS. ' Tramps.' (*The Uncommercial Traveller* ; xi. 1861.)

61. MITFORD. ' The Old Gypsy.' (*Our Village*. 1824-32.) Miss
Mitford's village is Three Mile Cross in Berkshire.

63. STEVENSON. ' Beggars.' (*Scribner's Magazine*. 1889.)

64. J. ROBERTS. Groome (*In Gipsy Tents*, chap. iv.) gives this title to
a passage in a letter to him from John Roberts, the Welsh
Gypsy harper. The original, as one may see from the early
copy, printed with many mistakes by George Smith of Coalville in *Gipsy Life* (pp. 209 *sqq.*), contains several Romani
words and sentences which Groome has translated. I change
his ' comrades ' (for *chovolay*) to ' children,' as the word
' comrade ' is never used by Gypsies and now seems to have
been appropriated by the propagandists of Communism.

66. BUNYAN. *Pilgrim's Progress* ; Pt. I.

66. MEREDITH. Kiomi speaks. (*The Adventures of Harry Richmond* ; chap. vii. 1870.)

67. JEFFERIES. ' Just before Winter.' (*Field and Hedgerow*.)

68. EIFION WYN. Translated from ' Y Sipsiwn ' (*Caniadau'r Allt*,
1927) by J. Glyn Davies. I quote the first stanza in the
original :—

' Gwelais ei fen liw dydd
    Ar ffordd yr ucheldir iach,
A'i ferlod yn pori'r ffrith
    Yng ngofal ei epil bach ;
Ac yntau yn chwilio 'r nant
    Fel garan, o dro i dro,
Gan annos ei filgi brych rhwng y brwyn,
    A'i chwiban yn deffro'r fro.'

68. S. BOSWELL. A translation from the original Anglo-Romani,
given as a specimen of the speech in Smart and Crofton's
Dialect of the English Gypsies.

69. BLUNDEN. From *The Shepherd and Other Poems of Peace and War*.
1922.

70. WORDSWORTH. ' Gipsies.' (' Poems of the Imagination.'
1807.) Hazlitt's criticism which follows misses the chief

Y

point, though it scores another. The 'wild outcasts of Society' whom the moralist resents finding seated round their camp-fire in the evening, as he had left them in the morning, were, it may be presumed, not inactive during the whole interval. The error may have been suggested to his mind by the immovable attitude of the Gypsy in repose, which, however, is succeeded by a sudden and irresistible energy when he is aroused. The poem in fact throws a stronger light on the temper of Wordsworth himself than on that of the Gypsies.

71. HAZLITT. 'On Manner.' (*Round Table*, no. 12, note 2. 1815.) Hazlitt, who has both understanding of the Gypsies and sympathy with their love of freedom (cp. pp. 31 and 210, and *passim* in his own works), thoroughly enjoys this tilt at Wordsworth.

72. MASEFIELD. From *The Everlasting Mercy*. 1911. Mr. Masefield beautifully overcomes a difficulty which may have occurred to those who realize the difference between *Gavéngere* (city-dwellers) and *Théméskere* (dwellers in the country).

72. OLD IRISH SONG. The defence of a country life by Marban the Hermit, in a colloquy with his brother, King Guaire of Connaught, who wishes him to return to his rank of warrior prince. Translated from an Old Irish poem of the tenth century by Kuno Meyer. (*Four Songs of Summer and Winter*. 1903.)

75. WALTON. *The Compleat Angler*. 1653.

75. BRIDGES. From *The Testament of Beauty*; Bk. 1. ll. 65-107—a passage which Dr. Bridges generously contributed to my *Festschrift*. (*J. G. L. S.* 3rd ser. vii. 3-4. 1928.)

77. LYLY. From *Alexander and Campaspe*. 1584.

77. OLD IRISH SONG. *Four Songs of Summer and Winter*. Trans. Kuno Meyer.

79. KEATS. Sonnet written Dec. 30, 1816.

79. CLEAR. From *The Eldest Sister and Other Poems*. 1927.

80. WORDSWORTH. Composed 1802; published as one of the 'Evening Voluntaries.' 1807.

80. DAFYDD AB GWILYM. This monachal figure comes from a fourteenth-century poem of Dafydd ab Gwilym, chief bard of Glamorganshire, entitled 'Aflwydd y Bardd ar nos Dywyll, a Mawl i'r Ser a'i Goleuodd yn Ddiogel,' 'The Mishap of the Bard on a dark night, and Praise to the Stars that lightened him safely.' Trans. J. Glyn Davies (*Cymmrodorion Trans.*, 1912-13).

81. HUDSON. *Hampshire Days*. 1906.

81. STEVENSON. *Travels with a Donkey in the Cevennes*. 1879.

82. GOETHE. In a letter to Frau von Stein, Sept. 1780. This translation of the ' Wandrers Nachtlied ' is by Longfellow.

IV. GYPSIES AND GENTILES

85. BLAKE. *Marriage of Heaven and Hell.* 1790.

85. ROMANI SAYING. In deep Gypsy: *Kushké si kherá kherengeréngi,* or in Anglo-Romani ' The *ker* is *kushko* for the *kerengero.*'

85. BORROW. From ' Book of the Wisdom of the Egyptians.' (*Romano Lavo-Lil.*)

85. BORROW. *The Zincali* ; Pt. II. chap. i.

86. BORROW. *The Zincali* ; Pt. II. chap. iv. The reference is to the Gitano Rhyme no. 75 ; cp. p. 168.

> ' Io no camelo ser eray
> Que es Calo mi nacimiento ;
> Io no camelo ser eray,
> Con ser Calo me contento.'

> ' O I am not of gentle clan,
> I 'm sprung from Gypsy tree ;
> And I will be no gentleman,
> But an Egyptian free.'

86. SACKVILLE-WEST. *Orchard and Vineyard.* 1921.

87. HOUSMAN. From *Last Poems* ; no. xii. 1922. The remainder of the poem runs :—

> ' And how am I to face the odds
> Of man's bedevilment and God's ?
> I, a stranger and afraid
> In a world I never made.
> They will be master, right or wrong ;
> Though both are foolish, both are strong.
> And since, my soul, we cannot fly
> To Saturn nor to Mercury,
> Keep we must, if keep we can,
> These foreign laws of God and man.'

87. SYMONS. ' In Praise of Gypsies.' (*J. G. L. S.* n.s. i. 298. 1908.)

88. DEED OF 1596. From a deed belonging to the family of Seys of Boverton Place in the county of Glamorgan. Printed in full in *Archaeologia Cambrensis,* 4th ser. vol. xiii. 1882 ; and thence in *J. G. L. S.* n.s. ii. 336. The Acts which rendered it capital to be one of the people calling themselves Egyptians were not repealed until 1772.

89. JEFFERIES. ' Country Places.' (*Field and Hedgerow.*)

PAGE

90. BORROW. *Romano Lavo-Lil*; p. 131.

90. LELAND. I omit the two penultimate stanzas depicting forms of gentile boredom. From *English Gipsy Songs, in Rommany with Metrical English Translations*; by Charles G. Leland, Professor E. H. Palmer, and Janet Tuckey (1875). It was of this publication that Palmer wrote to his collaborator, suggesting an appeal *ad misericordiam* to the public: 'You are earnestly requested to subscribe to the above work; it is the composition of a blind orphan who is deaf and dumb and has no use of his limbs. Unless 50,000 copies at a penny each are taken by a Christian and sympathising public, the book will remain unpublished, and the writer will have no resource but the workhouse or dishonesty.'

92. SHAW. *Cashel Byron's Profession*. 1886.

92. PALMER. From *English Gipsy Songs*. Except for a few 'minute particulars,' every line of this poem rings true both in Romani and in English.

93. HAZLITT. 'On Personal Identity.' (*Monthly Magazine*; Jan. 1828.)

93. HUDSON. *A Shepherd's Life*. 1910.

93. BORROW. *The Romany Rye*; vol. i. chap. v. 1857.

95. FIELDING. *Tom Jones*; chap. xii. 1749. I omit the monarch's somewhat tedious description of Gypsy Polity, which, it may be noted, has its sole derivation in *Bampfylde-Moore Carew*, published four years earlier (see note to p. 15). A trace of Fielding's personal acquaintance with the broken speech of the English Gypsies is found in the dialect of the King, who uses *d* for *th* ('de,' 'dose,' 'dey,' 'vid,' etc.), and is doubtful as to his pronouns—solecisms not found in Carew.

99. CRABBE. 'The Lover's Journey.' (*Tales*; x, ll. 141-203.) 1812.

99. LENAU. *I.e.* Nicolaus Franz Niembsch von Strehlenau: 'Die Drei Zigeuner,' trans. C. G. Leland in *The Gypsies*.

100. SCOTT. *Guy Mannering*; chap. viii. Jacques Callot (I amend Scott's 'Calotte') takes rank as one of the earliest and foremost of Romany Ryes. Running away from his father's home in Lorraine at the age of twelve, with the intention of studying art in Rome, he travelled with a band of Gypsies as far as Florence; and it is these people whose costume and customs he so graphically depicts in the four plates for which he is famous. He was in their company for six or eight weeks, and the plates were engraved eighteen years later, in 1622.

102. S. ROBERTS. *The Gypsies*. 1836.

102. SCOTT. *Quentin Durward*; chap. xvi. In drawing the character of the Gypsy Hayraddin, Scott may have been influenced by Shakespeare's Barnardine in *Measure for Measure*, ' a Bohemian

NOTES 341

born . . . That apprehends no further than this world, And squares his life according.'

104. KINGLAKE. *Eothen*; chap. xii. 1844.

105. HUDSON. From *A Shepherd's Life*. 1910.

105. WORDSWORTH. ' Peter Bell '; Part First. Composed 1798; publ. 1819. Wordsworth probably drew this portrait from some of the travelling potter class, whom he may have encountered in the Lake District more frequently than true-bred Gypsies.

106. PENNELL. *To Gipsyland*; pp. 211-12. 1893.

107. LISZT. *Die Zigeuner und ihre Musik in Ungarn*; chap. xiv. 1861.

108. BORROW. *The Zincali*; Pt. II. chap. viii. Borrow's translation of the Gospel of St. Luke into Spanish Romani, published in 1837, was, he tells us, treated by the Gitanas as a charm to bring them luck in their thieving expeditions. ' Ustilar à pastesas ' is defined by Mérimée, in *Carmen*, as ' voler avec adresse, dérober sans violence.'

109. SITWELL. *The Visit of the Gypsies*. 1929. The tapestry which Mr. Sitwell here describes formerly hung in the Château d'Effiat, and was embroidered at Tournai about the end of the fifteenth century. It therefore gives us a contemporary picture.

110. MURRAY. 'English Gypsy Dress.' (*J. G. L. S.* iii. 115-19. 1892.) Philip Murray was an old Irish tinker, who spoke both Shelta and Romani. Marrying a Gypsy woman, Harriet Smith, he lived among the ' old 'stablished Romani-chals ' until her death, and thus had unique opportunities of obtaining curious information as to the manners, dress, and super-stitions of the English Gypsies of a hundred years ago.

113. JOHN. ' Russian Gypsies at Marseilles and Milan.' (*J. G. L. S.* n.s. iv. 217. 1911.)

113. SKELTON. 'Elynour Rummynge.' *c.* 1517. See Crofton's comment on this passage. (*J. G. L. S.* n.s. ii. 209-10.)

114. WORDSWORTH. The first three stanzas of ' Beggars '; composed 1802, publ. 1807. From Dorothy's description of Gypsies she had met near the quarry at the head of Rydal Lake.

114. AUSTEN. *Emma*; chap. xxxix. I take my title from Borrow's ' Mang, Prala.' (*Romano Lavo-Lil.*)

115. THOMPSON. *J. G. L. S.* 3rd ser. iv. 139-42. 1925.

119. MARSTON. *J. G. L. S.* n.s. i. 191. 1907.

120. OMAR KHAYYAM. *Quatrains of Omar Khayyam*, from a literal prose translation, by Edward Heron-Allen, of the earliest known manuscript; done into verse by Arthur B. Talbot; quatrain 115.

V. THE ROMANY CHYE

PAGE
123. S. ROBERTS. *The Gypsies.* 1836.

123. BORROW. 'The English Gypsies.' (*Romano Lavo-Lil.*)

124. NAIDU. From *The Golden Threshold*, written, as Arthur Symons tells us (*J. G. L. S.* n.s. vii. 151), by an Indian lady of ancient family, whom he knew as a girl of seventeen—'as wise as she was young.' By 'Indian Gypsy' perhaps we should understand the Jat, who are a pastoral people.

124. CERVANTES. 'La Gitanilla de Madrid.' (*Novelas Exemplares.*)

125. ALFORD. 'The Gypsy Girl.' (*Poems.* 1845.)

125. WATTS-DUNTON. *Aylwin*; chap. iii. 1898.

126. EWING. 'Father Hedgehog and his Neighbours.' (*Brothers of Pity and Other Tales.*)

127. WATTS-DUNTON. From *Idylls of Gypsy Dell* (*Athenaeum*, June 1895); repr. in *The Coming of Love.*

128. GROOME. *Kriegspiel*; Bk. ii. chap. 10. 1896.

128. MEREDITH. *Harry Richmond*; chap. vii. 1870.

130. WHITE OF SELBORNE. From a letter addressed to the Hon. Daines Barrington, dated Selborne, Oct. 2, 1775. (*The Natural History of Selborne*; Letter xxv). Cp. p. 283.

131. EMERSON. *Poems.* 1846.

132. PAGET. *Hungary and Transylvania*; vol. ii. chap. viii. 1855.

133. MÉRIMÉE. *Carmen*; chap. iii. 1845.

134. HUGO. *Notre Dame de Paris*; Bk. i. chap. vi., Bk. ii. chap. iii.

135. SYMONS. 'Souls in the Balance,' no. x. (*Images of Good and Evil.* 1899.)

135. COLERIDGE. 'A Sapphic.' (*Morning Post*, Dec. 1, 1801.)

136. SACKVILLE-WEST. From *The Land.* 1926.

136. HODGSON. 'Flying Fame Broadsheets.' 1913.

137. BORROW. *The Romany Rye*; vol. i. chap. x.

139. BORROW. *Ibid.*

140. BORROW. *The Romany Rye*; vol. i. chap. vii. The original song is in Romani, of which Borrow himself gives no translation.

140. TRANSYLVANIAN GYPSY FOLK-TALE. Translated from Wlislocki's *Vier Märchen der transsilvanischen Zigeuner* (1886).

141. TRANSYLVANIAN GYPSY LAMENT. 'Gypsy Songs of Mourning'; translated by A. Herrmann from Wlislocki's *Totenklagen* (*J. G. L. S.* i. 294. 1889). A *Keshalyi* is a hill-fairy who sits

on the high mountain peaks and lets her mile-long hair blow down through the valleys, which causes the miſt.

142. BORROW. *The Zincali*; Part III. chap. i. nos. lvii.-lix. 'Flamenca de Roma' signifies a Gitana. See note to a passage in Mérimée's *Carmen* (chap. iii.) : ' Allons, il y a remède à tout, quand on a pour bonne amie une *flamande de Rome*,' viz. : 'Terme d'argot qui désigne les bohémiennes. *Roma* ne veut pas dire ici la ville éternelle, mais la nation des Romi ou des *gens mariés*, nom que se donnent les bohémiens. Les premiers qu'on vit en Espagne venaient probablement des Pays-Bas, d'où eſt venu leur nom de *Flamands*.' In 1540 we find the name ' Flemyng ' (or ' Femine ') among the Scottish Gypsies who rebelled againſt John Faw, recognized by James V. of Scotland as ' Lord and Erle of Litill Egipt.'

142. TCHINGHIANÉ LOVE-SONGS. Translated from scattered fragments of love-songs in Paspati's *Études sur les Tchinghianés* (1870), some of which may have had their origin in popular Greek poetry.

143. HUNGARIAN GYPSY SONG. Translated from a song contributed by J. Podhradský to Miklosich's *Beiträge zur Kenntniss der Zigeunermundarten* ; IV. ii. 1878.

145. TRANSYLVANIAN GYPSY SONG. Translated by W. E. A. Axon from Hugo von Meltzl's *Jile Romane*. 1878.

145. HUNGARIAN GYPSY SONG. Taken down by David MacRitchie from Julie Lakatos of Neu-Pest ; the air recorded by F. Heltai.

146. ANNUAL REGISTER. 1769. (Chronicle for Sep. ; p. 128.)

146. A PROCESSION. In every land of Europe Gypsy girls rejoice in beautiful and sonorous names. My examples are culled from those met with among English Gypsies. See also Paspati (*Études*, p. 63) and Liebich (*Die Zigeuner*, pp. 89-90).

VI. GYPSY CHILDREN

149. TRANSYLVANIAN GYPSY SONG. Translated by W. E. A. Axon from Wlislocki's *Haidebluten*. 1880.

149. GROOME. *In Gipsy Tents* ; chap. ii.

149. BUNYAN. *Pilgrim's Progress* ; Part II.

149. BORROW. *The Zincali* ; Introduction.

150. SACKVILLE-WEST. *Orchard and Vineyard.* 1921.

151. HOWITT. *Rural and Domeſtic Life of Germany* ; p. 387. 1842.

152. GAUTIER. *Voyage en Espagne* ; xi. 1840. The *Zorongo* is a lively Andalusian dance akin to the Fandango.

153. E. THOMAS. ' The Gypsy.' (*Poems.* 1920.)

PAGE

154. SYMONS. ' In Praise of Gypsies.' (*J. G. L. S.* n.s. i. 297. 1908.)

154. ARNOLD. From *The Strayed Reveller and Other Poems.* 1849. The Gypsy child was probably one of the Boswells, who settled in the Isle of Man in the middle of the nineteenth century, *pace* Groome, who hails her as ' Lavinia Lee.' (*In Gipsy Tents*, p. 22.)

156. HOGG. *The Life of Percy Bysshe Shelley* ; vol. i. chap. vi. 1858.

159. MEREDITH. First published in *Macmillan's Magazine*, Feb. 1869.

161. R. SMITH. *Gipsy Smith, his Life and Work, by Himself.* 1902. Rodney Smith, the Free Church Missioner, born in 1860, was the son of Cornelius Smith and Mary Welch, both Epping Forest Gypsies. In this reminiscence of his childhood, the narrator seems unaware that the burning of the dead wife's tent by the husband, though represented as an accident, was part of the regular ritual of a Gypsy funeral.

162. WATTS-DUNTON. Sonnet suggested by an anecdote of the child ' Lavinia Lee ' [? Dorelia Locke] given in Groome's *In Gipsy Tents*. (*J. G. L. S.* ii. 1. 1890.)

163. DAVIS. Prayers taught by Mrs. Patience Davis, a pure-bred Romany woman, to her grandson, at Hambridge, 1908. (*J. G. L. S.* n.s. iii. 77. 1909.)

VII. STURT AND STRIFE

167. BORROW. *The Zincali* ; Part III. chap. i. ; nos. 3, 5, 10, 19, 29, 30, 31, 41, 75. The rhymes, except the fifth, sixth, and seventh of my arrangement, are of course separate canciones. ' The shirt which binds my frame,' is Borrow's unfortunate rendering of ' *El gate de mi trupo*,' a cliché which he elsewhere (no. 60) translates ' The goodly shirt I bear.'

168. BORROW. *The Bible in Spain* ; vol. i. chap. x. 1843.

169. SCOTT. *Quentin Durward* ; chap. vi.

172. PARSON HABERDYNE. This sermon, which is described as ' larky ' by Dr. Furnivall (*Early English Text Society*, Extra Ser., no. 9) and taken by him from the MS. Cotton Vesp. A 25, leaf 53, occurs also in the Lansdowne MS. 98, leaf 210, where the introduction reads : ' A Sermon made by Parson *Haben uppon a mold hill at Hartely Row*,' etc., Hartley Row being situate on the South-Western road past Bagshot, where the stretch of flat land was used as a galloping place for coaches that had to make up time.

174. RUMANIAN GYPSY PRAYER. From J. A. Vaillant's *Grammaire Rommane*. 1868. A *Modoran* is a footpad, or highway robber.

174. LAMB. Letter to B. W. Procter, 1829. (*Letters of Charles and Mary Lamb*, ed. E. V. Lucas ; no. 474.)

176. BURNS. *Poems and Songs.* 1788. James M'Pherson, a cateran
and freebooter of notable strength and prowess, was the son
of a beautiful Gypsy woman by a member of the family of
Invereshie in Inverness-shire. After his father's death he
joined his mother's tribe, and for some years daringly defied
the magistrates, until in 1700, with others of his Gypsy gang,
he was captured by the Laird of Braco at Keith Market,
and being haled before the Sheriff of Banff, was hanged at
the Town Cross on November 10th.

176. MORWOOD. *Our Gipsies, in city, tent, and van*; chap. xv. 1885.
Buckland kicked off his shoes to avoid the reproach of having
died in them. A similar story is told of a Scottish Gypsy
named Charley Graham (Simson : *History of the Gipsies*;
p. 143).

177. GILDEROY. Percy's *Reliques of Ancient English Poetry*; Bk. III.
no. 12. Gilderoy, though not, like M'Pherson, of Romani
stock, must have ranked as a hero among the Gypsies, since
we find his name perpetuated as a praenomen in several
Gypsy families. 'Gilderoy Gray' was the travelling name
of a certain President of the Gypsy Lore Society.

179. THE GYPSY LADDIE. See *Child's English and Scottish Popular
Ballads*; vol. iv. pt. viii. no. 200. This traditional ballad,
of which there are many versions, is related of Johnnie Faw,
the Gypsy chieftain, and Lady Jean Hamilton, Countess of
Cassilis, in the first half of the seventeenth century. It has
been translated into deep Romani by Sir Donald MacAlister
(*Romani Versions*, p. 29), and an English Gypsy variant has
been recorded from the family of Robinson. (*J. G. L. S.*
ii. 84.)

180. BORROW. *Wild Wales*; vol. i. chap. xiv. 1862. By the
Gwyddelod—Lavengro, *more suo*, gives us two other render-
ings of the plural—or Irish, we are to understand the tinker
clans, who still infest Wales, though the rivalry between them
and the Gypsies is less acute than in Borrow's day. The
guide's 'Paddy Gwyddel' may denote either Irish Gaelic
or the ancient cant known as Shelta. Nowadays Irish tinkers
such as the Furys commonly speak both Shelta and Romani ;
cp. note to Philip Murray, p. 110.

182. BORROW. *Wild Wales*; vol. iii. chap. xxx. 1862. 'Ingrines'
is a mistake for 'Ingrams,' a Gypsy clan who entered Wales
with the family of Wood in the early eighteenth century.
Damaris, the daughter of Abram Wood, married William
Ingram's son Meredith, who was born in 1759.

184. SHAW. *Cashel Byron's Profession.* 1886.

184. BUNYAN. *Pilgrim's Progress*; Part II.

185. BORROW. *The Zincali*; Introduction. It was Thurtell who
taught Borrow the use of his fists as a schoolboy at Norwich,

PAGE

1817-20. The fight took place in a field near Eaton Church, a few miles out of the city.

188. BORROW. *Lavengro*; vol. i. chap. xxvi. 1851. The fateful '*dukkeripen*' was that of Thurtell, who was hanged at Hertford in 1824 for the murder of William Weare. In *dearginni, grondinni,* and *villaminni* Borrow has preserved three very archaic impersonal verbs, now loſt in Anglo-Romani.

190. TRANSYLVANIAN GYPSY. The opening lines of a long lament taken down by Professor Herrmann from Mojsa Ćurar in the prison of Brasso (Kronſtadt).

190. J. ROBERTS. Autograph letter to F. H. Groome, dated March 23, 1880, and introduced into his *In Gipsy Tents,* chap. ix. The name of the boy who was drowned at Aberdovey is Loverin, son of Black Billy and Mary Wood.

191. BORROW. ' The English Gypsies.' (*Romano Lavo-Lil.*)

VIII. BLACK ARTS

195. SCOTS RHYME. *Denham Tracts*; vol. ii., 9 (*Folk-Lore Soc.,* 1895). Thus rendered by Leland in his address to the ' Congrès des Traditions Populaires,' held at Paris, Aug. 1889 :—

> ' Des fées, des Tsiganes et sorcières,
> Ma nourrice me chantait ;
> A mon tour je chante les sorcières,
> Les Tsiganes et les fées.'

195. LELAND. *Gypsy Sorcery and Fortune-Telling*; p. 260. 1891.

195. SCOTT. *Quentin Durward*; chap. xvi.

196. NOËL. Composed by Le Sieur Nicolas Saboly, Maître de Musique de l'Église de St. Pierre d'Avignon ; and firſt publ. in his *Recueil de Noëls,* 1670. Reprinted, with some slight corrections, from *J. G. L. S.* i. 135-8.

202. DRYDEN. *The Satires of Decimus Junius Juvenalis,* translated into English verse by Mr. Dryden and several other Eminent Hands. 1693. Satire vi, ll. 698-708. This freely-translated passage of ll. 542-47 in the original is evidently inspired by the piĉture of an English Gypsy fortune-teller.

203. MORE. *A Dyalog of Syr Thomas More Knyghte*; Bk. III. chap. xv. 1528. This is the earlieſt reference to the Gypsies in England, made at an inqueſt held in 1514 respeĉting the death of Richard Hunne in the Lollard's Tower. Since Lambeth is also mentioned in this conneĉtion by Pepys (see note to p. 211), a Gypsy colony may have exiſted there from the beginning of the sixteenth century.

204. BORROW. *The Zincali*; Pt. I. chap. vii. The song, which Borrow also gives in the original, is quoted by Longfellow in his *Spanish Student* (Act III. sc. 5). *Busno,* properly ' a goat,'

is used by the Spanish Gypsies to denote a savage or gentile, one not of Gypsy ſtock. I correct Borrow's Roma*n*iks to Roma*n*iks, preserving the Slavic termination he has affixed to the word.

207. SCOTT. *Guy Mannering*; chap. iii. Scott tells us in the Introduction that 'the individual gipsy upon whom the chara&ter of Meg Merrilies was founded was well known about the middle of the laſt century by the name of Jean Gordon, an inhabitant of the village of Kirk Yetholm.' In a letter to Simson he writes : 'My father remembered Jean Gordon, who had a great sway among her tribe, and possessed the savage virtue of fidelity in the same perfe&tion as Meg Merrilies'; adding that he himself as 'a little boy' had met one of her granddaughters, 'a woman of more than female height dressed in a long red cloak, on whom [he] looked with no common degree of awe and terror.'

208. CLARE. *The Village Minſtrel and Other Poems* ; vol. i. 1821.

209. J. ROBERTS. Autograph letter to F. H. Groome, dated Jan. 14, 1878, and introduced into his *In Gipsy Tents* ; chap. ix.

210. HAZLITT. Hazlitt's title to the whole Essay. (*Round Table*, no. 12.) 1815.

210. BROWNING. 'The Flight of the Duchess' ; se&t. xv. (*Dramatic Lyrics.*)

211. PEPYS. *Diary.* 1663. Five years later, Aug. 11, 1668, Mrs. Pepys, with 'Mercer' and 'Deb,' had their fortunes told by some Gypsies at Lambeth (probably at Norwood), though on this occasion we do not hear the *dukeriben.*

211. MILTON. *Apology for Smeƈlymnuus* ; se&t. x. 1642.

212. ADDISON. *Spe&tator,* no. 130. July 30, 1711.

214. ROGERS. *Pleasures of Memory* ; Pt. 1. 1792.

214. GAY. 'Tuesday, or The Ditty.' (*The Shepherd's Week.*) 1714.

215. HERRICK. *Hesperides* ; no. 166. 1648.

215. BEN JONSON. *A Masque of the Metamorphosed Gypsies.* 1621.

216. NARCISSUS : A Twelfe Night Merriment. 1602.

216. GYPSY SONG. A fragment sung by Ethelenda, wife of Joshua Gray. (*J. G. L. S.* iii. 203.)

217. GOLDSMITH. *Vicar of Wakefield* ; chap. x.

217. PLATO. *Republic* ; ii. 364 B ; trans. A. D. Lindsay.

218. XII. CENT. MS. Translated from the Georgian *Life of Giorgi Mtharsmindel* of Mt. Athos, by M. Tchoubinof (Miklosich, *Mundarten,* vi. 60). I take my version from Groome (*Gypsy Folk-Tales*), who cites this passage as an early illuſtration of the use of poison by Gypsies.

348 · NOTES

PAGE

219. BORROW. *Lavengro*; vol. iii. chap. iv. The prototype of the Mrs. Herne who poisoned Borrow is understood to be Martha, the wife of Reynolds Herne and mother of Sanspirella who married 'Jasper Petulengro,' *i.e.* Ambrose Smith; but the sequel of her hanging may be a Borrovian figment. (*J. G. L. S.* n.s. iii. 165.) The poison used seems to have been water-spar, probably obtained from the Shropshire lead-mines at Minsterley, in the neighbourhood of the famous Dingle (*J. G. L. S.* n.s. ii. 205).

227. BORROW. *The Romany Rye*, vol. i. chap. vii.; where the Romani original is sung by Mrs. Chikno. According to Knapp this song is built up from a prose draft, three separate versions of which occur in Borrow's MSS.

228. SHAKESPEARE. *Othello*; Act III. sc. iv. Cp. Furness in the *Variorum* ed. : ' Presents of this kind from Gypsies proper occur in Italian poetry ; thus Ariosto : " About her neck a jewel rich she ware, A cross all set with stones in gold well tried ; This relick late a *Boem pilgrim* bare, And gave her father other things beside." Cp. also Ben Jonson, *Sad Shepherd*, II. i., where Maudlin describes her " browder'd belt " which " A Gypsan lady, and a right beldame, Wrought by moonshine." This, Elze says, Ben copied from Shakespeare.'

229. DEFOE. *A System of Magick*; chap. iii. 1727.

230. R. SCOT. *The Discoverie of Witchcraft*; chap. x.

230. BORROW. *The Zincali*; Pt. I. chap. vi. Related to Borrow by a Jew of Fez, ' who had travelled much in Barbary '—perhaps the Hayim Ben Attar who was later confronted with Mr. Petulengro (see p. 26).

232. SCOTT. Note to stanza xxii. of ' Christie's Will ' (*Minstrelsy of the Scottish Border*, Pt. III.) beginning: ' Besides the prophetic powers ascribed to the gypsies in most European countries, the Scottish peasants believe them possessed of the power of throwing upon bystanders a spell, to fascinate their eyes, and cause them to see the thing that is not. Thus, in the ballad of " Johnnie Faa " (see p. 179) the elopement of the Countess of Cassilis with a gypsy leader is imputed to fascination :—
" As sune as they saw her weel-far'd face,
They cast the *glamour* ower her."
. . . The receipt to prevent the operation of these deceptions was to use a sprig of four-leaved clover.' (See also Scott's *Letters on Demonology and Witchcraft*, no. iii.)

232. LYSTER. See *J. G. L. S.* n.s. ii. 50, 1908 ; and *The Gypsy Life of Betsy Wood*, chap. xii., 1926. ' Siani ' is Betsy, wife of Howell Wood ; ' Taw ' is the by-name of Saiforella, mother of Matthew Wood.

234. CORNHILL. From ' The Wedding : a Gypsy Tale.' (*Cornhill Magazine*; Aug. 1922.) The heroine of the episode was a

youthful daughter of Bohemia Boswell—nameless here for evermore.

235. BORROW. *Lavengro* ; vol. i. chap. v.

240. 1 *Samuel.* In the view of Byron this tale of the Witch of Endor is the finest ghost story in the world. *Tot homines quot sententiae.* Lang gives his vote for ' Wandering Willie's Tale,' and Borrow his for a tale of terror in Lope de Vega's *El Peregrino (Wild Wales,* iii. xxxi.).

242. APULEIUS. *The Golden Ass,* chap. v. ; trans. Adlington. 1566. This African tale of black magic, which has held spell-bound every Gypsy audience to whom I have recounted it, has, of course, no Indo-European pedigree. But in the diffusion of folk-tales strange things happen ; and I myself have heard the story of Jonah and the Whale told me in a guise in which the prophet of Nineveh figured as *O Churo Jak* or Poor Jack.

247. RUMANIAN GYPSY FOLK-TALE. Constantinescu : *Probe de Limba și Literatura Țiganilor din România* ; Basm no. x. This story of The Red King and the Witch, Groome considered the finest in his collection, comparing it, in its kind, with Dürer's ' Knight,' or the csárdas of some great Gypsy maestro.

251. SHAKESPEARE. *Cymbeline* ; Act IV. sc. 2.

IX. A GYPSY BESTIARY

255. BORROW. *The Bible in Spain* ; vol. i. chap. ix.

255. BLAKE. From the *Pickering MS.*

255. LISZT. *Die Zigeuner und ihre Musik in Ungarn* ; chap. ix.

257. BORROW. *Lavengro* ; vol. i. chap. xiii.

259. RUSSIAN GYPSY SONG. Trans. from the *Kisilefskie Žigane* of Mr. U. N. Dobrowolski by D. F. de l'Hoste Ranking.

260. BORROW. *Lavengro* ; vol. i. chap. xvi. Borrow has antedated the parading of Marshland Shales, at Tombland Fair, Norwich, by nine years to suit the purposes of his story.

261. CUNNINGHAM. ' Adventure with the Gypsies.' (*Blackwood's Magazine* ; vii. 1820.) The Marshalls were a Tinkler clan of mixed Gypsy descent ; see Simson : *History of the Gipsies,* and M'Cormick : *Tinkler Gypsies of Galloway,* passim.

263. BORROW. Borrow's statement (*Zincali* ; Pt. ii. chap. i.) that the older Spanish Gypsies entertained a belief in the doctrine of metempsychosis has received little corroboration, and is, by his own account, laughed to scorn by the Gitanos of to-day : ' We have been wicked and miserable enough in this life,' they said ; ' why should we live again ? '

263. S. ROBERTS. *The Gypsies.* 1836. Clara ' Vanis ' or Heron, when a girl of fourteen, was for a week or so a guest in the

PAGE

house of Samuel Roberts, the philanthropist of Sheffield, and communicated a vocabulary of 250 words to the daughters of her host. A quarter of a century later, on Derby Day, Borrow met her on Epsom Downs ' as a full-blown Egyptian matron with two very handsome daughters flaringly dressed in genuine Gypsy fashion ' (*Romano Lavo-Lil*, p. 293).

264. EWING. ' Father Hedgehog and his Neighbours.' (*Brothers of Pity and Other Tales.*) On the name and important part played by the hedgehog in Gypsy life see Pischel : *Beiträge zur Kenntnis der deutschen Zigeuner*, p. 26. Among the Welsh Gypsies a pet name for ' Father Hedgehog ' is Udika Wood, humorously referred to as a member of their own family, about whom they delight to weave many droll stories.

265. HUDSON. *A Shepherd's Life.* 1910. According to Harry Wood, one of the Editor's Gypsy friends, hedgehogs whistle at night to each other when they go a-courting. For other curious habits of hedgehogs related by ' Gypsy naturalists,' see Groome : *In Gipsy Tents*, p. 163.

266. LIEBICH. *Die Zigeuner in ihrem Wesen und in ihrer Sprache.* 1863.

266. GYPSY LEGEND. Related to the Editor by Noah Young, as explaining why *Márengro's Čai* (Baker's Daughter) is one of the Gypsy names for the owl. Shakespeare's commentator Douce gives a version of this legend from Gloucestershire, with the substitution of a cake of dough for the draught of water. Here the girl, blaming her mother for the generous size of the loaf, exclaims, ' Heugh ! heugh ! heugh ! ' when she sees it swelling in the oven.

267. E. THOMAS. *Poems.* 1920. The ' melancholy cry ' which moved the heart of Edward Thomas was that of the screech-owl, the Welsh ' aderyn corff ' or ' corpse bird,' known to Gypsies as the *merimásko čeriklo*, and universally regarded as a bird of evil omen.

268. BERNERS. *A Treatyse of Fysshynge wyth an Angle*, first printed by Wynkyn de Worde in *The Boke of Saint Albans.* 1496.

269. COTTON. The first stanzas of ' The Angler's Ballad ' (*circa* 1686). To ' troll with a pink ' is to fish with a minnow on a running line.

271. ENGLISH FOLK-SONG. This famous poaching song is included here as embodying the Gypsy's attitude to the Game Laws, though the only apprenticeship he recognizes is the life-long one to Nature.

272. GROOME. *In Gipsy Tents* ; chap. ii. In Germany also the water-wagtail is known as the *Romano tschirkulo* or Gypsy bird (Liebich : *Die Zigeuner*).

272. GYPSY LEGEND. I quote from the version in ' Table Talk ' (*Gentleman's Magazine*, July 1876).

PAGE

273. Gypsy Proverb. Adopted as the motto of the Gypsy Lore Society.

273. Groome. *In Gipsy Tents*; chap. i. Another Welsh Gypsy superstition concerning snakes is that of ' Blowing the Ring ' (cp. *Folk-Lore*, xxxii. p. 268, xxxiii. p. 118).

273. Groome. *In Gipsy Tents*; chap. vii. ' Appy ' or ' Happy ' (by-names of Absolom) Boswell is our Romani Münchhausen, to whom scores of Lügenmärchen are accredited by Gypsies from all over England and Wales. He is perhaps best described by his *gâjo* stepfather as ' the rummest ole liar as ivver walked Gawd's earth.' The son of ' black ' Ambrose and Trēnit Boswell, he was famous throughout the North Midlands for his grinding barrow of German silver, from which he was supposed to chip solid blocks whenever he found himself in pecuniary straits. Among other ' lying tales ' attributed to him are ' Appy Boswell's Monkey,' ' Appy Boswell's Dog ' (seven distinct variants of the anecdote related in my text), ' Appy Boswell's Donkey,' ' Appy and the Conger Eel,' and the delightful story of Appy's reason for begging the skin of a dead sheep from a farmer—' to wrap around my nose for to keep it warm.' (See *J. G. L. S.* n.s. v. 160, viii. 198-9, 227-33 ; 3rd ser. iv. 29-31, v. 120-5.)

X. EGIPTE SPECHE

277. Borrow. *Romano Lavo-Lil*; title-page. There are many versions of this ditty : one, noted by the Editor from the singing of a young Gypsy girl, ends with the explanatory lines twice repeated : ' Said the *Romani chai* to the *Romani rai*,' i.e. ' Said the Gypsy girl to the Scholar Gypsy ' (*J. G. L. S.* ii. 81-2).

277. Borrow. ' Book of the Wisdom of the Egyptians.' (*Romano Lavo-Lil*; p. 131.)

277. Johnson. Letter to William Drummond, dated Aug. 13, 1766, in support of a ' scheme of translating the holy scriptures into the Erse or Gaelic language.' The title is Johnson's own, reported by Boswell in his *Hebrides*, Sept. 18, 1773.

278. Paspates. The opening sentence of his famous *Études sur les Tchinghianés*. 1870.

278. Borde. *The Fyrst Boke of the Introduction of Knowledge.* 1547. Under the impression that he is giving us examples of the tongue of Pharaoh, Borde has here recorded the earliest specimens of Romani in any dialect, obviously collected from English Gypsies. Though printed in 1547, and edited by Dr. Furnivall for the *E. E. T. S.* in 1870, this fact was not perceived until its discovery by an Austrian professor, Dr. Zupitsa, in 1874. I correct the misprint *susse* to *tusse [tusa]*.

PAGE

279. JONSON. *A Masque of the Metamorphosed Gypsies.* 1621.

279. SHAKESPEARE. 1 *Henry IV.*; Aĉt II. sc. 4—in which reign, of course, there were as yet no Gypsies in England. Probably, as Scott supposed (see p. 284), Romani is meant by the Tinkers' language, though Leland has conjeĉtured it may refer to Shelta. Cp. note to *As You Like It*, p. 59.

280. HARRISON. *Description of England.* 1577. In this fiĉtitious account of the invention of Cant, Harrison would seem to refer to the notorious Cocke Lorrell, whose leadership of the Regiment of Rogues is celebrated in *Martin Markall* by S[amuel] R[owlands], 1610.

280. HANSARD. In the Debate on the Repeal of the Penal Laws againŝt the Gypsies, April 19, 1772. Following Ribton Turner, Mr. Ongley's reference to Romani has been commonly misprinted ' an *obscene* and myŝtical language.'

280. BORROW. *The Bible in Spain*; vol. i. chap. ix.

282. H. WOOD. In conversation with the Editor.

282. BORROW. *Lavengro*; vol. ii. chap. xix.

283. WHITER. Preface to *Etymologicon Magnum, or Universal etymological diĉtionary . . . with illuŝtrations drawn from various languages . . . Hebrew, Arabic, Persian, Sanscrit, Gipsey, Coptic, etc.* 1800. An earlier work than his *Etymologicon Universale*, which firŝt drew Groome's attention to Whiter's knowledge of Romani. For Borrow's mention of the philologiŝt, see p. 306.

283. WHITE. Letter to the Hon. Daines Barrington. *Petalengro*, not ' *Curleople*,' is the usual Gypsy name for Smith.

284. SCOTT. The firŝt portion of this passage is taken from two letters addressed to James Simson, the ' individual ' referred to (*Hiŝt. of the Gipsies*, pp. 60 and 66), and the latter from the note to chap. vi. of *Quentin Durward.* 1823. Cp. note to p. 308.

284. LEUPOL. An anagram for F. É. Leloup de Charroy, of whose *Jardin des Racines Sanscrites* this sonnet forms the dedication. 1870. His ' rimes ' are a *memoria technica* to Sanskrit roots.

285. GROOME. *J. G. L. S.* i. 374-5.

286. CHAMBERS'S JOURNAL. April 13, 1878.

286. MEREDITH. *Adventures of Harry Richmond*; chap. vii. 1870.

286. PHILLIPS. ' A Morning's Walk from London to Kew.' (*Monthly Magazine*, Jan. 1817.) Cp. pp. 23-4 for another passage from the same article. The laŝt sentence is amusingly charaĉteriŝtic of the parsimony of the vegetarian publisher, and recalls his good advice to the youthful Borrow to abŝtain from meat, and live on bread and cheese, or, if cheese coŝt too much, to live on bread alone : ' As good men as yourself have eaten bread alone ; they have been glad to get it, sir. If with bread and cheese you muŝt drink porter, sir, with bread alone you can, perhaps, drink water, sir.'

287. NORWOOD, Vicar of Wrenbury. *On the Race and Language of the Gipsies*: a Paper read before the Brit. Ass. at Leeds, Sept. 1858. (*J. G. L. S.* n.s. iii. 209.) The amiability of Mr. Norwood's character is attested by his lifelong devotion to the Gypsies having arisen through their theft of his pet donkey, when he was a small boy. Thenceforward he was an eager student of them and their language. In 1863, on meeting at Cheltenham racecourse the old Gypsy Edwin Buckland, who introduced him to deep Romani, he records the *trouvère* in his Diary with the grateful entry : ' Thank God for such a measure of good fortune as this was.'

287. GRAFFUNDER. *Über die Sprache der Zigeuner* ; p. 52. 1835.

287. BORROW. *Romano Lavo-Lil* ; p. 13. Translated from the Romani beginning—

> ' *Coin si deya, coin se dado ?*
> *Pukker mande drey Romanes,*
> *Ta mande pukkeravava tute . . .*'

Borrow states that ' the first three lines of the above ballad are perhaps the oldest specimen of English Gypsy at present extant, and perhaps the purest ' ; but this is disproved by the corrupt form of the original.

288. BORROW. *Lavengro* ; vol. i. chap. xvii.

291. SMART AND CROFTON. *Dialect of the English Gypsies* ; pp. 275-6. The Gypsy speaker is the famous Isaac Heron, whose impression of Borrow is given on p. 308.

292. BORROW. ' Kirk Yetholm.' (*Romano Lavo-Lil.*) The Gypsy Queen was Esther Blyth.

294. JUBILEE BOOK. *Jubilee Book of the Philosophical Institution of Edinburgh.* 1897. The argument, reported almost verbatim, is that of my old friend, Noah Young *alias* Heron.

294. BORROW. *Romany Rye* ; vol. i. chaps. xi. and xii. Borrow seems to have been unaware that the deep Anglo-Romani of two hundred years ago had been preserved by the Welsh Gypsies ; nor indeed in travelling through Wales twenty-nine years later did he make this discovery. *Patteran*, a trap for the bogus Rai, is a dissyllable pronounced *patrin* (cp. *Romano Lavo-Lil*, p. 233).

296. LELAND. *English Gypsies* ; Tale xxii. p. 227. *Jōter* (Smart and Crofton's *jŏlta*, Welsh Gyp. *dyūta*) is the name of the peculiar Romani whistle on the two notes—

Z

XI. SCHOLAR GYPSIES

299. BORROW. *The Zincali*; Introduction.

299. WORDSWORTH. 'The Cuckoo.' I cite these lines of Words-worth's poem (which some might deem irrelevant) with a backward glance at Mr. Petulengro's parable of the Gypsy and the cuckoo (see pp. 6-8).

299. SYMONS. In a review of *The Day-Book of Bethia Hardacre*. (*J. G. L. S.* n.s. i. 280.)

299. GEO. SMITH. From *Gipsy Life*; Pt. III. (1880)—a passage which would seem to show that even Brother Stiggins was capable of moments of vision. For the effect on the Gypsy mind of one of his letters to the Press, see p. 317.

300. BORROW. *Lavengro*; vol. ii. chap. xxvi. The song, of course, is improvised nonsense.

301. GLANVILL. *The Vanity of Dogmatizing.* 1661. Two points stand out in Glanvill's precious story. One is, that it was by the 'insinuating subtilty of his carriage' and by 'the preg-nancy of his wit and parts' that the Scholar endeared himself to his Gypsy friends, showing them that he was no dull-witted Gaujo, but one worthy of sharing their Gypsy secrets. And the other is this, that while there are two kinds of occult power possessed by the Gypsies, rightly distinguished by Scott (see note to p. 232), the hypnotic one of casting 'glamour,' or imposing one's imagination upon others 'so as to make them see the thing that is not,' and that of divina-tion, thought-reading, and prophecy, it is of the former only that the Scholar speaks, though he does not claim to have divulged the whole mystery to his friends. Both powers, it may be said, are believed in by the Gypsies themselves : ' they are,' as an old sibyl once confided to the Editor, ' *o bita baxtiben te dids 'men o beng*, " the little gift with which the Devil has endowed us." '

302. ARNOLD. *The Scholar Gypsy.* 1853. Arnold's reflections on the ' oft-read tale.' The poet's plan, which makes Oxford the centre of the picture and the spectral Scholar a constant haunter of old scenes, tends to obscure the truth that he ' came to Oxford and his friends no more.'

305. ARNOLD. The concluding lines of ' Thyrsis,' *i.e.* Arnold's friend, Clough.

306. BORDE. *The Fyrst Boke of the Introduction of Knowledge.* 1547. Andrew Borde, by some supposed to be the original of our ' Merry Andrew,' in verse which he rightly characterizes as ' ryme dogrel,' makes many shrewd observations on the people and lands he visited. Thus of the Welsh he says :

'North Wales and Sowth Wales do vary in there speche,
and in there fare and maners . . . but for all the variaunce
of the premisses, they can not speke x wordes to-gyther of
Welshe, but " deauol " that is to say " the deuyl " is at the
ende of one of the wordes.' The same is true to-day.
Cp. note to p. 278.

306. BORROW.   *Lavengro*; vol. i. chap. xxiv.   Cp. p. 283.

307. BURNEY.   *Diary and Letters of Madame D'Arblay*; vol. ii.   1788.
Jacob Bryant, the mythologiſt, who made his collection of
Romani at Windsor Fair in Auguſt 1776, was one of the firſt
to eſtablish the Indian origin of the Gypsies.

308. OFFOR, the biographer of Bunyan.   In *Notes and Queries*.
' *J. S.*,' I may explain, to prevent possible misunderſtanding,
ſtands for James Simson, the publication of whose *Hiſtory
of the Gipsies* was warmly encouraged by Sir Walter Scott.

308. BORROW.   ' Lines to Six-Foot-Three.'   (*Romantic Ballads*, no. 25.
Norwich, 1826.)   Borrow's portrait of himself as a youth.

308. HERON.   Verbatim in a chat with the Editor.

308. HENLEY.   *Views and Reviews*.   1890.

310. BORROW.   *Wild Wales*; vol. iii. chap. xxxii.   1862.   ' Plas y
Cadno,' Fox's Court, perhaps ſtands for London.   The inn
where Borrow ſtopped on his way to Swansea, Nov. 11, 1854,
was at Gutter Vawr [*recte* Quarter Mawr, 5 miles S.E. of
Llangadock].

311. PENNELL.   *Life of Charles Godfrey Leland*; vol. ii. chap. xiii.
We owe this description of the ' merry race ' to the pen of
Mrs. Elizabeth Robins Pennell, Leland's niece, herself a true
Romani Rawnee (see pp. 318-21).

311. LELAND.   *Ibid.* ii. 201 ; from a Letter to David MacRitchie,
written May 1888, on the accession to the Society of the
Archduke Josef of Auſtria.   Leland himself was elected
President, and Mr. Henry T. Crofton Vice-President, the
other two members being David MacRitchie the founder and
Editor, with Francis Hindes Groome as his collaborator.
The firſt number of the *Journal of the Gypsy Lore Society* was
published in July 1888.

312. KARĊIC.   Translated from a Romani tale, recorded by Wlislocki.
Numerous other legends have sprung up about the Archduke
Josef.

313. PASPATES.   Dr. Alexandre Paspati was the collector of the pureſt
dialect of Romani, that spoken by the Gypsies of the Ottoman
Empire.

314. LELAND.   *The Gypsies*; chap. iii.   1882.   These old Welsh
Gypsies belonged to the Lee family.

PAGE

315. HARDY. From a Notebook of T. H. dated July 29, 1879. (*Early Life of Thomas Hardy.*) Leland has himself related the same anecdote in *The Gypsies*. The first President of the Gypsy Lore Society, Charles Godfrey Leland may be regarded as the most popular writer on the Gypsies since the time of Borrow. Amongst his many excursions into untrodden fields, he gave to the world *The Hans Breitmann Ballads, Tales of the Algonquin Indians, Pidgin English,* and *Gypsy Sorcery and Fortune-Telling.* He was also the discoverer of the ancient Irish jargon known as Shelta.

315. LELAND. Translated from the verses entitled 'Miro Pal,' appended to Walter Besant's *Life of E. H. Palmer.* 'The Palmer' was Leland's affectionate name for his friend Professor E. H. Palmer, orientalist, and collaborator with him in *English Gipsy Songs and Ballads.* Palmer's adventurous career was cut short through his murder by hostile Arabs, when on a secret Government mission to Egypt.

316. HITCHMAN. *Richard F. Burton: his Early, Private and Public Life.* 1887. Sir Richard Burton, explorer and oriental scholar, was the author of *A Pilgrimage to Meccah,* and *The Jew, the Gypsy and El Islam,* and translator of *The Arabian Nights.* There is an entire lack of evidence that Sir Richard was in any way related to the Gypsy clan of Burtons, though he himself apparently fostered the belief.

317. GROOME. *In Gipsy Tents;* chap. viii. Cp. note to p. 299.

317. J. G. L. S. iii. 199. Quoted in illustration of the pleasant imagination of Johnny Gray, who narrated to the Editor the three English Gypsy folk-tales of 'Bobby Rag,' 'De Little Bull-calf,' and 'De Little Fox.'

318. WATTS-DUNTON. Translated from a Romani elegy (*Athenaeum,* Feb. 22, 1902, repr. in *Old Familiar Faces*). Groome, an Oxford undergraduate, who married a Gypsy wife, was the author of *In Gipsy Tents, Gypsy Folk-Tales,* and *Kriegspiel,* and editor of *Lavengro.*

318. PENNELL. *To Gipsyland;* pp. 30-6. 1893. Cp. note to p. 311.

321. VICTORIA R. *The Girlhood of Queen Victoria: a Selection from Her Majesty's Diaries between the Years* 1832-1840. The Coopers are a South of England clan, who travelled chiefly in the neighbourhood of Windsor. The good Queen, who on her death-bed indignantly told the Archbishop that she would never dream of being introduced to King David, may well have felt some interest in the humbler Queen Sanspirella, whom she met in 1878 at Knockindale Hill and described in her *Leaves from the Journal of a Life in the Highlands.*

323. HEINE. Translated from a Romani adaptation of Heine's song. (*Heimkehr,* no. 15).

324. ARNALDOS. From Lockhart's translation of a ballad in the *Romancero.*

XII. ENVOY

PAGE

329. BORROW. *Lavengro* ; vol. i. chap. xxv. As a more peaceful
valediction, readers may care to recall the lines from Wordsworth's 'Old Cumberland Beggar' :

> 'Then let him pass, a blessing on his head !
> And, long as he can wander, let him breathe
> The freshness of the valleys ; let his blood
> Struggle with frosty air and winter snows ;
> And let the chartered wind that sweeps the heath
> Beat his grey locks against his withered face . . .
> As in the eye of Nature he has lived,
> So in the eye of Nature let him die ! '

Glossary of Romani Words

not explained in the text

acoi [*akai*], here. 124
adrey, dray, in, into. 127, 277
atch, stop. 119.
avali, yes. 288
avella, is coming. 227
bal, hair. 127
bar, pound sterling. 111
bebee, aunt. 223-7
bengui [*beng*], devil. 237
bitchadey pawdel, transported. 289
bitti, little. 112
boro, big. 112
bosh, fiddle. 277
Busné, Busnees, Gentiles. 85, 204, 280
canengri, hare. 36
chabo, chavo, boy, child. 36, 119, 183, 206, 289
chachipé, truth. 85
chai, chie, chi, girl, daughter. 7, 8, 123, 124, 183, 295
chal, Gypsy man. 7, 123, 295, 296, 329
chin, cut. 277
chirikel, bird. 127
chong, hill. 182
choon, moon. 127
chore, steal. 85, 138
chovakanon, chowahanee, witch. 118, 206
comly, dear. 128
cost, wood. 277
cukkerin, cuckooing. 7
Dabla! God! 127
danniers, teeth. 127
diklo, kerchief. 113
dinilo, foolish. 120
divvus, day. 26, 111, 124
dordi, dawda, there! bless me! 64, 69, 127
dosta, enough. 329
drab, drow, poison. 224-7
dray, see *adrey*
358

dui, two. 26
duk, dook, spirit, fate. 225, 226-7, 314
dukkerin, fortune-telling. 7, 138, 225, 289-90
dukkeripen, fortune. 189
duvel, dibbel, God. 139, 182, 290, 317 (Cp. *Dabla!*)
ei, i, oh! ah! 69, 127
Errate [*rat*], the Blood, *i.e.* the Gypsy race. 85
foky, people. 183
gaujines, Gentile talk, *i.e.* English. 68
gav, town. 182, 288
ghora, man. 112
gorgio [*gaujo*], Gentile. 117, 120, 139, 220, 221, 227, 288, 289-90
grandbebee, great-aunt. 219-221
gry, horse. 127
harko mescro, tinker. 219
Hindity mescrey, Irish. 183
hir mi devlis, [Borrovian for] By God! 219
hokkawar, lie, deceive. 138
hotchi-witchi, hedgehog. 36
idza, clothes. 111
jal, go. 277
jawing, going. 182, 290
jin, know. 118
jöter, Gypsy hail. 296
juggal, dog. 221, 225
juwa, wife. 183
kairing, doing. 124
kako, kokko, uncle. 113, 119
kana, when. 329
kaulo, korly, black. 128
Kaulo gav, Birmingham. 182
kaulomengro, tinker. 182
kekaubi, kettle. 219
ker, house. 289
kosko, koshto, good. 26, 124
latcho, good. 319
lel, get. 127

lil, book. 8
lubbeny, harlot. 138
makta, chest. 111
manricli, cake. 219, 234
mendy's, our. 127
mishto! good! well done!
    317
moey, mouth. 127
mush, man. 183
mushi, woman. 183
nash, hang. 183
nav, name. 182
nock, nose. 127
nokengro, glandered horse. 26
palor, brothers. 26
patrin, trail. 65
pen, sister. 119
penning, saying. 182
penning dukkerin, telling fortunes.
    289-90
poknees, justice, magistrate. 288-
    289.
posnakos, kerchief. 111
purro, old. 111
ran, cane. 223
ratti, night. 319
ratvali, bloody. 116
rawni, lady. 94, 318
rokkering, talking. 119
rokra, talk, speak. 26, 277
rokrapen, speech. 292
rom, husband, Gypsy man. 36,
    204

Romanes, in Gypsy, Gypsy lan-
    guage. 119, 294
Romany, Gypsy. 7, 127, 292,
    295, 296, 314-15
Romany Rye, Scholar Gypsy. 127
    182, 300, 311, 318
romni, romi, wife, Gypsy woman.
    36, 113
roringeras [*horingeras*], watch-
    guards. 110
rye, gentleman. 93, 94, 127-8,
    294, 317
sar, how. 113, 124
sarishan, how art thou ? 92
savo, what sort of. 182
shan, shin, thou art. 113, 124,
    182, 292
shoon, listen. 182
so, what. 124
staripen, prison. 277
tachi, true. 118
tacheno, right. 94
tan, tent. 127-8
tarno, tawny, young. 127, 239
tikno, tickni, small. 36, 111
trash'd, frightened. 118, 119
tringoruschee, shilling. 183
tu, tute, thou. 124, 182
vasavest, wickedest. 112
vover, other. 112
welling, coming. 182
yockers, eyes. 127
yuk [*yek*], one. 112

Index of Authors

360

Printed in the United Kingdom
by Lightning Source UK Ltd.
118420UK00001B/199